*WHY DID HE BREAK UP WITH ME?*

Also by DeBora M. Ricks

**Love Addicted:** *One Woman's Spiritual Journey Through Emotional Dependency*

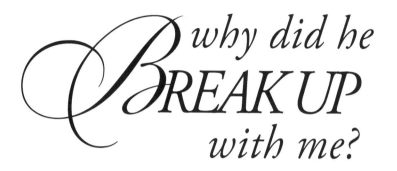

why did he
*B*REAK UP
with me?

Lessons in Love,
Loss & Letting Go

DEBORA M. RICKS

Sunny House Press

Library of Congress Control Number: 2010939868

ISBN 978-0-9764031-5-9
First Printing February 2013

Hair: Allan Van Johnson
Cover photograph: Kiara Whitehead
Cover & interior design: Carolyn Sheldraw

Publisher: Sunny House Press
For more books or information visit:
Web site: www.DeBoraRicks.com

PRINTED IN THE UNITED STATES OF AMERICA

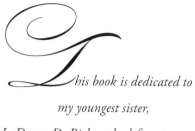
his book is dedicated to

*my youngest sister,*

*LaDawn D. Ricks, who left us too soon,*

*and Linda Patelle Lee, Sandra Woods' sister.*


*And to women everywhere who refuse to give up on love.*

# Contents

## DISCLAIMER

This book contains the opinions and ideas of its author, contributing writers, and interviewees. Neither the author, contributors, nor publisher are offering or rendering medical, health, psychological, or any other kind of professional services in this book. If the reader requires personal, medical, mental health, or other assistance or advice, she or he is advised to consult with a competent professional. The opinions of the contributing writers and interviewees are not necessarily that of the author, editor, nor publisher. Nor should the opinions of author and editor DeBora M. Ricks be ascribed to the contributing writers and interviewees.

This work is nonfiction. Names and identifying details have been changed to protect the privacy of those mentioned.

# Introduction

*POOF!* JUST LIKE that, without a word, he was gone. The man that Vickie was seeing months earlier had suddenly disappeared. She got no more calls, e-mails, or text messages from him. He didn't confess, "This just isn't working for me" or that he was seeing someone else. He didn't even bother to resort to that infamous cliché people so often use to spare the dumped person's feelings: "It's not you, it's me." My friend got nothing. Boyfriend did what so many cowardly men do when they're done with a woman; he simply vanished.

At the time, I too was reeling from a "breakup." A few weeks earlier a guy I liked a little too much had decided he no longer wanted to see me. The word breakup has quotation marks because I wasn't actually in a relationship with this man. I only wanted to be. Or thought I did. He seemed to possess so many of the things that I wanted in a man: tall, dark, and handsome, accomplished, financially and physically fit, a great conversationalist, on a spiritual path, and he had a helluva sexy smile. Yes, just my type. Turns out the feelings weren't mutual.

Years earlier, shortly after publishing my first book, *Love Addicted,* and anxious to get another book underway I'd go to the computer where I'd force onto the "page" a bunch of wooden, lifeless sentences. Consequently, my excitement for that book soon waned. I took that as a sign from Spirit to let it go. I turned my attention elsewhere.

Well, when I hung up the phone from talking to my friend Vickie on this cold January day I got a hot idea—*why not write a book about breakups? It's certainly a topic that I know a lot about.* After my nearly six-year relationship with my daughter's dad my intimate relationships seemed to have a much shorter shelf life. Consequently, I have had my fair share of romantic rendezvous. Some ended uneventfully. Others ended painfully. That's the "bad" news. The good news is this: *I now know enough about breakups to write a book about them.* I know how to get closure, grieve, heal, and gather myself so I can move forward with my heart open. I know the tools *and* tricks that usher in healing. I've also witnessed the pain, confusion, fear, depression, and inertia that other women experience during a breakup—up close and personal. And have watched women wrestle with the aftermath of a breakup.

Though Vickie's story inspired me to begin this book, it is my own intimate knowledge of and curiosity about love, relationships, and breakups that kept me writing. Quite frankly, I've had more breakups than I care to share. Still, I share my stories here. One day it occurred to me, with the help of my friend PeaJae, that learning and expanding through the ups and downs of love and intimate relationships must have been a sacred contract that I entered into before I incarnated. Since it is also my destiny to write, what insights and wisdom that I gain about love and life I am happy and honored to share with others.

Men experience hurt and confusion at the ending of a relationship too. Most men move on to the next woman quickly. Many pretend they're okay, while they're secretly despondent and brokenhearted. Because men have been socialized to believe it's a sign of weakness to show vulnerability, pain, confusion, and even sadness, rather than let on how much they are hurting they instead posture and act out. That is, they drink too much, use and abuse drugs, smoke dope, sleep around. This, they hope, will keep their heartache at bay, and maybe even heal it. Such escape measures will numb the pain, at least for a while, but they have not the power to heal. And yes, when some men experience a broken heart, they have a hard time opening their hearts fully to love when it beckons again. What a pity, since experiencing heartbreak and heartache are as integral to loving as death is to life. Few men, however, give up on relationships altogether. They might give up on love, but they seldom stop entering into new relationships.

This book is largely for women. If a man should find some healing and strength from this book that would please me greatly. However, the focus is on women. Why? Because women not only have the greatest difficulty letting go and moving forward after a break up, but far too many women, sometimes even decades later, remain hopelessly attached to their ex. Either they still love him. Or hate his guts. In a word, they are STUCK. They aren't living in the here and now but are floating around somewhere in a pastime "paradise." Some are still praying their ex will see the error of his ways and come back to them. Others can't stop wondering what went wrong, how did they fail and why weren't they good enough.

Then there are those women, after a series of toxic relationships, who are now bitter and resentful. They see men as "the enemy," and they hate their enemy. Let's be real, some women hate men. They have been burned too many times by "love," and now they are DONE, DONE, DONE. Finished. Shutdown. Checked out. Love and intimate relationships have no place in their life anymore.

Finally, this book is for all the women who have cried a river over some loser, cheater, traitor, or abuser, all because they believed they couldn't do any better. By the time you've completed this book, you'll know better than that. You'll know you deserve your deepest heart's desire in love and relationships. That is, you deserve to be loved and cherished.

Well, months later my friend ran into the guy that dumped her. It was a balmy spring day. Not one to make New Year's resolutions she'd nonetheless made one that year. Her New Year's resolution was to take one risk a day. That day's risk stood only feet away from her. She walked up to The Departed. After the standard exchange of pleasantries, she popped the question. Yes, she was clear that she could be inviting some pain into her life and that she risked being hurt by the answer. Still, she wanted, no, needed closure.

What did The Departed say? Keep reading, I tell you in Chapter Eleven.

I write this book with the prayer that something that I, or a contributor, offer will enlighten, inspire, encourage, support, lift, and free you from whatever bounds you. Too few of us know our worth. Consequently, we tolerate all manner of maltreatment and abuse to have a man. It is my prayer that this book will help you awake and step into your power and purpose. Perhaps something in this book will help you remember that no matter what you've endured, you are whole and complete, and that it is you, and you alone, who hold the keys to your happiness.

## Can You Keep Me?

Do not to your bosom take me
if you can not keep me.
If for some reason I become despicable—
a stench unto your nostril,
a slimy, creepy thing to be tossed away with a fling,
don't bid me come unto you if I can't forever cling.
Here is a heart for you—
mangled, trampled by transient bids.
Too shattered to seek another coupling,
too ill shaped for another grid.
Mold it as you will, pummel it to your conform—
purify, rectify, sanctify all.
I acquiesce to you.
But a covenant we must agree—
my heart to thee if thou can forever keep me.

—*Barbara Redfearn,* poet

# Inquiring Minds Want to Know

*"As long as one keeps searching the answers come."*
—Joan Baez

BLACK WOMEN LONG to understand black men. We want to know what drives black men's choices and decisions. What pleases them? What pisses them off? What draws them near? What pushes them away? Sisters want to know how best to love and support black men, how to get along with them, and how to make and keep them happy. We also wish we understood what forces cause so many of our men to go astray—romantically, socially, legally, and economically.

When a romantic relationship enters troubled waters or sinks women will often hold their sisterfriends hostage for days analyzing and dissecting the why, who, and what of it all. We particularly want to know why the man *we* love does what he does, behaves as he does, and treats us the way he does. We are baffled when men reject and leave us when all we offered them was our lavish love and support. Why, we wonder, do men talk right then walk left? How can some men treat love and relationships so casually, even irreverently, when for us love is what wakes us up in the morning?

Our need for understanding and answers increases exponentially when a man we love abandons the relationship. "What," a woman will ask herself, "went wrong? Why did he leave me? What's *wrong* with *me*?" Many even entertain the fantasy, even years later, that somehow if only they knew what broke they could fix it. The crazy in love even imagine they have the power to make another love them. Think the two Jennifers singing, *"I ain't going . . . and you're gonna love me!"* If only, some think, he'd give me another chance I could make him remember that he loves me and we belong together.

## DESPERATELY SEEKING ANSWERS

If we can't achieve reconciliation with the one we love, then we insist that, at the very least, we have a right to closure. In the absence of concrete facts it's not uncommon for women to get lost in their longing for answers to why a cherished relationship tanked. We insist that something from him will bring us closure. "Then I can move on," we moan. We forget that we can give *ourselves* closure simply by acknowledging and accepting what is—he's gone. It's over. Does it hurt? Yes. Do we wish things could be different? Sure we do. But do you seriously intend to put your life on hold until—which seldom happens—he hands you a satisfying reason for his change of heart? I hope not.

I've seen the need for "answers" immobilize intelligent, progressive women and keep once vibrant, passionate others from living vital, full lives. Not to mention, a woman's refusal to let go of her dream of happily ever after with one man can blind her to the love that abounds around her. Whenever we get stuck in the past, trapped in whyyyyyy, we block the blessings of the present moment. And so, we hope against hope, pine for understanding, and beg for closure from someone who simply doesn't give a damn anymore.

I'll admit, there are times when it's a smart, bold move to seek answers from The Departed. In fact, I'd say it's downright brave and bodacious. Plain and simple, it's Big Woman behavior. When an exit conversation with The Departed honors your authentic self and voice and therefore, grows your self-esteem and frees your spirit, then by all means make that call. I, however, caution you. If you're going to, check your motives before you push SEND. If you claim all you desire is closure, but you secretly hope the meeting will lead to reconciliation, think again. First, he will see right through you. You're hurting. You're afraid. You're vulnerable. You might even feel desperate. You're also transparent. Why? Because we are energy. The energy of your spirit will betray your speech. Why you really asked to see him will show up in your body language, your eyes, and your voice. If you want to get back together, tell him. Yes, tell the truth, to yourself, then to him. Honor your truth.

Big Woman behavior isn't sneaky and manipulative. Big Woman moves are bold and bodacious and honoring of self and others. They are above board. When we walk in our Big Woman heels, we can say what we need to say and do what we need to do and not be *attached* to the outcome.

Another thing, if any of your hidden agenda items include getting even, making him feel bad about leaving, making him jealous, making him hurt as much as you do, then prepare yourself for more hurt. In the throes of vindictive acts the ego will have us believe our retaliatory behavior will "show him." Don't believe it. It's a lie. When we hurt others we hurt ourselves, for what we do unto another we do unto ourselves. Deliberately hurting another person is like angrily smashing your vehicle into your neighbor's car. Sure, their car took a hit and is now banged up. But so is yours.

Here's another thing, be prepared to accept his truth. It's where he is. It may not make a bit of sense to you, but it is what it is. I happen to believe that when a man walks, he'd been moving toward the door long before he stopped calling. Let him go. Let me say it again: LET HIM GO! After you've made it abundantly clear that you'd like him to stay and he's still bent on leaving, LET HIM GO! Get up off your knees, dust your beautiful knees off, and turn toward the open door that starts the healing process, the one that leads to self-discovery and recovery. He's gone. You're still here. It's time to heal. Even if the relationship was brief, if your heart was in it, you have some healing to do. Get started.

Yes, it can be risky business to ask a man why he jumped ship because, as evidenced by his absence, clearly he no longer wants you. Consequently, the care of your heart is no longer a priority of his. That may sound harsh, and yet, it's true. If you've been dumped, it's your new reality. Facing the truth and accepting what is is what's going to heal you, not more denial.

I want to help you grow in self-acceptance and love. I want to assist you in reclaiming your life. You cannot do this as long as you're denying what is, no matter how painful it is.

A friend of mine recently broke up with a man who lavished her with trinkets, travel, and even a tummy tuck. She loved him. Then one day, a year into the relationship, he started behaving strangely. She knew something had changed. She did some investigating and learned he'd started seeing another woman while on business in another city. She asked him to end that liaison. He refused. Instead, he said it was okay if she dated and slept with other men.

She looked up from her cell phone at me, blinked her eyes, shrugged her shoulders, and calmly said, "I knew then he was no longer into me. A man who loves you doesn't want you sleeping with other men."

I sat looking at her in awe. As I stared back at her I asked myself, "Is she for real?" I doubt that I've ever seen a woman face reality so readily, so as a matter of course, without making herself small and insufficient, or making the man wrong for a decision that hurt her. I attribute her poise and quiet acceptance of what is to her spiritual beliefs and practices. My friend is spiritually grounded, lives from a knowing that life is abundant, that there is no lack anywhere, and that includes love and men. My friend knows that the Universe fulfills her every heart's desire, just like It had when she asked for and got this man, a man who could, and would, lavish her with attention and gifts. Yes, accepting what is begins the healing process. So long as we can't stomach the truth of what is we keep healing and a sense of wholeness at bay.

It takes mettle and a healthy dose of self-esteem to invite feedback from an ex. Suppose he accepts your invitation? What then? What if he tells you the truth, the straight-no-chaser, no-holds-barred-truth? What if he was just itching for the right time to tell you what a guy told me once, "You just aren't the woman I thought you were." What if he spits, "I just can't get pass the rolls of fat on your back." What if he confesses, "I'm holding out for the *full* package," like a Regular Joe told a stunned sisterfriend when she asked why was he holding back.

If you are forward enough to ask, he just might be shameless enough to answer. What if he confesses, "I found someone better"? Or the man who'd whispered in your ear, "You're the best thing that has ever happened to me" tells you, "I'm ready to settle down, to get married." As the words you had longed to hear spill from his lips it becomes abundantly clear from the tone of his voice that you're not the one about whom he speaks. And, as if he really expects you to be happy for him, he adds, "And I think I've met her!" In other words, you're good enough to bed but, uh, not quite good enough to wed. Then what? Where do you go from there? Is it to the kitchen for a sharp knife? Just kidding.

Well, asking why is too big of a risk for most women to imagine, much less, take. It's safer to not know why your love went away. Safer instead to fabricate a reason or two that suits the beaten and bruised and battered heart of a woman spurned.

## DOES IT RING TRUE?

> *"There is more hunger for love and*
> *appreciation in this world than for bread."*
> —Mother Teresa

Valerie and her nearly-a-year lover were supposed to go danc-ing on Friday night. He, however, forgot to call as promised. He apparently forgot to call on Saturday, Sunday, Monday, and Tuesday, too. Then he conveniently ignored her numerous calls and texts. Valerie was beside herself with anger and grief.

A man who I thought was committed to me had recently gone missing for a couple of days. I was stunned. Confused. Hurt. A host of sister and brother friends held my hand through that wrenching holiday weekend. So when I saw the pain in my new friend's face, I immediately offered my ear and support. Valerie is yet another reason why I'd experienced what I had; I could now minister to another hurting soul. Had a man not recently broken my heart, I might not have fully appreciated how deeply Valerie was hurting and how significant another's support would be to her healing. This is why we're here, you know, to pour into another person's life. Our misery is supposed to become our min-istry. After we heal, we get to assist others in their healing.

Okay, back to my friend. Valerie decided that she, at the very least, deserved an explanation. So she chose to pay this guy a visit to get it. "As a human being, I, at least, deserve to know what happened. That's the least amount of respect he owes me!" she yelled through the phone.

The next evening, Valerie drove over to Gavin's house. He wasn't home. She was on a mission so she waited for him on his doorstep. A little while later he pulls up, parks, and emerges from his car. As Gavin approached, Valerie spat, "Why haven't you called? You said you would call me on Friday! We were sup-posed to go out! Why didn't you answer any of my calls?"

Gavin had an explanation. "My buddy's mother died. She was like a mother to me. I was in mourning," he said sadly. That's why he was unable to call the woman he'd been sleeping with and allegedly loving for almost a year. He was too overwhelmed with grief to retrieve her number and push SEND on his cell phone.

Then he asked my friend, "Do you still want to be in a relationship with me?"

"I do," she answered softly.

"I was a wimp," she told me later. "When he asked me that, I wimped out, DeBora," she conceded. Yet she hadn't gone over there with hopes that the relationship would continue. Or so she told herself. She simply needed, for her own good, to confront him and speak up for herself.

Was Gavin in mourning? Maybe. Was he so messed up over the death of somebody else's mother that he couldn't punch SEND on his cell phone and connect with the woman he claimed mattered to him? Seriously, I doubt it. Does his story ring true to you?

Okay, now what? When a man's behavior—forget his words—screams, "I'm just not that into you!," what's a woman to do? Well, we have choices. We can accept the truth of the situation, even as it breaks our heart, gather ourselves together, and move forward without him. That's what self-respect encourages when someone no longer wants you. Or we can cling. Cling to denial. Cling to the fantasy that he's just confused and afraid of commitment but with enough love he'll come around. Cling to false hope. Cling to him. Cling to the lie that the problem is you, that there is something wrong with you, wrong with what you desire. Or we can accept what is, know this too shall pass and let the healing begin.

Once we make a choice that's out of alignment with our true self, our heart's deepest desires, our legitimate needs, the mind will always find justification for that decision. Valerie decided that it wasn't that Gavin wasn't his word when he didn't call, but her *needing* him to call that was the problem. It wasn't Gavin's failure to respond to her many attempts to connect, but her *need* for connection that was at fault. Thus, Valerie's new intention was to shrink her need for attention, love, and affection. Because, she concluded, "Sometimes I *can* be needy."

What do I know? Maybe my friend *is* emotionally needy. Maybe she isn't. Then again, perhaps her needs are healthy. Maybe it isn't the quality of my friend's needs that's problematic at all. Rather, she need only attract a man who wants to be with her in the way she desires to be in relationship. Maybe my friend need only to choose to be in a relationship with someone who is willing and able to connect with her on the level and to the degree that she is willing and able to connect. Then again, she has already found that in Gavin.

You see, we attract what we are, where we are—not what we claim we want. Gavin's inattentiveness, absence, inauthenticity, and lack of integrity mirrored something in Valerie. Valerie would not have tolerated his lies and neglect had she not felt deserving of this kind of treatment. You might ask, "Why do you say such a thing?" Well, not only did Valerie attract this man, but she took up with him. And even when the Universe offered her a chance to escape, she chose instead to stay.

We cannot tolerate for long people who are not emotionally and energetically compatible with us. Choosing a mate is like picking a dance partner. A master dancer isn't going to settle for an amateur, one who tramples her feet with his every move. Soon, she'll send her partner back to the wall from whence he came and reenter the market for a more compatible companion. One who is in sync with her. That's precisely how it is with relationships. Those we choose are the perfect match for who and where we are at any given point and time in our lives.

Here's where I'm going with this. Ladies, be ever so careful about a man who handles your heart callously, one who disregards your feelings, wants, and needs—needs you've made known to him, perhaps again and again. If you want to be treated like the precious jewel that you are, demand that men treat you that way. Don't compromise. Don't settle. Even if standing your ground means he'll leave you. Better he leave than you lose yourself, your dignity, and self-respect, right? I hope you agree.

I invite you to employ a litmus test that I use, one you undoubtedly have used, unconsciously if not consciously. When a man tells you something—after he has betrayed your trust—ask yourself this, "Does what he say ring true?" Well, *does* it? Does what he say feel and sound right to you? What is your gut telling you?

Humans were born with our very own radar detectors. This "device" detects lies, deceit, inconsistencies, and bullshit. It's our *intuition*. The intuition knows stuff that our minds don't know. The intuition is your friend. Tune in to it. Listen to it. Trust it. Rely on it. It won't steer you wrong. Not ever. Even if you decide to give someone the benefit of the doubt, don't discount what you know you know. Honor you enough to tell you the truth, even when others lie to you.

Years ago I went out with a man I respected for his professional savvy. We had big fun talking, laughing, and dancing into the night. We made a real connection. Or so I felt. As he left me at my door, I felt pretty certain that I would hear from this one again, and soon. Well, a significant amount of time passed. I didn't hear from him, which surprised and disappointed me. Finally he called. He had a splendid excuse, uh, reason, for why he was slow to reconnect. I listened with my whole self. I remember thinking aloud, "I don't know, but what you're saying just doesn't ring true." I don't recall his rebuttal, but that was pretty much it for me.

What I know is this: if a man isn't interested or he's insincere, sooner rather than later this will be evident. If we're wrong about him (not likely, since our intuition doesn't lie but people do), and he turns out to be what he purports to be, his future actions will support that fact. Nothing more ever happened between Mr. Happy Feet and me. Thankful, nonetheless, for that one exciting night and the early signs that I should move on solo, I did.

Years later, I bumped into Mr. Happy Feet. We talked. He had a confession. I was spot-on about that situation. Yes, he had lied to me. He'd gotten back with an old flame. It was a messy entanglement, he admitted; he didn't want me embroiled in it. So you see, Mr. Happy Feet did me a favor by not calling me right away. I really liked him. Had he called, chances are quite good that I would have stepped into a pile of mess. See, what we so often think is a bad thing happening *to* us actually is a good thing happening *for* us. Only it can sometimes take a while for us to realize this. However, we can train ourselves to look for the good in every situation even as things unfold. Trust me; good is there. You just have to get present to it.

Had I not obeyed the "YIELD" sign, I'm pretty sure I would have lived to regret it. Stay alert, ladies. If it doesn't ring true, yield! If necessary, stop! Take care of you. Just like a bus, another man is just over the bend.


## THE OLE BAIT AND SWITCH

*"Do not make a person your priority*
*while they make you an option."*
—Bernadette Greene

Generally speaking, reconciling with a man who you broke up with isn't wise. I know, I know. Sometimes a man will abandon a relationship only to realize it was the best thing that's ever happened to him. He makes a quick U-turn back to you, the jewel he'd foolishly discarded. Or you might dump a fellow only to discover he was The One, after all. It's seldom smart to reconcile because, whatever was broken, unless it has been repaired, well, it's still broken. Of course, there are exceptions to every rule.

And yet, too often women crawl back into the same old arms that pushed them away, and we do so without any signs of a change in his head and heart. Say he dumped you, now he's knocking at your door again. If he hasn't shown regret or remorse for hurting you, hasn't demonstrated a commitment to repairing the wreckage he caused, and you don't see a renewed commitment to making love work, why are you taking him back? That said, if you must take him back, just do it with your eyes wide open. Whatever you do, do it for the "right" reasons. That is, do it because you really love this man, not because you really hate being alone. Do it because he's seen the error of his ways and realizes how much he loves you, not because his new "situation" didn't work out as well as he hoped it would. The other woman didn't want him so much after all. Or, now, uh, he needs a place to stay.

Another caution. If an emotionally immature man discovers how much a woman desires a relationship with him, he may confuse your love and desire for a commitment for desperation. If he's also arrogant, he may think he's got you just where he wants you, under his control. Because he's an emotional juvenile, he's unable to distinguish a desperate, needy woman from an emotionally healthy woman who takes her commitments to heart, and thus, is deeply committed to making love work with him. Such an insecure man is inclined to abandon an emotionally intimidating woman because he's ill equipped to love in a mature and committed way. So, he loses a lot of good women.

A couple of days, weeks, or months later, after he's had some time to miss you and reflect on what he had, your phone will ring. Stay alert here. Where once you got, or so it seemed, a whole loaf of fresh baked 7-grain bread, now he's throwing you a bunch of white bread crumbs. This man isn't malicious; he's wounded. His unaddressed childhood wounds render him emotionally unstable. This doesn't mean he doesn't want you. It's just that he doesn't think he's good enough for you, that he can meet your expectations and high standards. He'd rather step off and spare himself the shame and feelings of failure than stay around to see himself as a failure in the eyes his woman. If the sex was good and plenty, rest assured, he'll be calling again. Only now he's looking to reduce you to a booty call girl.

Although some are, the wounded man-child isn't necessarily a playa. Nor is he interested in a harem. He, like you, desires connection, love, and companionship. Only he's not emotionally fit for the responsibility that comes with a serious, committed relationship.

Just when a woman's expectation for a deeper, more committed relationship mounts, the man-child finds a reason to take a long bathroom break. Then he starts to creep back. He's looking for a cracked side door; someplace where you're vulnerable. There's a knock at the door. It's him. It's a man, but not *your* man—which means you no longer have the right to hold him accountable for his words and actions. Now you're "just friends." Oh, but wait, there are benefits. His. He's now got a *friend with benefits*. This bait and switch demotes you to just another woman that he sleeps with. Meanwhile, he continues to get what he most wants, sex, while your desire and need for emotional closeness and connection within a committed relationship go unmet.

The BS is one of the oldest tricks in the man-child's love and relationship book. Why do men keep using it? Uh, because it frickin' works. And it works quite well. Shucks, I'm so versed on it because it's been used on me a time or two. Then I stopped handing men ready-made excuses for their immaturity, and started paying closer attention to what men do rather than what they say. If you fall for the ole BS, you only have you, your low self-esteem, and fear of being alone, to blame. Decide to think better of yourself, learn how to be alone, and you won't easily fall prey to the BS.

## MIND, BODY AND SPIRIT LISTENING

*Guard your heart above all else,*
*for it determines the course of your life.*
—Proverbs 4:23 (New Living Translation)

If, after reading the above, you still have the hots for your ex, here's what I hope you do if he comes a-calling. Listen not only with your needs and desires, such as the desire for connection and companionship—but fully engage your mind, spirit, *and* soul in your listening. If you're desperate and needy, well, you're a sitting duck for insincere men, players, and emotional invalids.

A desperate woman is a wounded woman, someone bent on filling up those empty places inside with something or someone. Like an old playa friend once told me, "A man can smell a desperate woman a mile away."

No worries though. Desperation need not be a permanent state. It can be healed. You have the power to overcome desperation and fear of being alone. I speak from experience, and in later chapters I'll share with you how I overcame desperation and my fear of being alone. But I digress. Let's get back to how to negotiate the getting back together terrain.

How can you tell if your ex wants *you*, not just your body? Pay attention. Listen. More than you talk. Listen as much for what he's *not* saying as to what he *is* saying. And please stop making it so easy for insincere men to bamboozle you. Don't spoon-feed him the words you'd like to hear. Shut your mouth and let him talk. You listen. Notice when he calls. Are too many of his calls close to bedtime? How does he suggest you spend time together? Is he too busy with work, friends, and family to do dinner and a movie but is more than willing to make time for a little somethin'-somethin', regardless of the time of day? Observe what he talks about, what he says he misses about you. If he hems and haws about the degree to which he's willing to commit, chances are very good that he's no longer offering a whole loaf of bread, but now is banking on you accepting his crumbs. If you desire the whole loaf, you also deserve it. Girl, get what you desire and deserve!

## WE TEACH MEN HOW TO TREAT US

Take your time. Don't settle for less than you want, for less than you're worth. If your intuition tells you something's not quite right, then something's not quite right. Trust me, when a woman falls back into a relationship with a man who doesn't honor, respect, and love her, she's setting herself up for a letdown. A BIG letdown and more pain. If he's the same man you left, or who left you, and it didn't work then, what makes you think it'll work this time around? It won't. Trust me. In no time, he, rather than his "representative," will show up and help you remember why it didn't work the first, second, or third time. You know the "representative," right? It's who this man appears to be, the person he wants you to believe that he is, not who he *really* is. Yes, it might take you some time to learn, but it's better to be alone, with peace of mind, dignity, and self-respect than to settle for a man who isn't worthy of you. Or a man who just isn't that into you.

Remember, we teach men how to treat us. If a man creeps, cheats, lies, leaves you in a lurch, makes you feel like you're still single because he's frequently missing in action, uses and abuses you, and you STAY with him, then know this: *you're* teaching him to treat you this way. Yes, you! Here's how you know this is so. Remember the jerk who you parted ways with who you later heard was with another woman that he treats like a queen? Well, he treats *her* that way because she commands that kind of treatment . . . and won't tolerate anything less.

A man's treatment of us is a reflection of what we think of ourselves. When a woman thinks highly of herself, she won't tolerate disregard, disrespect and neglect. Will some of this show up even in the best relationship? Probably. Let's not forget, all of us are wounded to varying degrees. We're works in progress. You know, however, if you're tolerating an abusive relationship or working through "common" relationship challenges that's natural to being in relationship with another soul.

The end of anything is also the beginning of something else, something fresh and new. A breakup opens a new chapter in your life. Despite the possibilities it offers, still it's natural if a big part of you resists this new phase.

Change, even when what you are currently experiencing is painful, is hard and scary. Even when change is sought, planned for, anticipated, or needed, it can be daunting. It's human to fear change because change takes us into the unknown, uncharted waters. People fear what they don't know and can't plan for. Besides, one never knows until she's in those waters whether she's equipped to successfully navigate them. We wonder, will I sink or swim? This terror of the unknown is the reason so many people stay in toxic, violent, or just plain unsatisfying relationships. Driven by fear, we will so often choose a known discontent over the sweet possibility of peace and happiness.

## IT'S YOUR PITY PARTY YOU CAN CRY IF...

Whatever you do, be loving and compassionate with yourself during this process. Know this, it's okay to be scared. Crying is not only permitted, it's highly encouraged. Tears are cleansing and strengthening and healing. Resentment, anger, blame, hurt, fear—emotions that become toxic when unacknowledged and left to fester—are released through our tears. Reach out to loving, supportive family and friends. Treat yourself with loving care. Avoid the temptation to rush the healing process. Seek support. Remember, you're not alone. God is ever-present. Turn within to the all-loving, all-knowing, everywhere-present Power. It will keep you. You are supported also by family and friends— those who love you no matter what.

While your heart works to mend itself, tend to your body and spirit with warm baths, rest, prayer, meditation, journaling, sunshine, nature walks, nourishing foods, fresh water, touch, massage, fresh flowers, movement, soul music, time and conversation with loved ones. It's your party, you can cry if you want to. And do anything else that makes you feel loved and cared for. Never mind that someone leaving you seems to say, "You're not worth my time, not deserving of my love." You *are* loved. You *are* worthy. Treat yourself that way; give you the love and care you so deserve. Try not to, however, hang out at those pity parties you throw too long. Cry. Then be done with it. Turn your attention on what's good and sweet in your life, and be grateful for them.

There is a brilliant light at the end of the tunnel. Perhaps right now you can't imagine such a place, where light and love shine forth. But there *is* such a place, I promise you. And if you stay the course, you will get there.

## CELEBRATE YOUR SINGLENESS

In time, you might even consider what's possible for you as a single woman. Perhaps you will rethink this thing we women so dread, living single, and see the advantages it can afford you. Even in our couple-obsessed culture, there's no shame in being single. In fact, the single life does have its advantages and pleasures and delights. Unimaginable adventures await the woman who, rather than feeling less- than because of her single status, embraces and enjoys it. Stand in it. Take pride in it. Celebrate it.

Being single is neither good nor bad. It just is. It's a natural and necessary chapter in a woman's life. It's not a less-than place. You need not apologize for being there either. Like I once did. Until I realized I was whole and complete unto myself. The single life, just like partnership, brings both annoyances and adventures. Your perception of it will determine which of these create your dominant experience. Like my friend LaRue is known to enthusiastically exclaim, no matter the situation, "DeBora! Since you're making it up anyway! Why. Not. Make. Up. Something. That. EMPOWERS. You?" Since every woman is destined to be single at some juncture in her life, even if she were to marry and remain so for fifty years, while you're not hitched why not live richly, fully, and passionately on purpose? It's your choice. A choice you are fully equipped to make.

Sure, being in a juicy, loving relationship with a man brings a certain sweetness to a woman's life. And it's natural for you to desire that for yourself. And yet, traveling solo has benefits that the coupled life doesn't afford you.

When some women are in a relationship, it's not uncommon for them to put their dreams on hold while they "take care" of their man. Meanwhile, their life languishes from a lack of attention. So, what better time is there to forge a new path than when you're suddenly single? With no one else to consider in your decision-making, and no one else expecting any of your time and attention, this phase of a woman's life can be whatever *she* alone chooses to make it. It can be spectacular!

Consider this, while you're single you could start that business you've been fantasizing about. You could relocate to a new city. You could pour yourself into writing that book. You could set out on an "Eat. Pray. Love" experience and globetrot across continents. You could do an African safari, return to school, spend more quality time with your children and grandchildren, date without demands, resurrect a hobby, rediscover a passion that once brought you deep joy, get in optimal shape, read those books you've been putting off, change careers, spend your money as you please, even reinvent yourself. To paraphrase a recently happily divorced professor, you can buy another loaf of bread even though there's already bread in the refrigerator! You're single, you can do what you damn well please!

## YOU ARE AS HAPPY AS YOU CHOOSE TO BE

Okay, even after reading all my splendid suggestions on how to rock the single life, if you're still not convinced that singleness can be a plus, fine. At every moment, we choose whether to be happy or miserable. Just know that if you're miserable, you are choosing that. To choose to despise your life, just as it is, gets you no closer to the life you desire. In fact, the choice to embrace, and even celebrate, your single life actually increases your mate manifesting powers, because happiness is *attractive*.

No one else can complete us. No one else can love us so thoroughly that we need not love ourselves. So long as a woman thinks she needs a man or relationship to make her happy, to make her feel whole and complete, she kills her chances of attracting a healthy man into her life. Here's why. Healthy men don't volunteer to babysit seemingly grown people just to be in a relationship. Emotionally, mentally, psychologically healthy individuals don't rescue broken people so they can feel needed.

Real love isn't about need; it's about want and desire and companionship. Real love is about finding a playmate—someone who enhances the adventure of life.

Need creates a parent-child dynamic. When we take full responsibility for ourselves, for our experiences, for our feelings and wounds, and do the necessary work that makes us feel loved *even when we're not in a relationship,* then we are a powerful magnet for all kinds of good stuff, like men, opportunities, and money. You see, we teach men how to love us by the way we love ourselves.

If you're single but desire to attract a quality man, then stand proudly in your singleness. Fall madly in love with you and your life. Take good care of you and your life. If you haven't already done so, find your passion and purpose and live them!

From experience, I can tell you this: *A passionate, purposeful woman is a man magnet.* When a woman is happy with herself and her life, she leaves neediness and clinginess behind. Neediness repels quality men. While happiness, confidence and a lightness of being magnetize good men to you. Remember, you're a woman—magnificent, magical, magnetic. Live. Laugh. Dance. Play. Love. And quality men will flock to you.

# ℋerstory of love lost

*"Some people come into our lives and quickly go.*
*Some stay for a while and leave footprints on our heart,*
*and we are never, ever the same."*
—Anon

Do you remember your first true love? Next to the relationship that a girl enjoys—or endures—with her father, whether he was present or absent, the relationship that she has with her first true love powerfully shapes her life and expectations of future relationships with men. Zee bares her soul in this tender story about her first true love.

**BY ZEE**

I got pregnant, again, at age nineteen, by a handsome black Muslim lieutenant. I met him in a club I frequented that was located at Gwynn Oak and Liberty Heights. I loved this little spot. The music was good. The atmosphere was electric but cozy. One night Ricky walked through the door. It was like Billy Dee and Diana Ross in the movie *Lady Sings the Blues*. Remember how Lady Day looked at Billy Dee's character, Louis McKay, then fell to her knees? Well, that was me and Ricky. He was my first true love. To this day, he still is. And yet, as much love and happiness as we shared, that year I got pregnant turned my dream world into a nightmare.

I was thrilled to be having the baby of the man I loved so dearly. He wanted, however, to maintain his status as a

Nation of Islam lieutenant, so I gave in to having yet another baby sucked from my womb. Only this time, I knew what I was doing. I had agreed with Ricky that this was the best thing for us; at least, that's what I told myself. But inside, I was hurting so much. I wanted to have Ricky's baby. I sensed that I was carrying a boy; it would look just like his father, dark and handsome.

I was too far along to have an abortion in Baltimore so we drove to a clinic in Washington, D.C. I went through all the preliminary questions, including, "Do you want to go through with this?" I nodded my head up and down as I said yes in a whisper—while inside, to myself, I was screaming frantically—"Well, hell no, I don't want to do this! But what can I do?"

A few hours later I awoke to a chorus of moans and groans. I opened my eyes and looked around. I was in a room filled with women moaning in pain, echoing the pain I was feeling. Was it the physical agony that we were giving voice to or was it the emptiness and guilt we felt from knowing we'd discarded our babies that were finding an outlet? I believe it was a combination of the two. At least, for me it was.

We drove back to Baltimore in silence. He held my hand, which helped a little but not much. I wanted so badly to cry, but I knew I had to be strong. I didn't want him to feel bad about what we had just done. (Here I am again protecting someone else while overlooking my own needs.)

Again, I found myself sneaking into the house and up the stairs to my room, my safe haven, where I cried until there were no more tears to cry and the physical pain had eased. And yet, the mental, emotional, and spiritual despair stayed with me for years. Not surprisingly, things were never the same between Ricky and me. He didn't come around as much as he used to. He claimed it was because he was busy with school.

One Friday night, a little more than a month after the abortion, I cooked Ricky's favorite meal—Whiting, brown rice, and broccoli. Then I waited anxiously to see him, to again feel his strong arms around me. A knock came to my door. I went to it. Ricky stood there, outside in the cold air, motionless. On his face was a look that I shall never forget, and from his mouth came words I shall always remember. "I met someone, a girl in my class. I won't be coming back," he said. The tears—my tears—started to flow. I got nauseated, my stomach burned, I felt faint.

"Ricky," I begged, "don't leave me, don't leave me, Ricky." In silence he turned on his heels and walked down the steps and into the car of the woman who would later become his wife.

I stood there dumbfounded, breathless, and broken-hearted. The pain was worst than any physical pain I had ever experienced, including the abortion. It ran deeper and with more intensity. My love had walked out of my life. The love who I knew would one day be my husband had left me. Hadn't we talked about marriage? I had imagined it over and over again; one day I would be this man's wife. The love I'd given up a baby for, so he could save face and his job in the mosque, had left me. My love, my sweet precious love was gone. My life was over. What else was there for me to live for? What had I done? What happened? How could the man who passionately proclaimed, "I love you" just walk away from me without even an explanation, with little or no emotion?

I began to wonder if he'd been seeing this woman before the abortion, and if that was really the reason for him telling me, "We can't keep this baby." Could he really be so cruel? Who was this woman anyway? What did she have that I didn't have? How could she take my man, my life, my love? Tears of anger, rage, pity, hatred, and love came like a rolling river. Yes, I still loved him. I have never understood how life could be so cruel, especially to one so young. All I ever wanted was to love and be loved.

Years have gone by, and I have never seen or heard from Ricky. I think of him often. I still see his face and feel him. He was, and still is, my true love. Ours was a bittersweet romance that will live in my heart for a lifetime.

# Herstory of being played

*"Women might be able to fake orgasms.
But men can fake whole relationships."*
—Sharon Stone

*"Tell me who I have to be to get some reciprocity?"*
—Lauryn Hill

**AZYA MAXTON,** author of *Goddess 'n the Game*,
performance artist, poet, and educator, shares her story
of being played.

Tariq was a wonderful friend TO me throughout my freshman and sophomore years at Clark Atlanta. He helped
me through a pregnancy scare with my ex and taught me
how to deal with life's little blows in mature ways. Tariq
was from Brooklyn, and I admired him for his combination of intelligence and street smarts. When I complained
about a friend not paying me back on a ten-dollar loan,
Tariq said, "Cool, you never have to worry about loaning
him money again." End of story. Tariq also taught me the
motto I have learned to live by when it comes to cutting people off: "When you see them, it's Hi and Hello,
but they aren't anybody you want to conjugate your
verbs with."

Tariq and I could talk about anything. We spent
hours on end talking about philosophy, religion, and politics, but our favorite subject was relationships. Sometimes

we would talk on the phone for hours about my latest man problem or Tariq's issues with women.

At the end of our sophomore year I found it more convenient to spend late nights using Tariq's laptop to finish end-of-the-semester papers than to go to the library. If it got too late I would just stay the night with him in the boarding house on Matthews Street, which was walking distance to the Communications Building where I had all of my classes. Spending all of this time together I eventually found myself falling in love with my best friend. For a while I didn't tell him for fear that it would ruin our relationship. But on the morning of the last day of classes, after spending another late night struggling with a final paper, I awoke to Tariq's caress. I didn't want to say anything that might ruin the moment so I allowed him to make love to me without protest. When it was over I got up to shower as usual and headed for class feeling confused yet elated.

That night I arranged to meet Tariq at my apartment to talk about what the morning's events meant. With a strong breeze blowing through the partially open window we laid on my futon and pondered the new dynamic of our friendship.

"Tariq, do you find it the least bit odd that we haven't even kissed?" I asked.

"Yeah," he responded in his typical nonchalant manner, "we should probably do that." We leaned toward each other, our lips touched, and thunder struck. No. For real. There was a storm brewing outside, *and* I was definitely in love with my best friend.

At first, Tariq and I were closer than ever. The clearest memory I have of the depth of our love is that of pasta. I was working at city hall and had gone to lunch at a res-

taurant across the street called *Eats*. I had some slammin'
spinach tortellini with marinara and pesto sauce. It was so
good that I wanted to eat it all on the spot, but I found
myself wanting to share something this special with Tariq.
So I quickly wrapped up half of my lunch and decided to
take it to him after work.

When I arrived at his boarding house Tariq was sleeping, so I left the tortellini with his housemate and headed
home. A couple of hours later Tariq showed up at my
apartment. As I opened the door he kissed me on my fore-
head. He had been so impressed with my offering that he
caught the bus over just to thank me.

I used to tell Tariq that he was the best lover I had ever
had, because he was the only one I had ever truly loved.
Sometime during our sophomore year Tariq got deeply
involved with the Rasta faith, and during a particularly intense early evening lovemaking session I cried out for Jah
like a convert inspired by a righteous orgasm. But somehow, as the physical side of our relationship grew stronger,
the mental side suffered neglect.

In August, Tariq went away to visit some family. On
the afternoon of his return I picked him up at the pool
where he worked as a lifeguard. A feeling of frustration
overcame me as I was driving home, and I began to cry
for no apparent reason. When Tariq asked me what was
wrong I told him I didn't know. After searching for nearly
five minutes for words to suit my emotions, I realized
them and shared: *I don't trust you anymore.* We rode the
rest of the way to Tariq's boarding house in silence.

I don't know what it was that made me lose faith in
my best friend/boyfriend, probably woman's intuition, but
Tariq called me when I got home and told me that if I didn't

trust him I should "probably go with that." I played Lauryn Hill's *Ex-factor* a thousand times on repeat that night and cried myself to sleep. "*And when I try to walk away, you hurt yourself to make me stay. This is crazy, this is crazy.*"

In January of the next year, almost six months after our breakup, Tariq and I got back together. After reestablishing our fragile friendship, a road trip rekindled the romance. It was the beginning of Christmas break, and I was going to my grandmother's funeral in Cincinnati. Tariq had relatives in Ohio that he was going to visit as well so I asked him to ride with me.

My father telling me that my grandmother had died was the first time we had talked in months. I had stopped speaking to him after he refused to put me on his car insurance when a friend totaled my car, jacking my mother's rates up sky high.

In addition to losing my car and my close relationship with my father, my roommate Ricki had moved her crazy boyfriend, Hakim, back into our apartment. Even after I had put them out. She was pregnant, had quit her job, and I was paying all of the bills and trying to keep my head above water. I'd tried evicting them both. I'd even changed the locks, but Georgia law stated that if her name was on the lease I had to give her thirty days' notice before kicking her out. And if Hakim was her company, he could stay too, even if he did pee in bottles and leave the heat on in their room all day.

I was beyond vulnerable, and Tariq was still a good friend and listener. When things got really crazy at my place, I started spending most of my time at his. I do remember spending Valentine's Day at my place that year. After finding chocolates and a big singing gorilla on the bed in Tariq's room, I'd told him to get dressed up because we were going somewhere.

When he arrived at my apartment a few hours later, I changed into a slip dress that was really an undergarment to a dress I'd worn to coronation that year. I'd also made spaghetti, salad, and garlic bread, which I served with a cheap white wine on a blue plastic dinner set I'd purchased at Walmart.

On my futon Tariq found a six-pack of his favorite beer, Guinness, and a six-pack of Dutch Master blunts. I also remember being shocked when Ricki and Hakim interrupted our meal that night. For some reason I thought they were gone. Although Hakim was repeatedly disrespectful to me in my own house, and we argued constantly, he never broke bad when Tariq was around. My man definitely had that "I am not to be played with" type of energy.

When I was finally able to scrape up enough money between the three members of my immediate family to pay all of the late fees Ricki and Hakim had accrued and break my lease that March, Tariq helped me move. He didn't stay the night though. I recall being very much alone in that new studio before Jai came by with a sub and an offer to help set up my stereo, and a few bits of furniture. I'm not sure where Tariq was that night, but our visitations became less frequent as spring approached.

Then, a few days before my twenty-first birthday, Tariq revealed that although he had tried, he just could not bring himself to love me as much as I loved him. I replayed all of the if-only scenarios in my mind, trying to figure out where we went wrong. I recalled the day, while riding in the car a few weeks back, that I had asked Tariq,

"Baby, what do you want from me?"

"I want you to be more conscious," he answered, "and I want you to lose weight." Then he wisely added, "But you're already doing that."

"Conscious?" I thought to myself, *Negro, I'm breathing, ain't I? I know I'm black. I know I'm a woman. And I know I'm in love with your ass. But I guess since I'm not sporting an Ethiopian flag and a head wrap while quoting Bible verses, that's not conscious enough for you.* I didn't say any of this, of course, but I know now that this was the beginning of my revelation that who I was would never be good enough for the man whose children I dreamed of raising.

Tariq's ultimate goal was to open a school in Africa that would de-Americanize "colonized" blacks and live on a weed farm. Meanwhile, I was busy chasing my childhood dream of working in Hollywood. Tariq and I were both too stubborn to make any sort of compromise that would have allowed those two worlds to coexist, and so, my former best friend made the mature decision to let me go. He undoubtedly accurately sensed that the depth of my love for him might lead me to abandon my dream. The last thing he needed was some bitter would-be actress smoking up all his crop in a desperate attempt to drown out the could-have-beens.

Although I admired Tariq for his honesty, being in love with someone who does not love you back hurts like hell. I vowed never to allow myself to be hurt that deeply again. But, before I could pass go, I was back in the game.

So, er, um . . . my editor wanted me to address how I felt about Tariq's wanting me to lose weight. I wanted to lose weight too. Let's just say a recurring theme in my life's story is that, like other women raised on fairy tales where beauty is deemed the most important virtue, I find it natural to feel inadequate when your aesthetics are in any way unappealing to your partner. That is an eloquent and articulate way of saying, I felt like shit!

## playing myself

i revel in your essence
rebel in your presence
disguising the evidence
surprisingly relevant
my feelings for you
cherish dealings with you
hiding my face while i hang
on each word
play it back in my mind
won't repeat what i've heard
cause the meaning is lost
to those i call friends
keeping it real—
now a game of pretend
feigning confidence
in the face of rejection
false revelations
won't reveal my affection
though i treat you like a brother
fantasize you're my lover
taint my sisterly thoughts
would have sworn i was caught
when jealous eyes
focused on her hug
gotta maintain control
my most difficult role
playing myself
not in love.

—*Ayza Maxton*

# Boy Meets Girl

*"I know we just met, but, baby, could you love me
quuuiccckly, quuuiccckly. I want you to love me like
you know the world is about to ennnd, baby, quuuiccckly."*
—John Legend

TWO PEOPLE MEET. There's a spark. They call, text, and e-mail back and forth. A face-to-face rendezvous follows—maybe lunch, dinner, dancing or a movie. If sparks continue to fly, they get together again. Love is in the air. Later, or maybe sooner, they have sex. Experts say the infatuation phase of new love averages about two years. From my experience and observation, it appears to be closer to three to six months. In any event, once lovers' clothes end up on the floor, something starts to happen to their eyesight. Well, uh, it gets clearer. What once were tolerable, even adorable, quirks can suddenly mushroom into irritants, fatal flaws, even relationship deal breakers. What he once thought cute, so he let it slide, he now feels a need to point out. A new man's insistence upon singing out of tune at the breakfast table and chewing with his mouth open can abruptly mature into perfectly legitimate reasons to reconsider the whole thing. Like that, what looked so promising is finished. In the words of singer Chrisette Michele, you're *"done, done, done . . ."*

Sometimes a woman meets a mouth-watering hunk of a man for which the very sight of him makes her quiver. She's so smitten by him that she's sure he must feel as she does. Well, uh, but he doesn't. His libido is aroused, nothing more. She, however, is so into him that she doesn't notice that after sex she's the only one doing *all* the calling and *all* the asking, "Want to get together later?"

Women are legendary for building utopian relationships that exist only in their heads. For such a woman, it might not occur to her that sex in no way means a man has genuine feelings of love and affection for her. To her credit, though, one day she awakes. She sees, at last, that she was nothing more than a thing of pleasure to her "Prince Charming." She was just something to do. Someone to keep him warm on cold, lonely nights. Once she has awakened, she finds the strength and courage to let go and move on with her head up.

What about this scenario: A brother is in hot pursuit of you. He's sexy, charming, financially fit, attentive, available, and easy on the eyes. There's just one little problem. There's no energy, no spark. *You* ain't feelin' *him*. Not really. You want to, but you aren't. Your feelings, to be precise, are room temperature. A chilly room. You could take him or leave him. Well, what woman hasn't been there? C'mon, admit it. Just because a man looks real good on paper doesn't mean he's your Mr. Right. He's somebody's Mr. Right, just not yours. This can feel like such a misfortune, because this man seems to have everything you're looking for in a mate. Everything but that somethin'-somethin' that gets your juices flowing.

Every sister knows the challenges of finding Mr. Right, right? Pause. Now exhale.

Let me say a couple of things about the good black man shortage. There are more than 1.5 million black men in America's jails and prisons. A percentage of brothers prefer white women, particularly after they have achieved a degree of financial success.

Then there are the drug-and alcohol-addicted brothers. And let's not forget brothers on the Down Low. Oh, don't believe the hype that sisters have written these brothers off. They haven't. I worked three-and-a-half years providing legal advice and coaching to ex-offenders and recovering addicts and alcoholics. I saw with my own eyes how strong, accomplished black women—mothers, wives, lovers—stood by these men. And yet, generally speaking, when successful sisters think about marriage and children, it is not these men about which they think.

Okay, I'll admit what I hate to admit: there *is* a shortage of good, marriageable black men. However, I refuse to believe or accept that there are NO *available* good black men still roaming the planet. A man need not drive a new Lexus, work in corporate America, make six-figures, own his own condo, and be at least six feet, two inches tall to be deemed "good." A man who works in construction, takes care of his children, drives a hoopty, has a good heart, is kind to humans and animals, is who he professes to be, is spiritually grounded, respects women and loves children, is his word and is willing to be held accountable for his deeds, is a good man in my book.

What do you believe? And are your beliefs empowering or disempowering? Does it empower you to believe there are no more good black men in circulation? Does it feel good and right to believe this? If it doesn't, why must you persist in believing this?

We choose our beliefs and thoughts. Our lives are created by the thoughts we choose to think. Our thoughts and beliefs create our experiences. Scarcity thinking creates scarcity. Just because your best friend believes all the good brothers are married or gay, doesn't mean you have to believe those myths. You can stop tuning in to that same old song, "There's a shortage of good black men, and I'll always be alone . . . la la la la la" and write your own song. Why not affirm, "There is a right and perfect man for me." What we think about we bring about. What we think is true for us, IS true for us, individually and collectively.

The more we entertain the thought, "all the good men are gone," the more we'll attract "bad" men. We'll go where good men are scarce. Hang out in places where good men don't frequent. Surround ourselves with men we deem unfit for partnership and marriage. All the while believing that's just the way it is, when in reality, we're creating our experience.

I'll go even further and say the more sisters are convinced that there's a scarcity of good black men, the more there will be a scarcity. One time I told a sisterfriend of mine about a handsome, successful brother I was going out with. Her first question was, "What's wrong with him?" Her question troubled me. Because he was single there had to be something wrong with the man? Puhlease! If you believe a good catch is too good to be true, then, well, that will be your experience. Effectively, my sisterfriend was saying all the good brothers are taken. If he's single and available, he's no good, per her thinking. Well, she's left herself no chance of attracting a good, available brother. She may as well resign herself to being alone or being with only losers. She disempowers herself but blames her circumstances on the dearth of men.

Sisters who choose not to believe in scarcity in love don't experience lack and scarcity. Their dating calendar stays full. You know these sisters. Some of them work with you.

We're powerful, creative beings. Our thoughts create our universe. Our individual and collective belief in lack and scarcity create more of what we say we don't want—lack and scarcity in love and companionship. Choose to see abundance, in everything, including love and relationships.

Okay, if you're not interested in a committed relationship with a man, no problem. People meet for an assortment of reasons. He isn't your Mr. Right. To put it more accurately, he's not your partner or husband. He, however, could be the man that has come to help you remember you're a delectable and desirable woman. He could be the man to help you recall what it feels like to be adored, loved, and respected just because you deserve it. He could be the man to help you better understand the male mind, so when your beloved does appear, you'll be better equipped to love and support him. He could be the man to provide that delicious male energy that women naturally crave in their life.

Or how about this, he could have come into your life so that *you* might grow and expand him with your wisdom, love, and support. Every man serves a purpose in your life. Appreciate them.

## WHY HE BREAKS UP WITH YOU

I did an unscientific poll of a few brothers to find out what caused *them* to leave a relationship. In sum, they said:

- I caught her dirty, i.e., cheating
- She wanted to wear the pants in the relationship
- She stopped having sex with me
- She was a drama queen
- She was crazy
- She let herself go

Men leave relationships for many reasons. The reasons given above are not only obvious, but all, interestingly, point to the woman as the problem. But both women and men leave and avoid getting into relationships not simply because the other person isn't a good fit; they also do so because of where they are emotionally and financially and how they feel about themselves.

Below, I note additional reasons why, I believe, men leave or avoid committing to a woman:

- He has low self-esteem and doesn't feel he brings enough to the table
- His insecurities and feelings of inadequacy repel women
- He is needy; i.e., he needs more attention, affection, and assurance than one woman can provide

- He thinks she's "too" independent and self-reliant
- He's intimidated by her achievements, aspirations, high standards, expectations
- He fears she wants and needs more than he can provide
- He's doesn't want to do what's required to make a relationship work
- He was never really committed anyway (translation: he was a player, so he was playing)
- He fears commitment and responsibility
- He subscribes to the edict that "less is better," (translation: he needs to feel superior, but couldn't and being his woman's equal makes him feel inferior)

## WHY YOU BREAK UP WITH HIM

Remember, my inspiration for writing this book came from my friend Vickie's experience with being dumped. Over the years as I've talked with women and men about breakups, while gathering information about why men leave one beautiful mocha-colored, thirty-something-year-old sister told me that she's never been left by a man. "How could that be?" I wondered out loud.

"Well, I leave *them*. I'm always the one to leave," she said rather proudly. She admitted that she was persnickety about her men. She ended one relationship because she didn't like the way the guy sang off-key at the breakfast table. Her standards were impossibly high. That is, her tolerance for imperfection, quirks, flaws, and shortcomings was incredibly low. By any emotionally healthy person's standards, her standards were unreasonable. Consequently, her relationships had a three-to six-month expiration date.

I could relate to Nicole. There was a time when I'd jump ship in a New York second. As soon as my fear of abandonment reared its unsightly head I'd leave my beloved before he could leave me. Like I once did, Nicole wrestled with fear of abandonment. People who fear abandonment will often nitpick people to death, especially potential mates, until they find some "justification" for distancing themselves.

In *Love Addicted*, I shared how I dumped Chance, a man I was madly in love with, because I was certain he was going to leave me. Had he given me reason to believe he wanted out? No, he hadn't. My fearful self was simply convinced that once this smart, handsome man saw how flawed and damaged I was, he would leave me. The woman fearful of abandonment will often leave her relationships to prevent being left.

Of course, fear of abandonment isn't what causes all black women to leave a relationship. Just like men, women leave relationships for a multitude of reasons. Let me reiterate, when I say "leave," that also includes choosing not to enter into a committed relationship with a man, someone who may, at first glance, seem like a keeper. You've gone out a time or two, perhaps even slept together, but you soon decide he's just not doing it for you. He sees possibility; you see problems.

## NICE GUYS FINISH LAST

Many women love bad boys. Here's why:

- Women secretly like danger. Bad boys embody danger. It oozes from their muscles and pores.
- Bad boys make a woman *want* to be good to them, want to do what they want them to do; that is, they *inspire* a woman to give in to them.
- Women are nurturers. Women want to take care of the bad boy. Or tame him. Probably a bit of both.
- The woman who adores men love the masculine energy, bad boys showcase and exploit their masculinity in the way that they walk and talk.
- Women like to see, feel, and experience a man's strength

and maleness. In a man's presence we want to feel more like a woman. The more masculine energy a man exudes, the more feminine a woman feels. Bad boys are masculine.

- Bad boys are skilled at "talking dirty."
- Bad boys can be very vocal and demonstrative about their appreciation of the female anatomy. Even with their eyes a woman can hear them say, "Damn baby! You look gooood!"
- Bad boys can be elusive, emotionally. Women enjoy a challenge. Women like having to use their womanly wiles from time to time to get a man to buckle.
- Bad boys are FUN! Shucks, sometimes a girl just wanna have fun.
- Bad boys are raw. Raw can be sexy.
- Bad boys have swag. What is swag? Swag is confidence that borders on cockiness with a dab of aggression thrown in for good measure. The opposite of swag is timid. I don't know a woman alive who gets turned on by timidity in a man.
- Bad boys got flava. They sport their unique style, whether the world approves or not.
- With a bad boy a woman feels safe and protected, like if something crazy jumped off when they're out and about he'll take care of bizness.
- Last, but certainly not least, bad boys "promise" a woman she'll be satisfied in bed. No, it's not that they brag about it. It's in their swag. A man's swag tells a woman, "*If you ever let me touch you, I'll rock your world.*" Yes, sex is *that* powerful and compelling . . . as if you didn't know that.

This isn't an exhaustive list. But it should give the nice guy some insight into why women fall for bad boys . . . again and again.

Now, let me be clear. What some men call a nice guy is simply a self-absorbed, humorless, much too serious fella who lacks confidence in his masculinity and doesn't understand women. That said, *some* men who have spent a lot of years studying and working their way up the corporate ladder fall into the nice guy category. When bad boys were studying women and learning ways to get in their heads and please them in bed, the nice guy was studying business administration and computer technology. Consequently, the nice guy tends to be at a disadvantage when it comes to getting and keeping a woman interested in him.

In any event, here's why I say nice guys finish last:

- Nice guys live in their heads too much, rather than their senses, heart, and soul.
- Nice guys don't know when to ask permission and when to just take charge.
- Nice guys try too hard to please. That turns women off.
- Nice guys are generally FUN impaired.
- Nice guys believe too much of what women say about what we want. We lie, to ourselves, and to others about what we want. On paper, women want one kind of man. Meanwhile, in real life they choose very differently. Not always deliberately or knowingly do women lie. But women lie because we're not always ready to tell a man how we really feel. Plus women want men to intuit a lot of stuff. I know it doesn't make sense. But love and matters of the heart don't make much sense either.
- Nice guys aren›t mysterious or dangerous. Women like both.
- Nice guys talk too much about some things and too little about other things; like too much about themselves and their jobs and not enough about the woman, how delectable and fine she is.
- Even strong, independent, powerful women want to be swept off their feet and ravished in the bedroom. Women don't see a nice guy pulling such a feat off.

Like I said, all «nice guys» aren›t nice. That is, some so-called nice guys are educated, degreed, self-absorbed, arrogant, disrespectful bores who only label themselves nice guys because they need an excuse for why they›re not fairing so well with the ladies. By the way, real nice guys, once they tweak a few things that tend to land them in the dreaded «friend zone» can move to the head of the line with more mature women. After women have had their fill of bad boys.

Oh, and all bad boys aren›t all bad. Some bad boys are good boys in disguise. Yep, these guys wear bad boy gear, attitudes, postures and gestures because being bad is cool, and women like it. Other bad boys have a «come to Jesus» experience or just grow tired of their womanizing, thuggish, criminal ways and finally settle down. If they›re not all worn out from "the game" and still got swag left some woman will want them.

Women favor bad boys, partially, because of Hollywood. American movies glorify the bad boy. Think the parts portrayed by Will Smith, Tom Cruise, Brad Pitt, Harrison Ford, Jamie Foxx, Samuel L. Jackson and more and more, Denzel Washington. Women also love beautiful men like Idris Elba and Hill Harper. Though these men are often cast as good guys, because of their cool, masculinity, sex appeal, confidence and edginess they would most definitely receive the "Swag Award," if there were such a thing. For the record, a good man is not to be mistaken for the nice guy. They are two entirely different species.

The bad boy is the tough, confident man who goes after what he wants, accomplishes the impossible mission and ends up rich and famous, or at least celebrated. Bad boys do what they gotta do, by any means necessary. A do-what-you-gotta-do approach to life is a quality that women admire in a man. The admirable man gets and keeps the woman.

## OTHER REASONS WOMEN LEAVE

He wears the wrong kinds of shoes. He's got bad credit. He has no credit. He's has no vision or direction for his life. He's not on her level. He's out of her league. He's married. He's single, and she prefers married men. He has too many kids. He's got baby mama drama. Her family and friends don't like him. He cheated. He's dishonest. He's a liar. He's untrustworthy. He has poor personal hygiene. His "whatsaname" is small. His "whatsaname" is too big. He's boring. He's shallow. He's an "adult baby." He's ugly. He's pretty. He's effeminate. He's an emotional vampire. He's on the down low. He's emotionally unavailable. He has no BS, DDS, MD, JD, or MA at the end of his name. He's intellectually challenged. He's emotionally immature. He's a mama's boy. He's crazy. He's lazy. He's controlling. He won't communicate. He doesn't drive the right car. He's a player. He's a bad boy. He's a nice guy. He's verbally abusive. He's weak. He's physically abusive. He doesn't go to church. He goes to church. He's not a Christian. He's a Bible-toting, fire-and-brimstone Christian. He's not spiritual. He's broke.

The list continues. Here are more examples: He's not a pretty boy. He's prettier than her. He won't leave his wife. He won't dump his girlfriend. He's unreliable. He lacks integrity. He's doesn't know he way around the female anatomy. He's on drugs. He drinks too much. He's a workaholic. He's got no job. He has no sense of humor. He chews with his mouth open. He slaughters the English language. He can't/won't commit. He won't put a ring on it. He's a wimp. He's a thug. He's emotional high-maintenance. He doesn't own a car. He's an ex-offender. He has no swag. He's short. He's too tall. He's not American. He's not black. He's clueless. He's needy. He's greedy. He's a loser. He's too old. He's too young. He doesn't make enough money. He's fat. He's scrawny. He's afraid of commitment. He won't change. He keeps changing. He won't embrace growth and development.

He has health challenges. He's a health nut. He's never happy. He doesn't want what she wants. He's a wuss. He's just not that into her. He doesn't know what he wants out of life. He's not her type. He's got issues. He's got baggage. He slept with her best friend/sister. They grew apart. She outgrew him. He's all talk and no action. He disappears from time to time. He's a drama king. She thinks she can do better. She *knows* she can do better. And did I mention my personal favorite, he has poor hygiene.

Phew! That's quite a list, right? Sisters ask for a lot, or so it seems, when we're in the market for a mate. Then we meet somebody. If he's good looking, smells fresh, appears to have a little somethin'-somethin' and acts like he finds us attractive, well, things can start to drop off our list. Don't let us sleep with him and the sex turns out to be finger-lickin' good. Well, now, sisters are known to lose their minds. Not only does our checklist of wants and needs get tossed, but now, we're consumed by an emotionally expensive and time-consuming campaign to win his heart. Once hitched, too many of us turn a blind eye to cheating, neglect, disappearing acts, lying, and a host of other abuses from a man.

Perhaps you stand by your needs-and-wants list when it comes to picking a partner. Whatever your concerns, for *you* they are valid and legitimate reasons for saying no to a new relationship. Or for walking away from an old one. Who am I to judge? It's your call. If a man isn't trustworthy (too many men aren't), lacks integrity, fails to keep his word, leaves you in a lurch, abuses you in any way, he's a loser not a keeper. Show him to the nearest exit.

There *are* good and decent brothers yet unhitched. Besides, all you need is one, right? Surely, you can train your mind to believe there's at least one more good man out there, who is just right for you.

## WHEN WE FALL IN LOVE

When black women fall in love, we fall in hard and deep. Until we get fed up. Once we're fed up, well, uh, we're fed up. True, it takes a lot before many sisters get fed up. Until we fall madly in love with *ourselves*. Self-love makes a woman a whole lot less tolerant of the bullshit. Self-loving women aren't willing to endure disregard, disrespect, betrayal, and abuse from others, and men are no exception. I believe that's why more and more sisters are consciously choosing to be single; they're fed up with how little love and respect they get from black men. Truth be told, too many brothers have forgotten how to love black women. Consequently, the emotionally self-sufficient and self-loving woman knows when to hold 'em and when to fold 'em. She has a low tolerance for disrespect and neglect.

But too many women stand on shaky ground, emotionally speaking, when it comes to men. They're needy and longsuffering. These women tolerate all manner of madness and mistreatment to have a man in their bed. A man can cheat, hit, neglect, and betray them repeatedly and they stay with him.

Women who know their man ain't holding it down brag to other women about what a good man they got. Meanwhile, they're living in quiet desperation with the truth. Put another way, they have a delicious, enviable relationship—only it's all in their heads. It's the ideal relationship on paper. They may have the house, luxury cars, two-and-a-half children, dog *and* cat. Or they might not have any of the material trappings, but he comes through, at his convenience, so they can "connect." Know what I mean?

How do I know this? Well, I've been this woman. Yes, I've been the woman bragging about what a good guy I had because he showered me with trips abroad, designer bags, and expensive social outings. Okay, it wasn't all bad, though he was a rascal. Actually, he was undeniably generous, supportive, and reliable.

But when it came to those intangibles that make for a loving, trusting, high-caliber relationship, ours didn't measure up. To be fair, neither he nor I had integrity in the relationship. He cheated and lied. And I sometimes flirted a little too much with my guy friends. That is, I was emotionally unfaithful.

I also know this needy, desperate woman because I call some of them "friend." I've also dedicated a lot of work hours as a coach, counselor, advocate, and attorney to women who don't love themselves. Women who would rather be beaten than be alone. Women who stay with emotionally and physically abusive men under the guise of love. These women are more committed to "loving" and supporting their men than they are to themselves and their own well-being. This might describe you. If it does, you *can* change.

Love isn't supposed to hurt. Your lover ought to be your best friend, not your closest enemy. Ask yourself, "Am I enduring this man? Am I suffering in this relationship just to have a man? Is my man attentive, tender, loving, kind, supportive, caring, nurturing, thoughtful, and fun? Or is your man selfish, harsh, impatient, unsupportive, neglectful, shaming, blaming, distant, cold, callous, and physically abusive? Now look honestly at yourself. Are you inflicting emotional or physical abuse on your beloved? Are you the bully, cheater, chronic complainer, liar, abuser? You need not tell anyone but yourself the truth. Be honest, are you?

# Herstory of being blinded by love

*"The purpose of relationships is not
happiness, but transformation."*
—Andrew Schneider

**By Kenyatta**

It was spring 2001. I was a freshman at Livingstone College and too excited that I was now on my own in the real world. Well, it was not long before the real world would slap me in my face. Overwhelmed by my new independence, I was open for anything. Then one day, there he stood—large in size, big Afro, muscles the size of boulders. I was in love. Or at least that's what it felt like.

After about a week of seeing him about campus I was itching to know who he was. While en route to lunch, there he sat eating a banana. I had never been close enough to gaze into his big brown eyes and feast on his full, fat lips. To my delight, he was sitting at the table with family, my older cousin. So I ventured over.

"Hi, my name is Gordon," he said, introducing himself to me.

At that moment all my senses abandoned me. "Hi, my name is Gordon!" I mistakenly spat out. To this day, if you let him tell the story, he would boast that he had me at "Hello."

We started hanging out more and more. I caught rides home with him and his friends. It was so much fun. They lived about thirty miles north of me, so he was too happy to take me home. Six months later, I was falling in love with this man. When I woke in the morning he was on my mind. When I went to sleep at night he was in my dreams. I didn't know what to do with myself. Then one day our eyes and lips met. What a day to remember. His lips were as soft as fresh rose petals; my heart pounded like a dribbled basketball.

We started to talk more and go out. He would pick me up from campus and take me to his place. In the beginning, it was fantastic. I could not believe how beautiful love could be. There was a time when I was the one who got the short end of the stick. But this time, I was getting the whole stick, and boy, did I become stick crazy.

This wonderful relationship would last for five years. During those five years, we created a relationship, home, bills, assets, and lots of special memories with each other. Toward the end of it, I fell ill. I could no longer do the things I once did or handle my normal daily tasks. This was hard on us both. I started working seven days a week and was off seven days a week. This took a toll on our relationship because he missed me.

Our communication virtually stopped. I was losing control of my health and the love of my life. I thought if I did everything I could for us that it would work out and we would live happily ever after. That was not to be. Happy was nowhere in our future together.

After I graduated college, I knew I wanted to continue my education. I also wanted to marry this man. Who knew my life would change in the way that it did. Our relationship was hurting, and my physical health was failing. There were so many things that came down on us all at once. The pressure was real hard. My man could not stand to see me sick and working hard. Then his father passed away unexpectedly, and I got accepted into a master's program in Washington, D.C. Moving to the city was not an option for him while *not* going was not an option for me.

It was fall 2006. Since my health was not improving we decided to move back home with our families. This was the hardest thing I have ever had to do. We talked about what we would do and how things would go. He would go home, be with his mom, and help take care of her. I would focus on getting better and preparing myself for school, which was a major challenge. He never did talk about my going off to school. I wish he had been able to say, "Baby, I don't want you to go, but I understand." Or something like that. But he never did.

Two months later I tried to connect with him. I called. There was no answer. After about the fourth call I left a message. I was headed to Rocky Mount, I said, where he was staying with his mom. My man suffered from diabetes, and I thought something had happened to him. So I planned to see what was going on.

Soon after leaving that message my phone rang; it was him. The conversation was not meant for the phone. This is when the real world punched me in the face. The man that I had loved, cared for, provided for, worked to understand, fought, prayed, and sacrificed for was leaving me, no explanation given. His only words were, "I can't do this anymore." I was mad as hell. I saw red. I cried for months.

After several attempts to talk to him, to gain a better understanding, I just stopped. And surrendered. Because the more I called the more he ignored me. Each time I died a little bit more. It would be almost two years before I would see or hear his voice again.

This experience taught me that love can be blind. I believe so much in unconditional love and so wish the world we live in did too. I hate having to live with a guarded heart just because one man who promised he'd always love and be there for me lied. That sucks.

I am twenty-five years old. My very first love happened when I was twenty. I was young and in love. If I had it to do all over again I would make sure that God was at the forefront of my relationship. I only wish I hadn't given him everything. Wish I hadn't made him my whole world. I lost myself in this man. And the love I had for him pushed him away. What did I learn? Well, it's never wise to love a man more than you love yourself. Why? Because, in the end he will leave you and all you will be left with are the pieces of your broken heart.

I was doing it for him all the time. I now know I have to do it for me. That I am a good enough reason to do whatever it is that I want to do. It took a long time before I could talk to another man, be with another man, and trust another man. Truth is, first I had to trust myself again. Being in love is its own greatest gift. I used to be mad as hell. But now it's okay. I realize that sometimes we have to get what we don't want for us to understand what we do want.

## RELATIONSHIPS DON'T FAIL

*"Our deepest need is for the joy that comes with loving and being loved, with knowing we are of genuine use to others."*
—Eknath Easwaran

Why do relationships fail? Well, actually, relationships don't fail. "Relationships," says Marianne Williamson in *A Return to Love,* "are eternal." Relationships are eternal because they are not of the body but are of the mind. Yes, our relationships exist in our minds. They last forever, even as the form that they take changes. They end, or they seem to, when two people separate physically. Someone we may have hoped we'd spend happily ever after with leaves. Our "soul mate" has a change of heart. We fall out of love with our beloved. So we separate. We choose to stop sharing our day-to-day life with this person. They move out. We move across town. Countries come between you. Did our relationship fail? No. Not only did it not fail, but it also didn't end. Only the appearance and form that it took changed.

Every meeting and sharing is purposeful. We are to love, learn, and expand from every encounter and relationship. Every relationship serves the purpose for which it comes, even when we don't recognize its purpose. Every encounter you have, regardless of its duration, comes bearing divine gifts. That brief liaison was no accident. That seven-year-yet-no-ring relationship was not a waste of your time. That ten-year marriage that left you reeling when he asked for a divorce was not a mistake that you need now sob, "I gave the best years of my life to." You got something from every engagement. You changed because of them. As author Octavia Butler says, "What we touch, we change."

We are forever changed by those that touch our lives. We are not the same people we were before our beloved graced our life. We've *become* someone we wouldn't be because of the people we've allowed to touch our life. They came to show us to ourselves, to help us grow in love with ourselves and the world. Now, we might not *like* who we have become, but that again is our choice. We have the power to like, or not like, who we are. If you learned the lessons of love that your beloveds came to teach you, then you're stronger, wiser, more loving to self and others. If you aren't, no worries, as George Eliot declares, "It's never too late to become who you might have been."

As I maintain in *Love Addicted*, every person comes into our life to teach us something about ourselves and life. Where's the failure in that? Even if you don't recognize the lessons offered you by the Universe through your beloved, your soul remains on its spiritual path. If you're like most people, you need to take a "course" more than once or twice before you learn the lesson. Know this, just because a relationship doesn't pan out the way you want it to, imagine it should, or it falls woefully short of your expectations, doesn't mean you failed at love. You haven't failed. Nor has your beloved failed. Consider every relationship an opportunity to practice compassion, kindness, and loving. With the seemingly ending of one relationship, the Universe offers you another chance to deepen your commitment to grow in love. Another beloved is in your future; that is, if you can keep believing in love and life.

## IS HE THE ONE?

It's ridiculous for a woman to expect every encounter with a man, even the meaningful ones, to lead to happily ever after. Or to a commitment. Or to *anything* or *anywhere*. In fact, why would you even want every man to potentially be The One?

Men grace our lives for a multitude of reasons. To be our Significant Other is only one among many. Believe it or not, men are people, too. Seriously though, it's a gift to have a male friend who acts like the brother you wish you had. How sweet it is to have guy friends who can give you the 411 on men. It's a blessing to have a masculine shoulder to lean on when you need to cry or borrow another's strength. It's priceless to have a guy friend with whom you can see a movie, have a glass of wine, or hang out with. How delicious it is to have men around, to look at, talk to, play and laugh with, love up on, all in the name of pure friendship. And please, let's not forget flirting and compliments. What a sad and dreary world it would be if men weren't around to give us a smile, compliment, and a "Damn, baby! You sure look good in those jeans!" look.

Like me, I hope you find men delightfully entertaining, fun, and delicious to have around. I appreciate that they don't have to be *my* man for me to enjoy ribbing and joking with them in the gym, share a chuckle with in the supermarket checkout line, or take pleasure in a manly hug following Sunday service. Personally, I relish my light encounters with men because I can rag them in a way that I can't women.

Try this: *Let go of the hope that every good-looking guy that crosses your path is The One.* Instead, delight in the present moment. Give no concern for tomorrow. Don't worry if you have a future together. In fact, why not date? Yes, date. To date is to go out with two or more men simultaneously. That's a rather alien concept for many sisters because we tend to meet a guy on Monday, and, if we're feeling him, by Friday we've tried on his last name. Tsk, tsk! Meanwhile, he's still seeing and sleeping with other women. Yes, try dating, ladies. Have lots of fun but no sex on these dates. (More about sex in Chapter 13.)

Don't force anything. Allow things to unfold naturally. The One could be among those you're dating; only now, you'll discover him while having loads of fun along the way to coupledom. Yes, fun. Have fun. There is nothing wrong with wanting a committed relationship. You need not fixate on it, though, for it to happen. Relax. Sing this with me, *"Que sera, sera . . . whatever will be, will be. The future's not ours to see . . . que sera sera."* When you have this carefree attitude, you become a man magnet . . .because you'll exude confidence. And you know what men say about confidence, right? It's the sexiest thing a woman can wear!

I repeat, when you meet a man, seek to stay in the present moment. Relish it. Roll around in it. Sink every fiber of your luscious being into it. Lap it up. Relax and let the future take care of itself. If you can get that you need not know where it's going or what it's going to be for you to enjoy the ride, you'll be a much happier woman. And, I might add, more fun to be with.

## THE ROLES MEN PLAY

Oh, but don't be too quick to write him off. Just because he's not the leading man doesn't mean he's not meant to play a supportive role in the movie you're producing. He might make a good friend, confidant, coach, supporter, mentor, playmate, colleague, or teacher. Consider this: Maybe he came to support you in learning how to receive love and support without feeling like you have to sleep with a man? Perhaps he came to help you better understand the male mind? What if that man you don't immediately warm up to *is* The One, just not right now?

Love is a powerful, beautiful God force. When we don't feel deserving of something so magnificent, so of God, so healing, so blessed, we can't stand it. So we reject it. Push it away. Consider that the next man that comes into your life, or that is already present, could have been sent by God to teach you how to relax into love and let a man love you, without conditions. Or your men friends could be in your life to help you remember how lovely, adorable, and smart you are. Or to teach you something valuable about men so you'll be ready when The One knocks on your door. (That happened for my friend; one day, out of the blue, her Mr. Right literally knocked on her door) So, just lean back and relax and enjoy the juicy journey, trusting that it's ALL good.

As we are spiritual beings having a human experience, we are here to learn, grow, and expand. When an attractive man comes along, exhale. Breathe. In fact, take two or three deep, cleansing breaths. Remain calm, and nobody will get hurt here.

Seriously, there's no need to be so eager and impatient. Eagerness and impatience smell much too much like desperation. Like you're a little too willing to abandon all that you're about to be with him. Him who you know so little about. Can you be excited? Yes. Excitement is permitted. Thrilled? Sure, indulge yourself. Still, keep at least one foot on the ground.

## MY THREE BASIC TRUTHS ABOUT LOVE

When I finally embraced the truth about love and relationships, I stopped beating myself up when a romance didn't unfold according to my mental blueprint. I stopped thinking every appealing guy who showed interest must be The One. I quit trying to force-fit a man into my life. I gave up the belief that something must be wrong just because a so-called promising relationship ended, and sometimes quite nastily.

Relationships, like life, are forever becoming, shifting, moving, changing. They are unpredictable and uncontrollable. No matter how much you love someone, if they have no love for you, it's best to let them—and the dream of you and them—go.

And another thing, nothing's promised to us. If you have a need for certainty in a relationship, you're setting yourself up for profound disappointment, despair, and struggle. Actually, a need for certainty in *anything* is paralyzing and keeps us from seizing and relishing this unique moment in time. The need for things to be headed in a particular direction, i.e., to the altar, or to materialize like the picture in your head else you deem it a failure, keeps us from living fully in the present moment and loving the beauty of what *is*. What is right *now*.

I also discovered, to my sheer delight, that my recovery from disappointment, hurt, and loss hastened once I embraced certain basic truths about love, life, and relationships.

**BASIC TRUTH #1 – I am not to take his leaving personally.** When a man leaves I don't have to take his leaving personally. I'll admit, it took me years to nail this one down. Once I got that no matter what a man does it's not about me, I stopped taking his behavior personally, including his departure. Does that mean no crying is allowed? To the contrary. I cry if it hurts. If I love a man and want more time with him and he walks out of my life, in the words of Jill Scott, "I'll cry if I want to." I cry for me *and* him. I cry for him because I'm a good thing. From experience, I've discovered that if a man falls for me, in time, he'll likely regret his decision to walk. Especially if he did something stupid that ushered in the end of us. He'll start to miss me and want to come back.

Since I don't respond to booty calls, he's SOL; you know, shit out of luck. Once I'm done, I'm done, done, done. I also might shed tears if we gave it our best shot, but our best just wasn't good enough. You see, I love to see black people make love work, and it bothers me when I see "promising" marriages and partnerships disintegrate. Even when I'm a party to it. But does that mean I think I'm deeply and irreparably flawed because a man leaves me? No, not anymore. Once upon a time I entertained such foolishness. I can assure you of this as well: there's not a thing wrong with you either. Never mind what your ex says about you or the negative things you say to yourself about you. This doesn't mean you and I didn't help abort the relationship.

Remember, all parties to a relationship contribute to its success or "failure." No matter how irresponsible, inconsiderate, or selfish he was, you are not a victim. You played your part. To say there's nothing innately wrong with them and us means just that. *Nothing's intrinsically wrong with us.* Sure, we got baggage. And issues. Who doesn't? There are no issue-free people on the planet. It matters not how fit, pretty, accomplished, rich, or celebrated you are. You have some stuff with you. Yep, you got baggage. As do I.

Speaking of issues, there are people with *issues*, then there are people with issues who are *aware* of and at work on healing their issues. I say the best we can do is choose to spend time with people from the latter group. They're more awake. Thus, they'll be a whole lot easier to love. And decide to belong to that latter group. Oh, people in this group leave you, too. People move on. In fact, they might move on faster . . . because they're likely more emotionally healthy. This is called life. That's a right we all have. Why begrudge another for doing that? Bless them instead. Still, their leaving isn't about you; it's about them seeking to fulfill their desires and needs. Remember, who is for you will be with you. If he decides to leave, if you so desire, you will attract another one.

**BASIC TRUTH #2 – I am responsible for my happiness.** Boy, was it enlightening—though initially scary—to learn that it is I, not a man, who is responsible for my happiness and wholeness. Sure, having someone special to walk this journey called Life with is a beautiful and blessed thing. It, however, isn't a magical elixir. Having a man will NOT make me a happy woman. When we're not partnered, many women secretly imagine that once they are, that every facet of their existence will magically fall in place. "I won't do so and so until he gets here . . ." might be the lonely woman's mantra. Then reality knocks you upside your head. You then realize, hopefully, that a relationship will not, because it cannot, make you happy.

Though a loving man can certainly enhance your happiness, a relationship cannot transform you from an unhappy person into a happy one. In fact, if we're not a happy person while we're single, we undermine our chances of attracting a great guy. If you're miserable before he comes, you can forget about being happy once he's here. You'll simply be an unhappy person *in* a relationship. And you'll be in one with another unhappy person, since we attract not what we want but what and who we are.

I know you've heard it before but it's worth repeating: Happiness is an inside job. I spent many precious years trying to find happiness in a man, with no success. I failed again and again. Take my word for it, happiness isn't "out there somewhere" in another person or thing. Rather, joy and happiness are by-products of a well-lived, rich, and full life that shines with meaning and possibility.

**BASIC TRUTH #3 – I am the one I have been searching for.** I once wanted a man more than I needed self-respect, more than I valued peace of mind, more than I cherished me. Why? Remember, I believed a man was the key to my happiness and fulfillment. For years I believed this, even with volumes of evidence to the contrary. Stupidly, I held fast to that belief. Even when I got a man, and that fact didn't translate into a happy me, I still clung to the false notion that a man could make me happy. I needed only to get the "right" man, then I would surely be happy. Or so I believed.

With every "failed" relationship I got closer and closer to seeing the light: *I am the one I have been searching for.* The emptiness, fears, and gaps that I desperately sought to fix or fill with a man started to dissolve as I rediscovered who I was, realized my worth, and tapped into my own power. This is true for you too. No one outside of you is the key to your happiness, peace, or prosperity. *You are the one you've been searching for.* Stop looking out there. Turn within. You will find Goddess there. Now, pour all your love into you. The love you give to you will make you happy and bring you supreme peace. It is from this place that you will then attract a man who will love you the way you deeply desire and deserve to be loved.

# Relationships Are Assignments

*"Human relationships are the perfect tool for sanding away our rough edges and getting at the core of divinity within us."*
—Eknath Easwaran

Relationships are sacred assignments that we accept so that we might grow and expand. That is, they have a divine purpose. They are designed to evolve us, grow our souls, to make us more loving and compassionate people. Our beloved is our teacher—and student.

Can we learn and grow outside of intimacy? Sure, we can. And yet, the people we attract and couple with are divinely equipped with just the right mixture of stuff—sex appeal, perks, wounds, and baggage—to trigger and, thus, force to the surface what is in need of accepting, integrating, healing, or releasing. The Universe, in Its infinite wisdom, sends us the people most suited and skilled, so to speak, at "motivating" us to become the best rendition of ourselves. It's, however, totally our call whether to take on this challenge. Seemingly promising relationships will often end when one or both parties decide they're simply not up for the challenging work required for evolving their souls.

They also end, or change forms, when the work has been accomplished. It takes courage and commitment to stay with it—when a relationship forces you to face painful, ugly stuff inside of you. Choose to be courageous.


## YOUR SOUL MATE

A man catches your eye. You're animated by his very presence. The mere sight of him quickens something in you. You feel strongly attracted to him. You feel at home with him. You fall in love, or think you have. You know what? You *are* at home because your beloved is your soul mate. That is, your soul and his, before you were born, agreed to meet, connect, and work out some soul kinks together. He has something you need to grow. You possess something for his spiritual evolution. That something is both sweet and sour. The sour stuff—unfinished childhood business, secret fears of not being good enough, doubts that you're lovable, abandonment issues, deep longings—when triggered, rises to the surface of your life in need of your attention, healing, integration, forgiveness, and release.

It takes commitment to emotional healing and spiritual expansion to hang in there with someone when fear and darkness replace the glow of romance and love. In our throw-it-away-and-replace-it, rather than repair-it society, it's tempting to drop the relationship when it gets hard and real work is required. It's so tempting to scurry off, in search of an easier assignment. Maybe we'll get lucky and find an assignment that won't require anything more than that we show up; it'll allow us to sit back and relax. Well, uh, good luck with that

In this school called Life, we get out of it what we put in it. If we sleep in or skip class, throw spitballs when we should be problem solving, and don't do our homework, we can expect to repeat that class. We only advance once we've learned the lesson.

We learn the lessons when we are good students of life, when we pay attention, and stay with it even when things get hard and messy. Have you noticed how your next relationship seems to pick up where your last one left off? That's no accident. You can't skip lessons, you learn and advance . . . or you repeat that course. No exceptions.

By the way, I don't believe we have just one soul mate. I think we have many. And they aren't all lovers. Anyone can be a soul mate. My daughter, Adia, is one of my soul mates. We meet hundreds, maybe thousands, of people in our lifetime. Many just pass through. Our soul mates, I believe, are the people that stay and play a while. For a reason, season, or a lifetime.

## HE IS YOUR TEACHER

Ask yourself, "Who am I *being* in my relationships? Am I *open* and *committed* to growing and expanding in love with my beloved? Or am I closed, rigid, and set in my ways?" Do you often imagine that your beloveds—certainly not you, need to change if your relationships are to work?

We can't help but expand, if we choose to see all that happens in our relationships as opp ortunities for growth and as lessons that life has come to teach us. We can attune ourselves to the God in our beloved and us by embracing our beloved as our mirror and teacher.

What about when an assignment ends badly or abruptly? Painful endings can be so incredibly humbling. They have the power to crack our hearts wide open and consequently make us ready and available to needed change. Sure, at times, we get stuck in despair. But within each of us lives a Power that, if turned to, that will comfort and move us through the darkest of times.

Can we evolve through happiness, pleasure, and success? Sure, we can. But, interestingly, we most often choose pain and woe to transform us. Maybe because woe shakes, then wakes us up, as it makes us more willing and ready students of life. Disappointment and darkness have a way of grabbing our attention and shaking us awake to who we are and what is truly important.

Remember, the men in your life have come to teach you something about you. They are teachers that your soul attracted to move you closer to your best and most powerful self. Forget about what you think they are there for; that's an illusion. When they depart, they always leave you with a lesson or two, don't they? You want to learn the lesson so you can forge ahead with a healed and open heart, onto the next adventure, lesson, and love.

For the lessons, get present to who you were being in the relationship. Take time to explore and examine what transpired between you and your ex. How did you feel about him? Did you place him on a pedestal, above you? Did your admiration of him cause you to tolerate behavior and treatment that chipped away at your self-esteem? Did your fear and resistance to being alone cause you to stay in the relationship much too long? Did you feel incredibly lucky to have met someone like him, someone that you secretly felt was out of your league? How did he treat you? Were you unhealthily dependent upon him emotionally and/or finan-cially? Did you silence your authentic voice to be with him? Did you tolerate physical and/or emotional battery? Did you justify otherwise intolerable behavior to stay in the relationship? Do you admire qualities in him that, if you were to develop in you, would make you feel more empowered and successful in the world?

Consider that your beloved came to show you to yourself, to give you another view into you. He was your looking glass, your mirror. His treatment—good and bad—was but a reflection of how you treat yourself, what you believe you deserve. Those char-acteristics that you praise about him, that, when you're with him, seem to make you feel whole and complete live in you awaiting your loving attention and cultivation. To get present to the gifts that your beloved brought you is to expand and grow yourself into a more powerful version of you. Everything you love and admire in him is in you. Tap into it. Embrace it. Nurture it. Use it.

## TALL, DARK AND HANDSOME

I met a man at a personal growth seminar. He was fiiiiinnne! His expensive, stylish clothes hung just right over his tall, gangly, fit frame. I eyed him moving about the room, standing, sitting, drinking water. Restless and energetic. There was something utterly dynamic about him. High energy in a man is supremely sexy to me, and compelling. He knew he was fine too. I wanted to meet him, get to know him.

About six months later, we ended up in another seminar together, both as participants this time. One evening I went to the microphone on behalf of a friend to ask the room to assist my friend in paying the balance for a course she'd enrolled in. I also did something out of character for me and invited this brother to sit next to me, so during one of the exercises we got to talk. Later, at the end of the night, we exchanged business cards.

He called me. Boy, was I excited. He left a message saying he wanted to meet and talk with me. I said yes. We had breakfast in a nice hotel restaurant. He shared that he'd been working on a project and asked if I might assist him. At once I was disappointed *and* delighted. I would not be dating him but there was money to be made. Wonderful! I might have wanted a man, but I *needed* money.

Every Friday, for two months, we met and worked together on his project. But for a glitch that occurred before we got clear about what he wanted and what I could bring to the process, it went swimmingly. I thoroughly enjoyed the process. It was intellectually stimulating and gratifying, and it paid handsomely.

I'd been self-employed several years by then, and it was always rewarding to generate income doing something that tapped into my natural passion and talents. Besides, I had a growing child that need to eat. Oh, by the way, he thought I was worth meeting and connecting with because, he said, anyone that would do what I'd done—that is, help a friend get the rest of the funds she needed to attend a personal growth seminar—was someone he wanted to get to know. That was my consolation prize, accolades for being a good friend. I accepted it graciously.

As the project drew to an end, I felt a bit sad that it was about to expire. And confused. Confused because I fully expected this guy to want me. I'd hoped that once the contract was fulfilled we would start dating. I'd been paid handsomely, and he was pleased with the product. We thanked each other and went our separate ways.

While I'm here, let me say something about mixing work with pleasure. It's a bad, bad, BAD idea. I learned the hard way, not from Preston, but from a similar situation. A businesswoman must be the consummate professional when she's both attracted to a man and out to secure his business. First, secure and fulfill the contract. Then, once the business portion is completely satisfied, if your interest in him persists, you can let your desires be known.

About a month later a phone conversation led to a dinner date. I was thrilled. Actually, a bit too thrilled. Though I would have never uttered these words out loud back then, I secretly believed he was out of my league. He was a successful entrepreneur, lecturer, partner in a business, and owner of a beautiful home and top-of-the-line vehicle. Though I was a lawyer, I was struggling to stay afloat financially after having left the practice of law to write my first book. My self-esteem teetered and tottered. The time we double-dated with his equally successful friend and his girlfriend, in their presence I felt awkward, inadequate, and unattractive. Besides having an awfully bad hair day, I was fighting valiantly to feel good in my skin and a dress I so wished was crisp and new. Well, uh, the dress won. When they ordered a bottle of wine and entrees from the menu, without regard for the prices while I stood by painfully aware of my inability to contribute to the bill, I knew then that that night was destined to end disastrously.

After we returned from the theatre, Preston walked me to my car. I knew whatever we were doing was done. I could feel it. It was in Preston's stiff walk. At my car, we stood in the cold in silence. Then Preston spoke, his words many degrees colder than the night air. "This isn't working. Take care of yourself." Then he turned and walked back to the restaurant to join his friends for another drink. I was mortified. Hurt and embarrassed, I slid behind the wheel of my Volkswagen. I was too cold and numb to cry. In silence I drove home. I couldn't get home fast enough; home to the safety of my four walls and the warmth and comfort of my familiar bed.

## WHAT'S WRONG WITH ME

Preston was the man about whom I spoke in the Introduction, who inspired me to write this book. I was so smitten with him. I felt so powerfully drawn to this man. So when he suddenly didn't want anymore to do with me, all I had were questions: Why didn't he want me? What was wrong with me? What went wrong? What had I done? Why wasn't I good enough for him? These were the questions I asked myself. But alongside these questions was a quiet knowing: *Preston* was *not my Mr. Right.*

And still, after that "breakup," I had some healing to do.

As I worked through the "what happened" doldrums, I got present to some things, helped by a couple of wise confidants who confirmed what I intuitively knew all along: *Preston hadn't come into my life to be my man.* Rather, he came to help me see more clearly who *I* was meant to be. In time, I accepted that more than I wanted to be *with* Preston, I wanted to *be* Preston, to be *like* him. I wanted a more abundant, adventurous life, like the life he seemed to be living. He was successful in his work. He traveled frequently for both work and pleasure, jetting from this city to that country. He went home to an exquisitely decorated house in an eclectic neighborhood. Doing what he loved for a living he was able to pay the mortgage, travel, and dine at pricey restaurants. Yes, I wanted that kind of life. Preston came to help me remember that I wanted it, and could have it when I truly believe in me, and what is possible for my life.

I pined for that kind of life. I'd long stopped dreaming it should come secondhand, i.e., through the man in my life. No, I was to create it. Well, Preston was the mirror I needed shoved in my face to wake me up.

Less than a month later, in a conversation with a life coach whom I will forever be indebted to, I got present to what I was doing to my life and why I was choosing failure over success. All my life my family members had harshly judged me for reaching for the good life, for chasing my dreams, for, they said, thinking, "You're better than us!" Sure, I'd achieved some things—a law degree, a house, trips to Europe and South Africa, wrote and published a book, and yet, some part of me still craved my family's approval and love.

But as I sat on my old sofa in my Mt. Washington apartment, tears of realization streaming down my cheeks, I decided *I would cease to care what my family thought of me.* Besides, even during those times when I didn't know how I would gas up my car, these same family members continued to withhold their love and approval from me. Then and there I resolved to reconnect with my power. I would create a life I can love. Let them kick rocks. Yes, I remember it like it was two weeks ago. The coach's words were the wake-up call I desperately needed to remember who I was. She helped me appreciate that my living poorly served no one, not even my family. I realized that I have an obligation to live brilliantly, abundantly, and powerfully. I owe this to myself, and my family.

About a year later, I ran into Preston. We chatted over the phone a few weeks, then started hanging out. It was different this time. I was on more solid ground, psychologically, emotionally, *and* financially. My self-esteem was no longer in the toilet. Uh, I had some. In fact, I was feeling pretty good about DeBora. No, I was not a hundred percent there, but I was well on my way to feeling like this man's equal. He no longer intimidated me. Nor did I feel like he was doing me a huge favor by spending time with me. Yes, I was enough, good enough and worthy of a quality man's time and attention.

# *Herstory* of marriage and love addiction

*"In real love you want the other person's good.
In romantic love you want the other person."*
—Margaret Anderson

*"What do you do when the only person that can
stop your tears was the one that made you cry?"*
—Unknown

**By Sadé**

It was my twenty-fifth birthday when my husband left me—his pregnant wife—and two children. It was September 24, 1980. "I need to find myself, I need some time," he said. I was dazed. I was so in love with him I wanted him to do whatever he needed to do to get his head on straight. He wrapped his clothes in a green paisley sheet, hurled them into the back of our brand new red Cordova sedan, and sped off. I sat down at the dining room table, stunned. There was no build-up to the breakup. No warning. I trusted this man to be there, and he just walked out of our home, just like they do in the movies. It was a house we were renting to own. Damn, I was too scared to be mad. Later that night I kept returning to the window to see if he'd come back. He hadn't.

I took all the knives in the house downstairs to the basement, as a precautionary measure. I didn't trust myself. I don't know how I came to be that sane in such an insane situation. I knew I wanted time to think, to push everything far away from me. I was in a daze for months. I never worked outside the home before, so I wasn't prepared financially. It was cold as hell the next couple of months, and I had no heat, so I used the gas. Luckily, it was still on. I blocked off the kitchen with a blanket so the heat would rise up to the second floor to keep my kids warm.

I finally told my parents that Wayne had left me. My dad, who was seventy-four years old, was fiery mad to see me trying to stay warm by the kitchen stove. I use his famous words when I recount my story to others. He said, *"Gal, you are on love and need to come home and detox."* Yes, that's right, a seventy-four-year-old man describing his daughter as being *on* love, an addict who would do anything to stay in a relationship. I mean, how on time was he to tell me that what I needed was a detox from love? I thought I was in a healthy relationship because my man put the key in the door every night. I was very naive to have that kind of trust.

During this time I had the first of many court cases. I saw a hearing officer who set the terms of the child support order at $400 a month.

While at my parents,' my father resorted to his brand of therapy: tough love. He would bark things like, *"How do you spell MAN?"* Then he'd add, *"That's right, you haven't seen that many to tell the difference."* Real witty, my dad was. Yet, all I could think was, *"Why did he leave? What did I do?"*

While staying with my parents I found out he'd gone to his mom's. My dad wanted me to see what my husband was made of so he insisted that I take our children over to stay with their dad's mom. I agreed. I placed the kids on the porch with their little suitcases, rang the doorbell, and rushed back to the car. I still remember their little faces, how they looked at me with those mommy-don't-leave-me eyes. In tears, I pleaded with my father not to drive away and leave them. My dad insisted that I would miss out on a learning opportunity if I never found out what Wayne was really made of; that is, I wouldn't get to see if my husband's father instincts would kick in. My dad even laughed at the thought of the kids being back at his house before we even got back there.

I had all of $200. I spent about $2 every few days. I was trying to get public assistance, but my parents refused to sign the paperwork. They feared someone would take their hard earned home. Eventually, they did sign the paperwork so I could get money to re-establish myself, on my own.

My children started showing signs of stress. My five-year-old daughter mouthed the words, "Mommy, I want to kill myself." These weren't even words I used. Nor had I cried or fully acknowledged that my husband was gone. My parents would speak in code around the kids. I was now really angry and scared that my daughter would have to have therapy. I made an appointment at the Child's Guidance Clinic, only to discover that in studies on divorce and separation, *I*, the parent, am deemed the patient. Consequently, the clinic never agreed to see my daughter. I was doubly confused. To think, I'd tried to get help for my kids but they are ignored because the counsellors want to discuss how *I* feel first.

### Fast-Forward

I gave birth to a daughter in March 1981 and moved out of my parents' house. My husband and I had a mini-reconciliation, and I gave birth to another daughter in 1984. He, however, left again in 1987. I then gave birth to another daughter whose father is an abuser, but I was complicit; I was using him as a stand-in because my other children's father wasn't there for me to fight with.

### 1990 to 1995

I date but don't fall in love. I used people as ego therapy. I was still unhealthy.

### 1996 to 2006

I have two long periods of celibacy. Five of those years I date one man without sex or intimacy. I was still in an unhealthy relationship because I didn't require him to be consistent. So I would love hard and sincere for both of us. The difference was that during that time I worked to build myself up and develop outside friendships. I was balanced. I just didn't know how to have a real give-and-take intimate relationship. It took my oldest daughter, who was five when her dad left, to help me see that it was my time that was the most precious, not my lack of sexual expression with this man. I knew she was right, but I was fighting an addiction. I was determined to *"stay and hang in there for the sake of love."* I also took this time to heal and speak life over myself. It was intensive care for my emotions. I became more spiritually aware; I was beginning to see my part and how I agreed to be mistreated.

### 2006 to the present

I have been in a serious relationship where both of us talk about love addiction and having separate and shared friends. We champion each other and help address our past wounds with love and understanding. We have the same foundational outlook on life.

Whatever happened to my children? Well, let's put a period at the end of a nearly thirty-year drama. Some things need clearing up, like getting the divorce papers served. But it's not toxic. I have released Wayne from the "should-have-been" and have accepted that he was a teacher with a very long lesson plan for me that I can say I have now passed.

# Knives

We could be together, don't you see
Because remember you promised me . . . forever and for
always
Don't you see? Baby, it wasn't the end of you and me
We could be together for eternity
Longer than a minute, longer than a day

Baby, I'll cast this life away
Because in the gates of heaven we'll be together always
You ended this
Because you hated it, hated me
Sometimes I wondered if I would ever really see
The real you, the one who said he loved me
But did you ever?

Baby, it doesn't matter
I hold my wrists
I'm not afraid of this
Your love cuts deeper than these knives can go
I'd bleed to death nice and slow
If it meant we could be
Because, baby, you promised me
Goddammit, you promised me
Can you hear it?
Drip. Drip. Drip.

Baby, I bleed for you
I ride for you, I die for you
I love for you, I lie for you

Did you ever love me too?
When you took those pills did you think about me?
Well, baby, this is a different kind of ecstasy
Drip. Drip. Drip.

I'm not afraid of this
Death is permanent but so is love
I can see you with my eyelids closed
You're all I want, all I need
And after all, you did promise me
Drip. Drip. Drip.

—*Adia Ricks Cummings*

## SINGLE BLACK FEMALE

*"The purpose of relationship is not to have another*
*who might complete you, but to have another with*
*whom you might share your completeness."*
—Neale Donald Walsch

Why should black women care why their love connections crack and break? First this, when I speak about breakups, I also include short runs, that is, relatively brief relationships and even relationships that *almost* happen. Like going out a few times with someone that you really, really want, only for him to never call again. Such seemingly promising encounters can leave us wondering, "What happened?" A string of these false starts can affect a woman's self-esteem. These letdowns—though perhaps not as devastating as a multiple-year relationship breakup—can nonetheless be baffling and psychologically bruising. Admittedly, this view comes from a recovering love addict. But even for the non-addict, sometimes even a brief encounter with what feels like a soul mate—and it need not be sexually intimate—can feel so otherworldly in its rightness and perfection that it seems to alter your very DNA. You intuitively know you've had a deeply spiritual brush with a soul mate, and because of it, thank God; you'll never be the same. It was that powerful, that delicious, that divine.

Now, back to why women should examine the reasons why our relationships falter, fizzle, and fade. You might ask, "Can't a woman move confidently forward without that knowledge?" Or you might argue, "Why should any self-respecting woman expend any more mental and emotional energy on understanding a man who, in some cases, didn't even bother to say good-bye?"

Well, my motivation for writing a book on breakups—and how to recover from them—is massive. For one, simply stated, I am not happy about the current state of black love and relationships. Research indicates that we are the most uncoupled group of people on the planet. Between 1950 and 2000, the percentage of African American women who married dropped from 62 percent to 36.1 percent. During this same period, the percentage of never-married black women more than doubled, from 20.7 percent to 42.4 percent.

I believe we can do better at loving and coupling with one another. Although I've ceased to see singlehood as a tragedy, still all across America there are beautiful, single black women who deeply desire to be in a loving, lasting relationship with a good man. I am blessed to call some pretty amazing women "friend," loving, generous, creative, spiritual, kind, funny, and beautiful women. Most of them are single. The majority of them pine for a love of their own. Sure, these women have foibles, flaws, fears, and barriers to loving and being loved. But, who doesn't? It's not uncommon for black women to peer across the divide at black men to assess and scrutinize what they are and are not doing to make love work. I understand. There've been times when I've been among these women.

However, as we gaze at our brothers, we must look even closer at ourselves, to see who we are being and how we love ourselves and them. As Dr. Phil is known to say, "Either we contribute to or contaminate our relationships." Black women not excepted. So I ask you to ask yourself, "What would be the quality of my unions if I would spend more time in self-examination than I do finger-pointing? What might be possible for me in love and partnership if I was more willing to see my part in all of my experiences with love and relationships?" Think about it. I invite you to journal your answers.

## MARS AND VENUS DIFFERENT

Let's say you habitually choose self-absorbed, emotionally abusive men who neglect to make you a priority in their life. Wouldn't you want to know why you keep attracting this kind of man? And just as importantly, wouldn't you want to know why you settle into a relationship with such a man? For sure, I think there's value in examining the roles that black men play in our love and relating. We will do that here. But not so we can absolve ourselves from responsibility or strategize on how to then fix them, though I and my contributors most certainly offer a few thoughts on how they might be better men.

Studying men makes sense to me because men are different from women. If I've not learned anything from my "MENtality guru" Steve Harvey, author of *Act Like a Lady, Think Like a Man*, I've certainly learned this: *Men think vastly differently from women.* Yes, men and women *are* different. Mars and Venus different. The sooner women accept and embrace this truth the less heartache we'll suffer and the more success we'll experience in relationships with men. Men think differently. Process information differently. Communicate differently. Their way is neither wrong nor right—just different. Different is not only okay and acceptable, different is good.

Besides, black men are who they are because we are who we are. Who we are impacts and shapes them. Not just as mothers, sisters, lovers, and spouses do black women shape black men. Who we are collectively molds the black man. Consider this, every time a sister says "hell no" to maltreatment and abuse, a brother gets a valuable lesson in love. He learns how to better treat women. Imagine if, say, seven out of ten sisters were intolerant of infidelity, violence, and verbal abuse. Do you think black men would treat black women with greater love and respect? Of course they would. Remember, they are who they are because we are who we are. And let's never forget, we teach men how to treat us.

How black men see, think of, and treat us impact and shape us too. Every time a black man loves and respects one black woman, he's loving and respecting ALL black women. Yes, how we see, think of, and treat each other is a reflection of how we treat ourselves. A black man who abuses black women is abusive to himself. If he loved himself, it would be impossible for him to raise his fist against a woman. Remember, we are one. What I inflict upon you, I do to me. What we dislike, can't tolerate, can't be with in others are the same things we dislike, can't tolerate, can't be with in ourselves. Through self-examination, we are able to see, own, embrace, and dissolve the blockages within that keep us from attracting, creating, and having the love we so desire. We have magic wands. They're called love, forgiveness, and compassion, for self and others.

# Herstory of toxic love

*"Love, I find, is like singing. Everybody can do
enough to satisfy themselves, though it may not
impress the neighbors as being very much."*
—Zora Neale Hurston, *author & anthropologist*

**By Neecy**

From the beginning my relationship with Donnie sent up
red flags. Five years after my sixteen-year marriage had
ended I felt I was ready to date again. Donnie showed up
and swept me off my feet. He was a smooth talker, conscious, spiritual, and fine. He said he was in transition and
wanted to move from his hometown, Savannah, Georgia.
Since I worked as a staffing specialist he asked me to find
him employment in the Augusta area. He said he would
move to Augusta with his family to take the position. He
frequently traveled between Augusta and Savannah to
visit me and job search.

After he had his final interview he decided that he
was ready to make that move. Now, we'd been dating approximately six months and it took a lot to even let him
spend the night. I had two teenagers, so I only permitted
him to stay over when my children were away from home.

This brother was in "transition." He had no job, no
vehicle, and no stable domicile, a fact I would later discover. I was so caught up in the whirlwind of love—after
all, we were so *compatible*—that I failed to see this brother

was hiding something—a lot of something. So many brothers say, "Sisters are difficult. They don't recognize a good man. They're all money hungry. And they ain't never satisfied. Blah, blah, blah, blah, blah." So in my quest to be more understanding and accepting I looked beyond this man's situation to see *him*.

When the brother moved to the area to take the job he said he couldn't contact his family in the area so he asked if he could crash at my place for a few weeks until he got it together. Well, two weeks turned into two years. Determined to be an understanding woman I let it be. After all, we were a couple. Now, he was not a "project" for me. I had been a wife for years. I knew how to run a household. I knew how to be good to my GOOD man. Consequently, I did not complain, nag, deny him sex, or go to bed looking like a beat-up soccer mom. I kept it right and tight.

I'm not saying my passivity was the answer. Nor am I placing all the blame on my ex because I refused to see the following: The brother had four jobs during the time we lived together. One time he was unemployed for seven months. Rather than work, he spent his time downloading booty (porn) and naked pictures of his Internet friends onto *my* computer. He had perverse sexual requests and often. He never introduced me to any of his friends. I only met his family by chance while picking him up in Savannah one weekend—they just happened to be outside. This man took pictures of his baby mama performing sexual acts on him with *my* camera and downloaded them onto *my* computer and used *my* computer, cell phone, and vehicle to hook up with other women *and* men. He clubbed three nights a week until 4 A.M., hid cereal, food, drink, whatever, from my children, and was only polite when I was passive and allowed myself to be controlled. Notice I said *allowed.*

I won't say he broke up with me. I think the relationship changed when I woke up and began to challenge him. I started meditating and going within. I never asked him, "Why aren't you working? Why won't you help out? Why the extra women?" Spirit revealed information to me and directed my steps. I gathered the information and prepared my escape. Yes, I felt trapped.

When we finally found him a decent job, one he decided to keep, he nonetheless refused to contribute to the household. He insisted that he deserved to shop for himself. I still didn't know him, his past, his friends, or his life outside of our relationship. On his job he started to solicit other women and men. I was his offsite supervisor but I never spoke ill of him to anyone.

I continued to look within. I knew I was bringing this negativity to me. I gave, gave, gave, gave, gave, and gave some more. A spirit of negativity hung over my home. My children were unhappy, and so was I. I'd never been in this type of relationship before. My marriage was basically a happy one that just came to an end because we grew apart—spiritually and culturally—which translated into irreconcilable differences. We have remained friends and co-parents.

The relationship reached a climax when my children and I took a trip to Virginia to retrieve my daughter's scholarship award for college. While there we were awakened by a phone call from my neighbor screaming, "The house is on fire! It looks pretty bad, and we're still trying to get them to come out!" As I hung on the line she repeatedly pounded on the door of my house. Out comes "my" man with another woman, from the house *we* shared!

When I returned to the city I had no place to go, no clothes, no renter's insurance, no food, no anything. On top of that he'd told the Red Cross that he was the only one residing in the home. In order to receive some assistance I had to go down to the Red Cross and prove that my children and I actually lived in the home. Needless to say, he didn't follow me to my new place. Even to this day he attempts to reenter my life. I realize that this was a highly toxic relationship, and I cannot, under any circumstances, revisit it. I believe the Spirit of Fire extricated me from this relationship.

Sometimes we avoid self-examination. My reason for staying in this lethal relationship was fear of embarrassment. I am a very private and extremely dedicated person. I rarely bring others into my circle. I felt betrayed because I'd opened my heart, my life, my home, my finances, my friends, and my family to someone. In the end I felt like I allowed the entire world to see my relationship fail—on the heels of a divorce.

My inability to let go was my stuff, and I blame him for none of that. What person wouldn't stay and get a free ride, feast on home cooked meals, and enjoy great conversations?

In his defense, prior to meeting me, he had never had his own anything—no house, car, apartment, nothing. Nor had he ever really held down a job. I have cut the apron strings, and he remains gainfully employed. Where he lives I have no clue. What I do know is that progress was made.

I take full responsibility for my part in my relationship with Donnie. It was a learning experience that has helped me to grow. It was simply another stone in my sidewalk of life.

## An Interview with
## *Life Coach*
## Christopher J. Gross

**DMR: What do you do?**
**CJG:** I am a Life Coach. I have been coaching for eight years.

**Do you work with couples; if so, what kinds of services do you provide them?**

I provide personal development and relationship coaching to individuals and couples.

**What kinds of relationship issues do you encounter?**

I encounter all types of relationship issues, all of which have their roots in childhood. Ultimately, the most common issue that couples present in their coaching sessions is a lack of trust. Under the trust issue is the real problem: fear. Whether it is the fear of being alone, the fear of being hurt, the fear of looking uneducated, or the fear of not having enough money, it all boils down to fear. By far, the biggest fear individuals and couples unconsciously present is the fear of not being enough. Not being enough to handle whatever comes up in, say, a difficult situation or conversation with their mate. Unconscious and uncontrolled fear causes people to physically and/or verbally attack or run away.

**Have you seen a recurring theme, problem or challenge with couples and singles around love and relationships?**

Yes. Here are two main issues that I see recur: 1) the lack of teamwork or the difference in each other's definition of teamwork, and 2) a failure to engage in personal development. Personal development is about work you do on you, not others. A lot of people want the other person to change, but personal development helps *you* develop *your* philosophy on what *you* need to do to make things better, not the other person. Furthermore, personal development help people see their blind spots, which are routinely exposed when conflict arises. When people constantly work on themselves, they are better able to have a healthy relationship with self and others.

### Are the challenges that black couples face any different from those of other races?

Yes, in the areas of finance and education, i.e., the lack of wealth and educational advancement. But the biggest difference by far is the effect that slavery and racism have had on the African American community. I believe that slavery and racism are the primary causes for the breakdown of the African American family and community. Slavery has planted seeds of distrust and disharmony in our community; this makes coherence and unity within African American relationships challenging.

### It is said that three out of four black marriages fail. What are your thoughts about why?

I believe there are two major reasons for this: 1) the lack of proper relationship planning—couples aren't talking about finances and how the relationship will operate, and 2) couples aren't dealing with their own emotional baggage before they say, "I Do." Most couples need two things to make love work: financial and emotional counseling.

### Why do black men say they leave relationships? Why do you think they do?

Based on my research, black men abandon relationships because of one or more of the following reasons: 1) he is ready to grow and feels that the woman is stagnated, 2) the woman is ready to grow and move the relationship forward while he's feeling pressure to but isn't really ready for growth, and 3) he isn't as interested in the relationship as the woman is.

**What are black men looking for in a woman?**

Based on my research, black men are looking for a woman who is supportive, emotionally stable, and attractive.

**If you have any advice for black men about how to make love work, what would that be?**

I'd tell them to seek understanding of self. Start with asking yourself, "Who am I?" Also, interview men who have made love work for at least twenty-five years. Make sure to get both sides—get what worked and what didn't work . . . and take great notes. If you seek truth, what you learn will show you how to make love work.

**If you have anything else to share with our readers about love and relationships, what would that be?**

All relationships are partnerships, whether good or bad they are partnerships. Look at the partnership as a mirror of you, one that allows you to discover more about yourself in a shorter period of time. So, don't run away from relationships. Embrace them and they will guide you on your path to true love.

# Sacred Contracts

*"Tell me whom you love, and I'll tell you who you are."*
—African Proverb

WE'RE ALL WOUNDED. Though, for sure, some are more emotionally tortured than others, every human being has some psychic and emotional unresolved issues that, if not healed, challenge his or her life and relationships. No one—not the richest, prettiest, fittest—escapes emotional wounding, much of which occurs during childhood.

And so, when two people are animated by each other, even if it is the curve of the woman's hips that catches the man's eye, it is not the relative smallness of her waist that ultimately hooks him. A woman might beam brightly with pride when she boasts about her new love, so pleased that at last she has found one worthy of her attention and admiration, someone she can look up to physically and financially. Yet, it isn't her beloved's lean, tight body and well endowed, uh, bank account that makes her giddy at the sound of his voice. (Though, I'm the first to admit that a man with his act together can be very compelling indeed.) Because there's far more to us than brilliant smiles, broad shoulders, and attractive bank balances.

We are spiritual beings having an in-a-body experience. That man you can't imagine life without has been divinely appointed to you. Yes, he is on assignment, to you. He is there to grow you spiritually. To help you evolve, to show you to yourself, to help you deepen self-understanding and move you closer to your best and highest self. There's nothing wrong with you. Neither are you broken. Thus, you don't need to be fixed. Consequently, he's not there to fix you. You, as am I, are wounded. We are in need of emotional healing. Thank God, we come to heal each other. Our beloved, our soul brother, comes to be healed by us, and that we might be healed by his presence.

In her book, *Sacred Contracts,* Caroline Myss teaches that before we incarnate into this realm we make agreements to meet and love certain people, to have certain experiences, and to do certain kinds of work. Consider this, when your heart leaps at the very sight of a delectable man, he is someone with whom you have a sacred contract. That spark you feel is your clue. Maybe that man you're so sure is your soul mate has contracted to walk this journey with you for six days, two months, ten years, or a lifetime. Heaven only knows. That electricity coursing through your body, that Myss calls *animation*, is a sign that a contract exists between you and another.

Our souls naturally gravitate toward fulfillment of our contractual agreements.

## SOUL CONTRACTS

Have you been with someone and worried that your love wouldn't last? You so wished you had a crystal ball so you could see into the future, to see just how long your beloved would be with you? Well, like business contracts, soul contracts have terms. We, however, don't recall what those terms are. Nor do we recollect how or when the contract will end or be satisfied. I think, like the contractual agreements we enter into on this earthly plane, our divine agreements can expire, be fulfilled, breached, or terminated by one or both parties...unfulfilled.

Have you ever felt like a relationship ended before its time, before all its terms were fulfilled? Like there remained unfinished business between you? Business you'd like to finish but were powerless to hold things together? Ever been party to an agreement where the other party decided they were done, and there was nothing you could do about it? What about the times you reconciled with someone after a breakup, only to see why it didn't work, then you ended it for good? That contract was over. A part of you simply needed to be sure.

We don't recall, so says Myss, the sacred contracts we enter into before we incarnated. So then it follows that we would have no recollection of whom we have contracts with, when they are to terminate, or how. I think it is by divine design that we don't know these details. As it is, we poke and meddle in a multitude of matters that are best left to God. Imagine if we had it in writing how long a man was supposed to devote himself to us? Hmmm, I smell a recipe for disaster. Some things call upon us to simply accept. And go with the flow and leave the details to God.

What did you agree to give, do, and learn from life, from love, and relationships? Do you know what your beloveds agreed to? Did anyone agree to love you faithfully, 'til death do you part? Did anyone agree to love you exclusively? Of course, you don't have the answers to these questions. In fact, you don't even know what *you* signed up for before you took a body--let alone what anyone else did. Nor do I know. But this I am sure of, every one of our contracts is designed to expand and deepen the love we have for ourselves and others. And though we may not recall the terms of our agreements, I believe the Universe is always guiding us toward our highest and best good. That still small voice and your intuition are your best guides. Trust them.

Let's face it, love and life aren't meant to be neat and pretty with clear, clean beginnings, middles, and endings. Life and love can be as unpredictable as the Chicago wind and as messy as a teenager's room. Still, life is on purpose. Trust it.

## Agreed?

Let's not talk about it.
Agreed?
Tacit agreements, contracts
entered into, mind and body.
It's best this way, don't you think?
Shunning difficult, messy, painful
truths for bittersweet little
white deadly lies.
Agreed?

But do let's stay together.
No meeting of the minds necessary.
Bodies bumping, colliding, clanging together.
Minds and spirits worlds apart.

Agreed?

—*DeBora*

## CHILDHOOD BUSINESS

We exert a pull on people who're equipped to help us heal unfinished childhood business. Harville Hendrix, PhD, author of *Getting the Love You Want,* insists that the purpose of "marriage is to help the two people in it finish growing up." That little girl fearful of abandonment, that little boy terrified of responsibility can, for a lifetime, live in us. Define us. Dictate our choices. And wreak havoc on everything that matters to us. Unless, of course, there's an "intervention." That is, until we do the necessary spiritual and emotional work to mend these wounds we can forever be slaves to them.

The men you draw unto you—mate with and marry—are perfect for you. They are perfect for you for they have come equipped with just the "right" warts and wounds for the woman that you are and are destined to become. All that stuff that you deny, hide, project, and reject, which keep you from being the all that you're meant to be stands ready for your attention, love, acceptance, integration, or release. The men that come into your life are there to help that woman emerge gloriously. I know, it doesn't always look or feel this way. That's beside the point. Here's the truth: *Every man is your teacher. If you will see him as such, you can also see the blessings in the form of lessons that he brings. Embrace them, use them, and expand.*

## BLACK WOMEN AND ABANDONMENT

> *"Women are made to be loved . . . not understood."*
> —Oscar Wilde

"Black women have been abandoned by so many black men," I shared with a brother-friend I was madly in love with, "that when we see a black man with a white woman, it can involuntarily evoke feelings of anger, sadness, and fear." In their youth, too many black women had no father to call their own because their father left them. Sure, these men may have believed they were justified in leaving a woman they no longer wanted or got along with, but sadly, most also abandoned their children. Fatherless black girls become women with children. Some of their offspring daddies then leave them to raise children alone. Men have been known to toy with women's minds and hearts, then leave them.

I speak from experience. My father abandoned me before I was old enough to speak his name. He left me emotionally, psychologically, and later, financially, to fend for myself. My father's leaving left a hole in my soul the size of Jupiter. I spent my youth and young adulthood grappling with the effects of his abandonment—the belief that I was damaged and unlovable, low self-esteem, fear of intimacy, depression, father hunger, the inability to commit to one man, fear of abandonment, trust issues, codependency tendencies, and a propensity to leave relationships to avoid being left. These are common challenges faced by people who wrestle with abandonment issues. Maybe you can relate.

## THE ROOTS OF ABANDONMENT

Fear of abandonment has its roots in childhood. Parents abandon their children when they are distracted, preoccupied with their own life, addicted, emotionally unavailable, unsupportive, mentally inaccessible, neglectful, callous, physically and psychologically abusive, and, of course, absent. A parent can abandon a child consciously, by packing his bags and leaving. Or she can abandon her child by dying. The impact is the same; the child feels abandoned.

Who suffers with abandonment issues? I will venture to say more black people suffer from abandonment issues than those who don't. Dating back to slavery, our families have been fractured, broken, and thrown asunder. Because abandonment need not be physical to damage a child, even when most black children had the benefit of a two-parent household, many, nonetheless, were emotionally and psychologically "deserted" by hardworking parents determined to make a decent life for "theirs" in racist America. During an era when children were to be seen but not heard, black parents struggling to survive and provide for theirs in racist America seldom had the time or interest in emotionally feeding their offspring. Too little attention, lap time, cuddling, communication, recognition, tenderness, quality time, and support can leave a child feeling utterly alone and abandoned.

## BLACK MEN AND ABANDONMENT

*"People are lonely because they build walls instead of bridges."*
—Joseph F. Newton

### Signs and symptoms of fear of abandonment in men
- "Macho" clinging, i.e., demanding, controlling, even violent behavior to get his partner's time and attention
- Has an excessive need for attention and reassurance
- Vies with children and family for the woman's attention
- Competes with the woman's work and career
- Frequent breakups and threats to leave
- Inability to commit and bond with one woman
- Fear of intimacy
- The inability to be alone with self
- Engages in emotional blackmail, i.e., "If you don't do this, I'll . . ."
- Low self-esteem/feelings of not being worthy masked by addictive behaviors like drugging, drinking, sleeping around

- Doesn't trust women
- Unconsciously engages in sabotaging behaviors
- Loves and gives with chains attached
- Tends to have a shallow, self-betraying relationship with self

Yes, men wrestle with abandonment issues too. Countless black men have never known their fathers. Or have had a hit-or-miss relationship with their dads. Others may have had fathers who were physically there but emotionally absent. Of course, some black men, in their youth, have lost their mothers through death, desertion, neglect, or abuse. Where do you suppose these boys, as they grow toward manhood, deposit their pain and longing for the parents they never had? How do these men handle feelings of unworthiness, loss, shame, hurt, anger, loneliness, fear of not being enough, good enough, and lovable? With this pain percolating in them, how do you suppose these men show up in their intimate relationships with women?

I'm not a therapist, psychologist, or grief counselor. What I know about men and abandonment I've observed and discovered as a professional, researched for this book, or experienced personally. For three-and-a-half years, I worked in a residential drug and alcohol recovery facility helping the residents, men and women, unravel their legal entanglements. My office was in the 120-bed, all-male, six-to-nine-month treatment program. On any given day, black men accounted for the majority of the population, between 80–95 percent. These men, who ranged from 20 to 65 years old, would candidly share their personal struggles with me. And I'd attend their many groups, where I'd hear their stories of loss and abandonment. Not surprisingly, most of these men were raised in fatherless homes; some by addicted mothers.

Interestingly, in my personal life, I have attracted my share of men who, in their youth, have lost their mothers to an early death. Mother succumbed to cancer or alcoholism, was gunned down by her man, went to prison, or just walked off. These are America's "lost boys." Even when dad, a relative, or the foster care system steps up to care for these boys, the loss of mother leaves a hole in their little souls. The absence of father leaves them no blueprint for manhood. These boys grow up and become the men black women endeavor to love, partner with, and marry, men grappling with loss, pain, and fear. Very often in secrecy and shame. So, you see, I have witnessed, sometimes up close and very personal, the havoc that parental loss wreaks on the lives of men.

A man isn't supposed to cry. Or at least that's what too many men believe. Society doesn't give them the green light to share their feelings and fears and few of them give themselves permission to be fully human. And still, these fears and feelings exist. If a man doesn't express his hurt, pain, loneliness, feelings of disconnection, fear of not being enough or lovable in words and tears, how, then, do these feelings manifest themselves? How, do you suppose? Well, they show up as anger, rage, irresponsibility, violence, betrayal, abandonment, addiction, womanizing, bed hopping, criminal activity, depression, suicide, imprisonment, and homelessness.

## THE DISTRUST OF WOMEN

Paul and his sister landed in foster care when his mother and father, down on their luck, could no longer provide for them. Mom visited twice in the two years that Paul lived in a New York City Boys' Home. Though his father also deserted him, Paul disdained his mother for abandoning him. Paul deeply distrusts and vehemently dislikes women, a reflection; I'm convinced, of how he feels about his mother. Consequently, all his closest friends are men. Paul is also aloof and cold toward women. He's a "Heterosexual Perceived" man, a HP. You see, though he's allegedly in a committed relationship with a woman, he sleeps with men.

One way some men, who are angry at their mothers and women, passively-aggressively "express" their anger toward women is to sleep with other men. Their message to women is, "Fuck you! I don't need you!" Until Paul forgives his mother, he'll continue to see women as the enemy, people unworthy of his love, trust and respect.

Emery, a married man I once loved, who I wrote about in *Love Addicted*, lost his father and mother to death. His father shot his wife, Emery's mother, then took his own life. Emery deals with his fear of abandonment by clinging to the familiar. His fear of change caused him to settle for a loveless marriage and a soul-crushing job. People who fear abandonment often crave closeness and connection, even as they shrink from intimacy. Everyday activities like going after a desired job or leaving a toxic relationship can be scary and feel risky, so they stay put with the familiar. Again and again, people who have experienced great losses as children will often choose the devil they know over the possibility of finding fulfillment and happiness by venturing into the unknown.

## HOW MEN DEAL WITH BREAKUPS

*"The only way to get over one woman is to get on top of another one."*
—Unknown

"How do men deal with breakups?" I asked my friend John.

John thought about it for a minute, then said, "When a man breaks up with one woman, to get over her he usually gets with another woman. Usually a woman with low self-esteem," John finished, as he used his right hand to indicate self-esteem, as if it were a short person. So the above quote sums it up. The typical man deals with a break up by quickly hopping into bed with another woman. The brokenhearted man gravitates toward women with low self-esteem because a breakup feels like a blow to his self-esteem. To this guy, this new woman is little more than a quick fix, someone to help ease the heartache and shore up his deflated ego.

Harvey, another guy friend, assured me that the rebound woman is nothing more than a Band-Aid to a brokenhearted man. Once he has finished using her, just like a used Band-Aid, she will be discarded. Steven James Dixon, author of *Men Don't Heal, We Ho,* writes extensively about the emotional instability of men who, rather than do the work to heal, opt to sleep around instead. Dixon even asserts that relationships break down because of the emotional instability of men. Yay! Finally, women get a break.

To my question, "How do men deal with breakups?" another guy friend answered with a question, "Has he been left or did he leave her?" Rick continued, "When a man gets dumped, if he's a sincere guy, in the next relationship he will be guarded." He continued, "Players don't get broken hearts." Then he thought more about it and decided that men will often become players in response to having had their hearts broken. Rick said some men will even turn to other men for sex and partnership after being repeatedly hurt and mistreated by women. Hmm, this seems to be a disturbing growing "trend." Something's not right about this. Are these closeted gay men, afraid to come out . . .so they blame their sexual proclivities on a broken heart and women? Something to think about.

A former coworker, Gilbert, weighed in on this issue. When a woman dumps a man, he said, "First, he gets angry. Then he gets introspective. He starts asking himself what went wrong. Next, in whatever way he usually copes, well, that's what he does." If he womanizes, then he quickly gets himself a woman or three. If he's a drinker, then he breaks out the Jack Daniels and drinks himself into a stupor. If his drug of choice is crack, then you'll find Joe hitting the pipe.

## A BLOW TO THE EGO

I went on Facebook and asked, "How do men deal with break-ups?" I got these responses: Felicia wrote, " . . . the brothers should speak up on this, but I know one way they deal is by shutting down . . . Once hurt their hearts close, it takes a 'special set of keys' to open it up again . . ."

Brother Essa wrote, "If a man hasn't taken some alone time to nurture his emotions, mind, and spirit without the aid or assistance of self-gratification and addictions, he'll probably use another woman, sex, drugs, or alcohol to suffocate, substitute, and abbreviate the healing process. Most men don't heal, they deal!"

Another male friend said being dumped is such an ego blow that it pushes all a man's insecurities and imagined inadequacies to the surface, and usually anger follows, whereupon some men might even become physically abusive.

Of course we know, men aren't the only people who use people to escape emotional pain. Women do it too. There was a time when I ran out of one relationship right into another to avoid having to feel the force of my pain. Consequently, I know the havoc that such behavior wreaks on all involved. So when a hurting man reaches for another woman, rather than stop, reflect, and heal, pain gets piled high and deep. Not only does this man ho around, but he tends to drink, drug, or overwork. All of which are enlisted to help him escape from himself.

A self he'll have to face eventually.

We cannot, however, escape from ourselves. Wherever we go, well uh, *there* we are. There we are worse off then we were before . . . because pain not healed waits for us up the road. Up the road there is illness, breakdowns and dis-ease—mental, emotional, psychological, financial, physical, relational, spiritual. The mind, body, spirit connection is real. Dis-eases that originate in the emotions have a way of showing up in the mind as mental illness and the body as a stroke, heart disease, hypertension, and cancer.

Sadly, too many men still believe it is a sign of weakness for a man to feel and express anything but anger. Fear, confusion, grief, sadness, and hurt are forbidden feelings, or so many men believe.

Since the range of feelings and emotions are all a part of being human, where do these feelings show up in the lives of men? Just because I don't acknowledge you, my emotions, doesn't mean you don't exist. Doesn't mean you aren't dictating how I think and behave. Just because I tell everyone, including myself, that you, my feelings, aren't important and impactful doesn't mean you aren't important and impactful. I'm convinced that our homes, communities, cities, and world would be a lot less violent if men could, at the very least, identify what they feel and tell someone. Violence against women surely would decrease if men could use their words rather than their fists to communicate their fears and frustrations.

Am I suggesting that men should be as emotional and emotive as women? Absolutely not! Men are different from women. These are differences I appreciate and respect and work to embrace. Quite frankly, such behavior in a man would be annoying, unnecessary, and extremely unattractive. I am, however, advocating a shift in how men handle emotional pain. Theirs and the health of our relationships, families, and communities would greatly improve if men would stop running from, stuffing, and anesthetizing their painful emotions and instead acknowledge, own, articulate and, where needed, heal them.

## MEN WHO DON'T HO BUT HEAL

The men who find the strength and courage to face their pain don't do it alone. They have friends, family, therapists, spiritual advisors, sponsors, life coaches, and, more significantly, a God of their understanding, helping them to navigate their inner landscape. When John's relationship fell apart, his Narcotics

Anonymous (NA) sponsor cautioned him against jumping into a new relationship. He was instructed to sit still so he could heal. Essa, who you'll meet very soon, has, for the first time, been willing and able to recover from a breakup without using women and alcohol. Both John and Essa have a cadre of wise and supportive confidantes to which they turn during emotionally tumultuous times.

When men, trapped in the false notion that real men don't need anyone, attempt to deal with life challenges alone—like the loss of a loved one—everybody suffers. Everybody. But when men are willing to face their pain, give voice to it, and heal it, everybody benefits. *Everybody.* You see, unacknowledged, unaddressed, unhealed emotions are either processed or expressed in healthy ways, or they, like grass pushing its way through the cracks of concrete, come out in places they don't belong, destructively, passive-aggressively, and violently.

Men can heal. And they must. Else they drag from one relationship to the next all their dirty, funky, dysfunctional laundry. And guess who is expected to help them with this mess? You guessed it; the women that love them. Which, by the way, includes mothers, sisters, daughters and friends.

If not for themselves, it behooves men to learn how to stop running from themselves for their children's sake. Addicted, womanizing, overworked men are unavailable men. They abandon their children, and the cycle of abandonment continues.


## THE REWARDS OF EMOTIONAL HEALING

Hurt, bitterness, unforgiveness, anger, hostility, resentment, and fear are lethal emotions when they harden. They weigh us down and make us heavy, dense, dark, and difficult people to love. Men and women who hold onto old pain make hellish partners because their unhealed emotional wounds make them crazy. Yes,

I said crazy. They become bona fide mental cases. They whine, complain, overreact, control, shut down, sulk, withdraw, disappear, manipulate, hide, fuss, fight, and find fault with everything. In short, they are allergic to happiness; consequently, they will do *anything* to keep happiness at bay. What makes the situation insane is that all the while they insist they want to love and be loved.

Think about it, if I ain't happy with me, how can I be happy with you? If I ain't happy, why in the world would I want you to be happy? If I'm miserable, how in God's name can I support you in being happy? It's simply an impossibility.

And another thing, unhealed men and women don't enjoy peace. Because of this, if it appears you're delightfully peaceful, they will do their level best to destroy it for you.

So, what are the rewards of emotional healing? The biggest reward is the lightness of being that emotionally healthy people enjoy. People on the healing path are kinder, gentler, more joyful people. They are more fun and a whole lot easier to love.

## A Conversation
## with Essa Ali
### *A Recovering Abuser*

**DMR: Tell us a little about you.**

**EA:** I am an African American man, forty-three. My single mother raised me. Much of my life I've been looking for a sense of significance, love, and validation because, I think, I lacked a strong, positive male presence in my life. At an early age, I gravitated toward the streets of Baltimore. I am not saying my mom and dad didn't love me; however, I didn't feel loved unconditionally. They did the very best that they could with what God blessed them with. They provided me with food, clothing, and shelter, while my emotional life and maleness was being fed and molded by my peers. Consequently, one of my core beliefs became: *if a man has money and women, then he has power and success.* This core belief led me to a world of sex, drugs, and violence.

I spent time in prison. Fortunately, I have always been spiritual and desired to improve myself. Today, I am committed to my spiritual, mental, and emotional development. I stopped breaking the law in 2002, got a job, and embarked upon a search for truth and soul development. My journey, I must confess, has been one of wrestling with childhood hurts, limiting beliefs, and addiction to women, relationships, drugs, and alcohol. It has been an uphill battle for most of my life; but today, I am grateful for my recovery. It took me decades to get comfortable with being single, without the assistance of women, drugs, and alcohol.

**What do you look for in a woman? Has that changed over the years? If yes, how so? And why?**

Being introduced to sex, drugs, and alcohol at the age of twelve, I learned to see females as objects. I believed women were for my personal gratification. A female, one of my drugs of choice, had to be someone that could make me feel significant, valued, and validated. That meant she had to be attractive, smart, loyal, down for whatever, sexually open-minded, honest, trustworthy, funny, healthy, and clean.

As I got older, what I looked for in a woman underwent a change. I fell into an unhealthy pattern with women. In ninety-eight percent of my relationships, I lied and cheated. I looked for a woman that was as codependent as I was, or more. I was a drama king and "king baby" to my core.

Yes, over the years I've grown. Today, I am not so caught up in the thrill of the chase and the novelty of sex. Nor am I as concerned with what a woman can do in the bed but am interested in what is in her head. Is she emotionally detached, jealous, insecure, and lazy? Does she place her friends before her man or relationship? Or is she spiritual, clean, drug-free, humorous, spontaneous, adventurous, and insightful? Is she emotionally available? Does she enjoy cooking and children? Is she honest? Can she express her emotions without anger? I am now interested in substance, rather than superficial characteristics. I want a soul connection not just a relationship.

**Largely, would you say your relationships have been successful or disastrous?**

I would have to confess that all my relationships have been a disaster because of my negative core beliefs, sense of male entitlement, codependency, and addictive personality. Unfortunately, I have never been in a successful relationship, and if you were to interview all the women from my past, they all would say I treated them the same way.

What does this mean? It means although I've been with a number of women, I have, nonetheless, been in the same relationship since I was twelve. Like a person has rollover minutes on their cell phone, well, I had rollover relationships. Like I said, I cheated and lied in ninety-eight percent of my relationships. I'm not proud of this, but I share it so you can see just how sick I was.

**Can you share a breakup story with us?**

Because all of my relationships have been essentially the same, this will be easy for me to do. Six months ago a relationship ended. It folded because of my insecurities, jealousy, and codependency.

The sister was a worldly woman with many male friends. I thought she had difficulty drawing the line between her male friends and our relationship. I had a temper tantrum whenever I thought she violated my "golden rules" of respect and male entitlement. I shouted, cursed, and used emotional blackmail in an attempt to make her feel the pain that I was feeling.

There was one older guy hanging around that was in love with her. At first, she denied that this man was in love with her. I, however, could see it. She wanted me to befriend him. When he learned of our relationship, he confessed his feelings for her. I thought she should put some distance between them, so he would see their relationship was strictly platonic. She told him I had an issue with their relationship. Consequently, they decided to put some space between them. That, however, didn't last long when she decided he should remodel her bathroom. As he worked on the bathroom, she would stay "under" him, all under the guise of being an apprentice.

Meanwhile, I was ignored. I told her how I felt. It was in vain. She told me she didn't want him, that there was nothing to worry about, and that she was making dinner for the three of us so we can eat together. I exploded, attacking her with some pretty cruel words. My words cut deep. She decided she didn't want anything more to do with me. Said she was tired of my controlling ways. Said she felt like nothing she did was right or good enough for me; that by being with me she was losing herself. I am not saying she had no shit, but I must own up to my shit, for the sake of my recovery and healing.

**Why do you think your relationships lacked longevity?**

Today, in retrospect, I believe my relationships lacked longevity because of my unconscious need to feel validated, valued, and loved by my significant other. Although I didn't realize it then, a core belief that I was a failure if I didn't have a woman or money was driving my destructive behaviors. Also, I was unemployed at the time; my woman, I believed, was my symbol of success. I used women like I used drugs. In fact, it was a woman's JOB to please Essa. She was to allow me to mold and shape her to fit my egotistical needs. Women weren't equals or human beings. Their sole purpose was to make me feel good. And still, I complained about everything. I complained because I lacked a sense of worth and self-love. What a job for them!

**When a relationship ends, how do you cope with that loss?**

In the past, whenever a relationship ended, I would cope with drugs, alcohol, and another woman. You see, up until today, I've never been single. It took me forty-three years to learn how to be alone and to embrace singleness. Actually, most of the time, even before the relationship ended, I had already gotten another woman. Meanwhile, I'd still be trying to manipulate and control my ex. In other words, I wanted to have my cake and eat it too. The pain of believing I was a failure was more than I could bear alone, so I turned to whatever made me feel better in an attempt to numb myself against it.

**Have your coping strategies changed over the years?**

Absolutely! It took me forty-plus years to acquire healthier relationship and coping skills. As I take full responsibility for the ending of my last relationship, I am also seeking help. I enrolled in the House of Ruth's Gateway Project for abusive men. I started therapy. I attended Narcotics Anonymous and 12-Step meetings for love addicts. I embrace my spirituality 100 percent. I am committed to uprooting this core belief in failure and heal my codependency. This has been a very painful and necessary process. Nonetheless, I no longer choose to avoid my emotional pain but to work through it. I absolutely refuse to one day be a lonely old man with nothing but memories of how I mistreated good women.

**Have you any regrets about who you were being in your intimate relationships?**

Absolutely! I regret every lie I told to women who only wanted to love me. I regret every abusive thing that I ever said to women who only tried to love me. I regret every emotionally abusive word or act that I ever inflicted on any woman that only sought to love me. I regret the cheating, the emotional blackmail, the complaining, and the codependency. Yes, I regret everything!

The only thing these women wanted from me was respect and reciprocity, to receive the unconditional love that they had for me. A few weeks ago I cried for the way that I had mistreated my last "victim." I felt ashamed. This woman did not deserve my wrath. To all the wonderful, beautiful women of my past I want to say, "I am sorry. Please forgive me!" I would never want my daughters to endure what I did to those women.

**What have you observed as common challenges that black men and women face in their effort to make love work?**

Too few of us are working to heal our negative core beliefs. Instead, in a desperate attempt to escape painful thoughts, emotions, and feelings, we fall prey to addictions. So many people stand on shaky ground in their relationship with a God of their understanding. For a sense of self and value, we seek the approval of others. I like to say we might have good personal hygiene, but our spiritual hygiene stinks. A lot of us wrestle with childhood traumas that show up as drama and chaos in our relationships.

Most black people could benefit from some form of therapy. Therapy could help them confront the underlying issues that cripple our relationships, families, communities, and us. We waste time looking outside of ourselves for that perfect mate who we think will complete us because we don't have the patience or commitment to spiritual growth and finding love within ourselves.

**What is the role of spirituality in your life and relationships?**

Spirituality plays a very significant role in my life. It is the driving force behind my willingness to change and ability to empathize with myself and others. Spirituality has assisted me greatly on my journey to self-discovery. Because of my faith in a power greater than myself, I have the courage to be honest about my issues and seek the aid of God. However, first, I had to admit that I was a man with control and jealousy issues, who didn't love himself enough, had male entitlement issues, and wrestled with addiction. In other words, I had to be completely honest with my Higher Power and myself if I intended to stop the cycle of self-abuse. I say self-abuse because every time I abuse or mistreat a woman, I am abusing and mistreating myself. We are one! I now realize that God is Love; therefore, I am love. This love is complete, whole, and powerful; therefore, I am complete, whole, and powerful. I need not depend on anything outside of myself to experience those qualities.

**I understand that you are a recovering addict. From what are you recovering? In addition to spirituality, what other tools and strategies are you engaged in?**

Yes, I am a recovering addict, and, outside of my deep personal relationship with God, I go to therapy, the House of Ruth men's program, and several support groups. I am recovering from sex and love addiction and drugs and alcohol.

**Black men tend to be antagonistic toward counseling and therapy. Why do you think that is?**

I think black men are reluctant to get therapy and counseling because of their fear of commitment and an aversion to changing directions. Largely, black men have pimped, played, and hustled our women for so long that we think it's the right and manly way to be in relationship with women. Therefore, being open, honest, vulnerable, and committed are the wrong, weak ways to be in relationship with women.

Sadly, more than a few women also think this way. Brothers think if one woman won't conform another one will. Entering therapy has been one of best things that I've done in my life. In therapy, I discovered that I've been in the same relationship for thirty years. I now see how my core belief "I am a failure" has been a magnet for the painful situations, circumstances, and conditions that I've created. I realize that all these years I've been a selfish, wounded little boy masquerading as a man. Thank God I'm on the road to recovery and true manhood.

* * * * * * *

## ABANDONMENT ISSUES AND RELATIONSHIPS

*"Fear of abandonment can create a pattern where you attract those who abandon you. Or you abandon them."*
—Laura Frisbie, M.Ed.

*"There is no greater barrier to romantic happiness than the fear that I am undeserving of love and that my destiny is to be hurt."*
—Nathaniel Branden, *Six Pillars of Self-Esteem*

Fear of abandonment sinks relation*ships*. Interestingly, the very thing the person wrestling with abandonment issues fears the most—being left—is what they very often cause . . . by driving their beloved away with their insatiable need for time, attention, love and reassurance. Like self-esteem expert Branden says, "There is no greater barrier to romantic happiness than the fear that I am undeserving of love and that my destiny is to be hurt."

A woman I know said she was in a relationship with a man that she adored. There was just one little problem. He complained constantly! He complained, "You don't spend enough time with me. You didn't call me back. You don't treat me fairly." She didn't do this. She didn't do that. It didn't matter that she was working, studying or spending time with her children, her man demanded constant attention. She soon lost the desire to see him at all. And noticed that her desire for his touch also started to diminish. "His neediness," she said, "besides being a nuisance was a turn-off." Finally, she broke up with him. He was like a leaky bucket. No matter how much she poured into him, because he had a hole in his "bucket," he always needed more, more, and some more. He simply wore her out.

This woman's ex didn't love himself. Consequently, he didn't feel worthy of her love. So he did what people with fear abandonment do, he sabotaged the relationship. See, as a child he had been abandoned by his mother. Until he patches up that hole in his soul that was created by his mother, he'll continue to attract women into his life who will love him and leave him. We heal by re-parenting ourselves. We give ourselves the love, attention, approval, validation, and reassurance that we so desperately seek from others.

People with abandonment fears will also leave relationships to avoid being left. Because my father left me, I was convinced that every man I loved would also leave me. And guess what? That's precisely what happened, over and over again. For years. Until I assumed full responsibility for my self emotionally, resolved to love me fiercely, and healed my fear of abandonment.

Whatever our dominant thoughts, out of them will come our experiences. My belief that men leave caused me to attract men into my life who did just that. And yet, as painful as it was to be left it was what my soul needed if I was going to heal my fear of abandonment. Men leaving forced me to learn how to be with and love me.

Both black women *and* men live with this ghost. And you can't identify them by the way they look, what kind of work they do, or how much or little money they make. If one or both of your parents left you, chances are, unless you've healed it, you are struggling with the fear of abandonment. Your up close and personal relationships triggers it.

Let's say you desire a committed relationship with a loving man. A good man comes along. Things are moving along nicely. Conflict arises, which is inevitable. You don't see eye to eye on an issue. He hurts your feelings. That is, he shows signs of being human. What's your knee-jerk reaction to this difficulty? Are you lacing up your Nikes and looking for the nearest exit? Are you ready to jet from reality with a bottle of wine, shop "therapy," a box of Edy's, another man? If you are, you just might be dealing with abandonment issues. If you can't trust your partner, even though he's given you no reason to distrust him, you might be wrestling with abandonment issues.

Here's another scenario: You meet a great guy. There's just one little problem: he has flaws and foibles. After all, he's a man, not *Superman*. You decide you can't live with him not being perfect, and so you kick his imperfect butt to the curb. Hmm, you just might be grappling with fear of abandonment.

You smother your beloveds. Your self-esteem is shaky. You desire intimacy even while you fear it. You opt out of a relationship with people for silly, insignificant reasons. Your need for attention, affection, and affirming never quite gets fed. That is, you're emotionally high maintenance. One moment you're clinging, the next you're threatening to leave. You secretly don't believe you're worthy of another's love and commitment. Secretly, your deepest heart's desire is to find someone who will prove you wrong.

When we can't relax into love because we are terrified that our beloved will leave us, we are bound to be high maintenance emotionally. We're like the leaky bucket; we can't hold anything because there's a hole in us. No matter how much our beloved pours love, attention, and time into us, we feel unloved. We are being loved, but we can't *feel* it. They're giving us love, but we can't *receive* it. They're showing us love, but we don't *see* it, don't *recognize* it as love. Love is running right through us. We don't feel loved because we don't love ourselves. We don't feel love from the inside. We don't see the love offered because we don't know love. Our ego has us convinced that love is something other than what we're getting; that love is about someone else completing us and making us feel whole, when authentic love really is about pushing those things to the surface that would have you believe you're broken and unlovable, so that they might be healed.

Fear of abandonment isn't healed by another's love, though others may support you in seeing yourself as lovable. Fear of abandonment is healed by the love we cultivate for ourselves. Besides, we can only see and feel the love of another to the extent that we love ourselves. I'm sure you've heard many times that you can't love another until you love yourself. Nor will you let another's love in until *you* love you.

## YOU ARE EMOTIONAL HIGH MAINTENANCE

About a decade ago, while visiting New Orleans, I met a tall, sexy world traveler. As I strolled down Bourbon Street, looking sophisticated in my jeans and shawl, he appeared from out of nowhere and started walking alongside me. He told me later that what caught his attention was how confident and self-assured I was. He was an interesting, capable man, who had a passion for life, the Blues, and great conversations. While he called northern Australia home, he traveled throughout Asia landscaping golf courses. Despite the physical distance between us, we discovered there was an emotional and spiritual connection. One time he flew in from California to visit me. When he left, I cried like a baby. Later, he flew to Wichita to tend to his deceased grand-mother's home. I met him there. Between visits, we sent each other long, lush e-mails.

Several months later, I got a "Dear Jane" e-mail from him. It wasn't working out, and he no longer wanted to see me. He wrote five words that I'll never forget, words that would change the trajectory of my life. After several painful paragraphs leading up to the final blow, I read, "*You are emotional high maintenance.*" I was floored. Stunned. Hurt. Devastated. Embarrassed. "Me? DeBora—high maintenance? How could he say such a thing? No, it's him. He's just emotionally stunted and unavailable," I argued to myself. "If he'd just learn to express *his* feelings, then I wouldn't be so emotional," so went my thinking. Until. Until I decided to stop railing against what felt like some truth.

*Was* I emotional high maintenance? Yes, yes, I was. Michael was spot-on. You know you're high maintenance emotionally when your beloved, who is traveling, responds to your e-mail with a phone call to say, "I'm thinking of you." You, however, only notice that he hadn't responded to your e-mail with an *e-mail.* Meanwhile, you can't even fully enjoy the phone call! Now *that's* emotional high maintenance.

When I look back on my relationships, I have to say I don't blame a few of my exes for leaving me. *I* would have left me. I was clingy and needy. Actually, I did leave me. We who wrestle with fear of abandonment abandon ourselves while we desperately seek the love and approval of others. How does this abandonment look? We're not faithful to our own needs, wants, dreams, and wholeness. Even as we look to another to fill us up with their love, we neglect to fill our cups with our tender lov-ing care. Remember, nobody can love you so much as to make it unnecessary that *you* love you. Commit to loving you. Love yourself deeply and fiercely and notice how easy you become to love.

## ABANDONMENT MAKES YOU *SWIRL*

Rejection can sting even the most self-assured person. But for the person grappling with fear of abandonment, rejection can feel like a blow to the head. The rejection of someone who doesn't want or love you can trigger your deepest fear that you're somehow irreparably damaged and unlovable. Rejection opens old, unhealed wounds that were created when our mother or father left us. The pain can be so raw and consuming that you'll do almost anything to make it stop. You so want those feelings of despair, desperation, unworthiness, and loneliness to stop that you seek to get back with people you know don't want you, aren't good for you, are even a danger to your well-being. You feel you can't live without him or her. Some even consider suicide as a way to make the pain go away. Depression too can also attend a breakup. And for the woman struggling with abandonment issues, depression and despair can be constant companions.

**Susan Anderson**, psychotherapist and author of *Journey from Abandonment to Healing*, writes that there are five stages of abandonment:

1.  **Shattering:** Severing of love-connection, devastation, shattering of hopes and dreams. The emotions are shock, panic, despair, feeling you can't live without your love.
2.  **Withdrawal:** You're in painful withdrawal of love-loss, as intense as heroin withdrawal. The emotions are yearning, craving, obsessing, longing for your ex's return.
3.  **Internalizing:** As you try to make sense of the rejection, you doubt and blame yourself. Idealizing the abandoner at your own expense, narcissistic injury sets in and fear incubates.
4.  **Rage:** Reversing the rejection and nursing retaliatory feelings. Displacing anger on friends who don't un-

derstand or are critical of the abandoner leads to more unhealthy action.

5. **Lifting:** Rising out of despair, life begins to distract you. You begin to open to love again and all its possibilities.

You **"SWIRL"** through all the stages over and over until you emerge from the end of the tunnel a changed person capable of greater life and love than before.

# Herstory of abuse and abandonment

*"When you hold resentment toward another,
you are bound to that person or condition by
an emotional link that is stronger than steel.
Forgiveness is the only way to dissolve that link and get free."*
—Catherine Ponder

**By Merci Hunt**

So why did I spend more than twenty years using, bashing, and manipulating men until they submitted to my will? Here is the truth. I was molested by a makeshift babysitter. C'mon, a male sitter for a six-year-old girl? Anyway, we had this really big cement basement, and this damn guy was a so-called carpenter. My stepfather paid him to apply paneling to the basement walls. There were other siblings playing in the basement too. But I was the one that he singled out. I remember to this very day how cunning and deceptive he was. Coaxing me to sit on his lap with a big, colorful, and round lollipop, the kind you get at the circus. He slid my panties down and immediately inserted his middle finger into my vagina. You know what? I still get a chill when I am finger penetrated by my husband.

I managed to tell this man that I wanted to get down. His hands did not move. I started to cry. My tears moved him to stop. I remember that my tears were bitter compared to the sweetness of the lollipop. This scene happened in the back of the basement, while my siblings were playing in the front. They were older than I, and no one cared that I was in the fucking back part of the basement in the dark? I was totally separated from them by the loud and noisy forsaken furnace. I remember that it was very cold outside, and I could see the frost and icicles hanging from the shutters. I also remember that his finger was cold, and that he had rather long fingernails for a man. He pushed me off of his lap and slapped my tail.

"If you don't tell anyone, I'll bring you a big bag of candy the next time," he said. How many children have been bribed with some frickin' candy?

Even though I was only six years old, I observed everything. My mom used to say I was too nosey. By the time I was sixteen years old I had been sexually molested many times, and so I decided that I would never trust a man. Instead, I resolved to always get over on them. I vowed to use, abuse, and kick their asses to the curb. That's right. I felt no remorse, no regret because my conscience had been seared by the invasion of unwanted lust, filth, perversion, and conditional attention.

I fell in love with a grocery bagger. He talked nonstop as he bagged my purchases. He was quite handsome; and I was impressed with his neckties. There was that "looking for a daddy shit" coming out. *Somebody save me, rescue me from myself.* Young and hot in my ass because of an early introduction to illicit sexual behavior, I gave myself to Peter. We openly fucked in the vestibule of my parents' home. My hymen was broken that night, and I got pregnant. Go figure, first time around fuck. Seven months later I gave birth to twin girls. Peter wanted to get engaged and then marry after we finished college. We were both really academic. He was planning to go to college to become a doctor, and I was going to attend the local college to pursue a career in nursing.

Unfortunately, this never came to pass, that is, the marriage. First of all, Peter's mom told me in the presence of their immediate family that he was not going to marry me. Even though he had given me a pre-engagement ring, Miss Sue said that it was just a friendship ring. I was shocked that this woman could be so bold, so cold, so callous about my feelings. Peter never uttered a word in my defense. I felt like I was going to faint from the rejection and abandonment.

Peter told me later, five fucking days later, that we were still going to date, and that he was going to marry me anyway. Well, anyway never came. Peter went off to college where he started having a sexual affair with his chemistry instructor. The bitch got pregnant. We both were pregnant at the same time. Her bastard girl was born first. Peter's family cooed over this child because she was jet-black and resembled Peter's deceased sister Roxanne.

My babies arrived two months too early, weighing in at one pound ten ounces, and two pounds eleven ounces. I believe it was an act of God's love that saved my babies. I was so stressed out. Most days I was depressed, though I functioned seventy-five percent of the time, since I worked as a secretary at Poly Western High School right up to two days before my seventh month of pregnancy.

I eyed my beautiful brown babies and promised those girls that I would forever protect them from MEN. I also promised them that they would never, ever be molested or touched inappropriately. So yes, because Peter dumped me, and I was sexually violated as a child, and experienced my share of broken promises, I set out to tear down the manhood, hope, spirit, and potential of any and all men I encountered. Why? Because mental pain can create an emotional imbalance that can lead to an icy, closed heart.

# Herstory of a father's abandonment

*"To get to forgiveness, we first have to work through the painful experiences that require it."*
—Christiane Northrup

## By Constance Delores Burrell aka Heritage

I was a young Lil' Kim fiend, walking around barking, "Fuck you! Pay me! Eat my pussy! Now politely leave, PLEASE!"

That mind-set, I believe, was the product of my relationship with my father. My father is a handsome, egotistical brother who is used to women answering to his every beck and call. Women have willingly surrendered their homes, bodies, and money to him. He called them smart because they were professional women. True, these women had degrees hanging on their walls. But in my opinion they were meek, naive, and flighty. That is, they were short on common sense. I watched and learned and decided I would be different. I wouldn't get so wrapped up in a man, since all men were like my father.

Interestingly, although I was but thirteen or fourteen at the time, my father's women would ask my advice on how best to handle him. I supposed they thought I would consider their feelings in my answers. They must not have read my résumé! I am the daughter of a single, strong-minded matriarch and a feeble-minded pimp whose intimidation and charm did not work on me. "You're just like your mother," he would say. In other words, I didn't take his shit. I was straight to the point with his women. "Open your mind, eyes, and close your fucking legs!" I would advise. My father's women saw me as an insolent, albeit astute, young lady. They seemed to silently wonder, "Why can't I be as strong and clever as you?" Clearly, my resilience and strength came from my mother.

At last, I have finally decided to tell the truth. Would you like to hear it? Well, here it is. In my adolescence and early adulthood I developed the Electra complex, which is a reversed Oedipus complex. I thought if I had sex with my father he would dump all of his women and give me the love a father should give his oldest daughter. However, when I grew into adolescence and my father still did not accept me, I turned to lesbianism. All the men who seemed to be attracted to me were chauvinistic like my father, and I was determined not to let a man treat me as my father had treated me. My father never nurtured me; this left me feeling distant and inferior. I have endured psychiatric wards in the best hospitals and been on anti-depressants since middle school.

Well, I now realize that I can change me. I have to let my negligent past be just that, the past. I accept that

I must let go and, as a result, I've grown more comfortable with who I am. I'm no longer afraid of developing relationships with men. I have gained a sense of self-worth and love that trump my traumatic past. I've also vowed to choose associates more carefully, love some people from afar, and love and be true to me.

## OVERCOMING FEAR OF ABANDONMENT

*"When I let go of what I am, I become what I might be."*
—Lao Tzu

I know the emotional and psychological carnage that fear of abandonment can create in an individual's life. I also know that the love of another, no matter how unconditional it is, cannot free us from this fear. You, my dear, have to do the work to heal this wound.

After you SWIRL through another breakup, what's important is that you survived it. You're breathing. You're still alive. What now? You have a choice. You can do what most people grappling with fear of abandonment do—run and jump into a new relationship. Unfortunately, though, so long as you carry the energy of rejection and loss in your mind, body, and spirit you set yourself up to attract yet another person who will leave you. You'll be hurled right back into the SWIRLing cycle. You, however, aren't powerless. Fear of abandonment can be healed. The Universe supports you in healing this wound. If you could latch onto another forever, you would, wouldn't you? But it doesn't work like that.

Meanwhile, that wound remains alive within you, wreaking havoc on your life, self-esteem, sense of self, and peace. Why? Because it's a painfully scary and precarious existence to expect another human being, who is both fallible and wounded, to make you feel whole and complete and loved. By the way, it cannot be done. Nobody or nothing outside of you has the power to make you feel whole and complete and loved. Only you can do that. The Goddess in you can do that. Are you ready to heal your fear of being alone, desperate, and codependent? It can be done. It takes work, but it can be done.

Adults who fear abandonment were once children who *were* abandoned. They were abandoned by their mothers and fathers, those charged to love, protect, and provide for them. We cannot go back into the past and change it. We can, nonetheless, change how we see and feel about that past. I offer you these eight strategies for overcoming your fear of abandonment.

## 8 STEPS TO DISSOLVING FEAR OF ABANDONMENT

Fear of abandonment is a wound. From childhood. If you want to be free of this debilitating fear, you must heal the wound. It's a process. It's work. It, however, can be done. These steps put you on the path to healing.

**1. Take Responsibility for You** – If you truly desire to be free from the fear of abandonment, you've got to stop looking "out there" for someone or something to give you a sense of completion, wholeness, and happiness. It's a futile quest anyway. No matter how much another loves you, nobody can make you feel secure, happy, and complete. That's your job. That emptiness that you feel can be healed, but only when you stop addictively seeking to fill it with another relationship, shopping, drinking, sex, drugs, or money. Take responsibility for your life, your emotional life included. We were born alone, with everything within us to feel whole and complete, whether we're in a relationship or not. Somewhere along the way, you lost sight of this wholeness. But it's still there. You simply must do the work to rediscover it. To reclaim it. To feel it again. Put down the bottle, chicken wing, piece of cake, pills, credit card, cigarette, porn magazine, joint, and tend to your inner world. Pray. Meditate. Fast. Journal. Sit with the pain. Pray some more. Find a loving, supportive spiritual community and be in it often. It's time to take care of you in every respect. Trust me, a sense of wholeness and completion can be recovered. Stay the course.

**2. Forgive Your Parents** – Your deepest wounds were inflicted in childhood, by your parents and caregivers. As you move through life, when you've not forgiven and healed old hurts you attract people into your life—lovers, friends, spouses, coworkers, colleagues, supervisors and managers who needle and strike at those unhealed places. Remember, your parents were wounded too. That's why they hurt you. Hurt people hurt people. If you're like so many people, you have yet to forgive your parents. Until you do, you will never be free. You are frozen in a painful past, doomed to repeat it. This isn't living. Instead, you're acting out fearful conditioning. Nor will you ever be in a new relationship so long as you hate your parents. It might look like a new relationship, but is it? He's a bit taller, darker, and wittier than the last one. But wait. He too is a controlling, emotionally unavailable cheater. Just like the others. Just like dear ole dad. So long as you hold a grudge, harbor resentments, nurse bitterness, you chain yourself to a painful past. Unwittingly, you've brought the past into the present. Consequently, your future probably doesn't look too inviting. We attract our "parents" into our lives because we bring about what we think about. We're powerful like that.

Our refusal to forgive hurts nobody but us. Meanwhile, the perpetrator is unaffected. Don't you think they've hurt you enough? By forgiving them, you stop "them" from hurting you further. Besides, an unforgiving heart is a closed heart. It keeps love at arm's length. You can forgive, with God's help you can.

**3. Shift Your Perception** – If you fear abandonment that means your parent(s) abandoned you in some way. It could have been desertion, divorce, death, abuse, or neglect. No matter how much you wish things had been different, things were what they were. You, however, have the power to change how you look at what happened and what it all means.

As a child, bestselling author Dr. Wayne Dyer spent some years in an orphanage. He didn't make that a bad thing. When new kids were delivered to the orphanage, crying, he'd be summoned to give them a pep talk. He said he didn't understand why they were sad, that they could do whatever they wanted; there were no parents to answer to!

I was no Wayne Dyer. In my youth, although I felt protected by some invisible force, I, however, didn't see the blessing in being abused and abandoned by my father. However, now that I'm on the other side of the pain, I'm clear that but for that difficult relationship with my father I would not be the strong, resilient, and wise woman that I am. My father's insistence that I'll "never amount to anything!" was fuel to me. Those words drove me to achieve. I had to prove him wrong. With very little support, I graduated high school and got a job in a nursing home as a dietician's assistant. Two years later, I went to college. Six years after graduating college, I went to law school. There's a blessing in every "bad" thing that happens in your life. If you look for it, you'll see it. That's how powerful you are.

**4. Re-Parent Yourself** – What kind of childhood do you wish you'd had? How do you wish your father/mother had treated you? Had talked to you? Were your parents harsh, cold, distant, silent, belittling, critical, abusive physically, emotionally unavailable, and inaccessible? Have you always wished you'd had warm, kind, tender, fun, protective, and available parents? Did your parents shut you down, close you out, and ignore you and your feelings? Okay, what are you going to do about it?

We've already discussed it. You can't go back and redo your childhood. But guess what you can do? To yourself you can be the parent you never had. Don't laugh. You can. In fact, you must. First, you've got to stop beating up on yourself. Give yourself a break and some long overdue tender loving care. It's time to smash those self-sabotaging tapes, you know the ones, the ones that demand to know, *"Who do you think you are?"* The ones that bellow, *"You'll never amount to anything! You're so stupid. That's dumb. You can't have that! Stop dreaming! You're not pretty enough to do that. You're fat and ugly. You always screw things up. Stay in your place. You'll only fall on your face. You can't."* You can have some compassion for *you.* Support you in everything that you do. You can show up for you. And when you stumble and fall, you can be there to pick you up.

Here's a novel idea: you can be your OWN parent. While you're doing that, forgive yourself for everything you've ever done or didn't do.

Last but certainly not least, have some fun. Play, laugh out loud, dance.

**5. Cultivate an Intimate Relationship with a Higher Power** – Whether you call that power God, Spirit, Divine Mind, the Universe, One Mind, Higher Power, Allah, Yahweh, Jehovah, Jah, I AM, or the Almighty, having an intimate relationship with this power is the key to healing *everything* that ails you! Trust me, I know. I've been through the relationship wringer, so to speak, and I'm still standing because I have an intimate relationship with God. Your parents might have abandoned you. Your man might sometimes misbehave. You might feel alone and lonely more often than you'd care to admit. But there's a Power that dwells within you that will never leave or fail you. This Power fills empty places, mends broken hearts, and restores us to wholeness in mind, body, and spirit. You need only turn to It.

To tell you the truth, I can't imagine attempting to weather life's storms alone, without God. Trying to live the good life without tending to your spirit would be like attempting to grow a maple with no soil, sun, and water. Without those things that nourish the tree, there is no tree.

**6. Change Your Perception of Relationships** – *A Course in Miracles* tell us that relationships are assignments. Given that, don't you think it's time we stop using relationships as hiding places, stop treating them like avenues to material wealth and success, and cease to believe they have the power to make us feel complete? If we'd be willing to see them for what they are, opportunities to learn, grow, and transform, we might have more compassion and patience with our beloveds and ourselves.

Having a man won't solve your problems. If you're miserable, he won't make you happy. A man, however, can help heal your wounds, if you are willing to do the work once evidence of them surface. We experience so much angst in our relationships because our expectations of what they can do are unreasonable. Your man is your mirror. Look deep into his eyes, see your soul, and instead of trying to fix him, turn your attention inward and heal you. Every relationship is your teacher. Learn the lessons that they come to teach you and advance forward. Every advancement gets you a little bit closer to the woman you are meant to be, a self-loving woman who knows her worth.

**7. Fly Solo for a While** – Be alone. Yes, I said it. Go it alone for a while. Your fear of abandonment alerts you to the need to be alone with yourself. It's a wound that's yearning to be healed.

Your attempts at healing it through getting in another relationship are merely a temporary fix, a Band-Aid. The wound is still there, only covered over by a relationship. When you encounter relationship challenges or it ends, you'll once again experience the emptiness. If you heal the wound, you won't need a Band-Aid. You can then be in a relationship minus the fear of being left. Though some of the fear may linger, no worries because you will have discovered how to be single and satisfied.

Another thing. If you've not fixed your "picker," you'll only attract the same kind of man over and over again. He may be a little taller and more financially stable, but emotionally, he's the same as the last one. And the one before that one.

When we fear abandonment, we tend to attract people who are ambivalent about commitment. Shoot, we're ambivalent ourselves though we swear we want to be in a committed relationship. Remember, what we think about we bring about. A fixation with someone leaving results in our beloved going away. So why not fly solo for a while? Don't get into another relationship right after a breakup. Put some significant space between relationships. Give yourself space to breathe. To reflect. To regroup. To examine the part that you played in the demise of your relationship. Get to know you, your inner landscape, through journaling, prayer, and meditation. Reacquaint yourself with you. Or get to know yourself for the first time. Resolve to get on more solid ground, emotionally, spiritually, and financially.

**8. Find Your Purpose and Live It** – Do you know why you're here? Why you took a body and incarnated? We each have a purpose. What's yours? My purpose is to teach, inspire, love, and encourage others as I grow and expand. I'm happiest when I'm doing one of those things. No matter how in love I am with a man or how much he loves me, I cannot be completely fulfilled unless I teach, inspire, love, and encourage as a speaker, writer, coach, friend, and mother. Those hunger pangs of yours can't be satisfied by the love of a man. Being a wife and mother are worthy roles to play on the planet. And yet, we are capable of more. Much more.

There's a call on every life. Maybe for some, being a wife and mother are their Calling. But for most women, those beautiful roles don't completely fulfill them. God has called them for more. Consequently, a man, no matter how decent and devoted he is, cannot satisfy your need for fulfillment nor take the place of a purpose-driven life. Like I said to a guy friend, is it any wonder that some women are a pain in the butts of men, always wanting more, more, and some more . . .because they put all their desire eggs into their love and relationship basket? Tsk, tsk! What a recipe for disaster.

Per Abraham Maslow's hierarchy of needs, the fifth need is esteem, not only self-esteem but the esteem of others. When we walk in our purpose, we enjoy the satisfaction that comes from being in alignment with God's plan for our life; we also get our need for the esteem of others met. This, by the way, curbs, and perhaps even cures, an excessive need for the attention, validation, and approval of our partners.

## HOSTAGE NO MORE

You need not continue to be a hostage to your fear of being left. Besides it being an utterly agonizing way to walk through life, like all fears, fear of abandonment makes you a magnet for more of the very things you don't want. You draw unto you men who experience closeness and intimacy as engulfment. And when the fear gets to be too much, they jump ship.

Men ambivalent about whether they even want a committed relationship find you attractive. Though they may appear to be ready, willing, and able to commit, they aren't. Ambivalent men leave you while they're with you. You get sick. They don't show up. They insist that you lean on them; then they let you down. They withdraw their love and attention under the guise of being overwhelmed with work. Just when you need them the most, they leave you in a lurch. They lie and cheat, other forms of abandonment and betrayal. Such men are but a reflection of your fear of abandonment and intimacy.

Your fear of abandonment compels you to run from anything that remotely looks like it could bring you pain. "Don't get too close," the abandonment ghost chants, "he's going to leave you just like all the other ones did. Just like your father did. Remember?"

Endeavor to heal your fear of abandonment so you can experience the freedom that comes from being secure within whether you're in a relationship . . .or flying solo. It's work. But you're worth it. And up to it.

# Breaking Our Silence

*"Our lives begin to end the day we become silent about things that matter. If it's important enough to complain about, it is important enough to take action on."*
—Dr. Martin Luther King, Jr.

WHERE I WORSHIP, one of my favorite parts of the service is a segment called, "It Works." During It Works we get to share how our spiritual practices and principles are working to transform our lives. One Sunday Shameeka Dream went to the podium. Her right arm was in a cast and sling. One of her eyes was black; there were stitches in her face. She said, "I was assaulted. When I was in the hospital my friends came, my minister came, and the police are looking for him."

Right before service ended, I went downstairs to the bathroom. Upon my return, Dream, still seated up front, was surrounded by a group of women and one man. I joined them. We held our beloved sister and prayed with her. She sobbed. I cried. Some of the Reiki practitioners did a treatment on her. I wiped the tears from her eyes. And mine. I felt compelled to pray for a healing between the sexes. I prayed for the hurting young man who'd brutally beaten our beloved sister, his ex-girlfriend, with an iron rod. Clearly my brother had to be hurting to have done something like this, to have broken a woman's arm in two places, put a deep gash in her scalp, and left her pretty brown face black and blue. While I prayed for that wounded young man, I also prayed for all hurting black men.

Dream gave me permission to share her story and her real name. She thinks it's time we break the silence around domestic violence. She's right. It's time to break the silence that seduces us into believing that black men don't beat and kill their wives, girl-friends, baby mamas, and exes. While we know they do! Every nine seconds a woman is beaten by a man who claims to love her. Maybe you have never been slapped, punched, body slammed, knifed, choked, dragged, spat on, burned, kicked, stomped, backhanded, or raped by a man who professed to love you. But you know a woman who has. A mother, daughter, sister, friend, coworker, neighbor.

Dream told us who had beaten her. "I won't be ashamed," she said defiantly, "and I'm not a battered woman. Yes, I was beaten up, but I'm not a battered woman." I agree. A woman who gets the beat down and keeps coming back for more is a battered woman. A woman who is beaten but stands forth un-ashamed, declaring, "I will not tolerate being beaten," is not a battered woman.

## LITTLE GIRL IN THE MIDDLE

From a deep sleep I awake to loud voices. A little girl is crying hysterically, pleading with her father not to hurt "Mommy." I can see her sweet brown tearstained face in my mind's eye. Her eyes full of fear. Her mother says plaintively, "Doug, baby, I love you . . . but I can't do this anymore! It's 3:12 in the morning. I'm annoyed. In less than three hours I've got to get up and get to work." *Should I call the police?* I don't. This is getting old.

Just weeks prior I was forced awake by Doug's obscenities. His wife was all kinds of bitches and whores. It was 3:22 A.M. The first night Adia and I spent in our new home our expectations of peace and quiet were suddenly shattered. Doug slapped Diamond around, ignoring the pleas of his little girl to not "hit my mommy." What irony. A battered women's shelter is in walking distance from us. Ten years ago I worked there, as an attorney, helping battered women secure protective orders against their abusers, husbands, boyfriends, babies' daddies, and exes. Before that, as a law clerk for Baltimore City's State's Attorney's Office first Domestic Violence Unit, I dedicated six years of my life to assisting abused women in prosecuting their abusers. I advised, counseled, coached, prepared, cajoled, begged, and pleaded with women to prosecute their abusers. *And yet, none of these early mornings did I call 911.* Why? You know, I didn't want to get involved. We never want to get involved. We're rather roll over, and go back to sleep.

But we can't sleep on domestic violence any longer. It's time to wake up. If not for anyone else, we must wake up and get involved for the children. Else the cycle continues.

We live in a society where violence against women is not only ignored and encouraged it's deemed good entertainment. Do you doubt me? Turn your TV on, any time of day or night. Go to the movies. What will you see? Violence against women.

Sister, you don't have to be a statistic. It's your birthright to live a violence-free life.

Violence, as you undoubtedly know, isn't limited to a fist upside your head. Loads of women who have never experienced the blow of a man's hand against their soft skin nonetheless are being abused. Many don't realize they're abused, while others are in denial about it. Still, other women secretly put up with abuse because they're infinitely more terrified of being alone than they are intolerant of emotional and verbal battery.

# The Emotionally Abusive Relationship

*"As a holistic being you shatter the illusion of your separateness and reveal your connection to everything. This empowers you in a way that the ego-driven self could never contemplate."*
—Dr. Wayne Dyer

TAKE THIS MINI quiz to see if you can spot emotional abuse. Circle the best answer(s):

    a.   You like to talk things out; he won't
    b.   He insists, "You're just too sensitive!"
    c.   He doesn't support you in achieving your dreams
    d.   He competes with you
    e.   All of the above

    a.   He yells at you, but only in private
    b.   He denies your reality, then hands you his
    c.   He frequently "needs" you when you need to focus on you, your work, your child(ren)
    d.   His jokes are at your expense
    e.   All of the above

The physically abusive relationship is easy to spot. Your man slaps, punches, pushes, bites, kicks, body slams, backhands, stomps, drags, bear hugs, spits on you. Your injuries are visible, sometimes for all the world to see. Other times, they're hidden under your clothes. Your flesh is black and blue, swollen, torn, broken, cut.

On the other hand, the emotionally abusive relationship can be harder to detect even by the woman in it. If you answered "e" for both sets of statements, then you're right. All of the above are forms of abuse. Emotional abuse. Which, by the way, always accompanies physical abuse but can be inflicted in the absence of physical abuse.

A guy I was with, who we'll call Dick, was emotionally abusive. I finally left him when he cheated on me the morning of my birthday. And yet, while with him, though I bragged to my friends about how wonderful he was I secretly suspected that I was tolerating abuse. He shut me down, put me down, and halfheartedly supported me. He pressured me to choose between him and my child, him and my commitments, him and my me-time. He lied to me, and broke up with me when I didn't comply with his demands for more attention, time, and submission to his perception of a good woman.

One day we were sitting in Dick's living room, talking and watching TV when, out of the blue, he grabbed me in the collar and started yelling at the top of his voice. I don't remember what he said, more importantly, I don't recall what triggered this assault. What I do remember is the terror that I felt. This six-foot plus, 230 pound man with a hand span the size of a football was tossing me around like I was some thug he had a score to settle with. I should have left him then. But, like so many women, I chose to act as if nothing meaningful had happened, made it insignificant in my mind . . . so I could remain in the relationship. Later, he laughed it off and said, "Baby, you know I was just playing with you." I wonder how many women have been kicked, punched, ridiculed, shamed, jabbed, put down, berated, dragged, called "bitch" . . . all under the guise of "Woman, you know I was just playing"? Of course, he was "just playing with me." That's the sort of thing abusive men say when a woman calls them on their violent behavior.

It wasn't until I happened upon Patricia Evans's book, *The Verbally Abusive Relationship,* that I could no longer deny the truth: Dick was an abusive man. By then I was done with him. Still, I was thrilled to finally discover that there were concepts that describe the dynamics of our relationship.

Evans writes about two kinds of power: *Power Over* and *Personal Power.* "One kills the spirit. The other nourishes the spirit," writes Evans. To read more about how these two kinds of power differ, get her book. But here's what I got from Evans's research and interviews with emotionally abused women. The Power Over way of being in a relationship, by definition, is abusive. How could it not be? Your mate seeks to have power over you. To dominate and control you. But you're a grown woman, right? Evans says this kind of power "is stolen power." The abuser subscribes to the edict that "if you don't have someone you have power over, you don't have power at all." My "aha!" moment came reading Evans's book.

After several months of being with Dick he suddenly stopped being willing to discuss important issues and, therefore, resolve conflicts. Equals communicate. Hear each other. They are willing to discuss and resolve conflicts. Their respect for the other—and their own thoughts, feelings, and opinions, is at the core of their ability to honestly share and listen.

A man bent on dominating and controlling the woman in his life refuses to see her as his equal, so he shuts her down. To him, what she has to say is of little to no value. If he can keep her from experiencing a sense of resolution and closure about the issues that matter to her then he has control, or so he believes. Consequently, the abused woman never feels like she's being heard and seldom feels like she has resolution and closure on issues. This leaves her feeling unsupported, invalidated, and alone.

Personal power is the other kind of power. Individuals who desire to live a life of power and purpose are committed to developing their personal power. To have personal power is to exercise control over your own life. Not over somebody else's life. In a relationship where the personal power of each party is respected, even encouraged, there's a spirit of cooperation, mutual support, and respect.

Evans says Power Over and Personal Power people exist in two different realities. It takes two people, says Evans, to create the relationship where personal power reigns supreme. And yet, it only takes one person to prevent Personal Power from being the prevailing culture of the relationship. Said in another way, if you're involved with a man who's so insecure and fearful that he must have power over you to feel powerful, then even if you'd like to create a relationship in which mutual cooperation and support are valued, you can not do it with this man. Unless, of course, he is willing to change. You, however, cannot change him. He must change himself. Dick's arrogance and self-righteousness told me he would never change. So I left. I, as do you, deserve to be with a loving, kind, and supportive man. And I hope you won't settle for anything less than that.

## BREAKING THE CYCLE OF ABUSE

I'm no victim. Nor was it an accident that I attracted Dick and all the other controlling men into my life. If you can relate, listen up. I wanted a loving, trusting relationship with a man. In the beginning it appeared I'd attracted it. It didn't take long for me to see that to stay with Dick would be to choose to be abused, disrespected, and invalidated. To stay with Dick would mean I was choosing him over me. Our relationship lasted seven months.

Once upon a time I would have given a man like Dick years. I've grown. I don't need a father. Nor do I want one. I demand that the man in my life be my partner and friend and lover.

A woman who has yet to heal her daddy issues is an incredible magnet for controlling, domineering men. Because such a woman is still emotionally a little girl desperately—though unconsciously—seeking someone to take care of her abusive men find her appealing. We, however, pay an exorbitant price to be "taken care of." We pay in personal power and freedom and self-esteem, some of which we willingly hand over. Remember, you are the architect of your life. Whatever goes on in your life you've invited, created, allowed, encouraged, or promoted. Know this, no man, no matter how controlling he is, can have power over you unless you give it to him.

A woman breaks the cycle of abuse by taking back her power. She endeavors to grow up. She willingly assumes the responsibility for herself. She becomes emotionally and financially self-reliant. Is this a contradiction of what author Stephen Covey maintains and I discuss in a later chapter—that the highest level of functioning is interdependence? No, it isn't. If two people are to function interdependently, both must come to the relationship knowing—no matter how they're currently showing up—they're already whole, perfect, and complete. Knowing it's not their beloved that CAN nor SHOULD complete them. Girls and boys in adult bodies largely bring needs to the table. However, grown people bring a sense of self, confidence, and personal power. When a woman stands in her true power, she will cease to tolerate abuse from anyone. Men are no exception.

The power is within you to take care of you. You were born with it. No man can take care of you better than you can. Quit looking for Prince Charming. Stand on your own two feet, in your personal power, and reserve the front-row seats of your life for genuinely loving and supportive men. Enough said.

"The new female and the new male
are partners on a journey of spiritual growth.
They want to make the journey.
Their love and trust keep them together.
Their intuition guides them. They consult with each other.
They are friends. They laugh a lot. They are equals.

That is what a spiritual partnership is:
a partnership between equals
for the purpose of spiritual growth."
—Gary Zukav

# *I'm a Strong Independent Black Woman*

> *"There can be no great disappointment where there is no great love."*
> —Dr. Martin Luther King, Jr.

SEVERAL YEARS AGO I did a *Men's Rap on Love* forum with a small gathering of brothers. Except for me, there were no women in attendance. Six men, ranging from twenty-five to fifty-eight years old, showed up at Wayne's apartment, my friend and co-facilitator. I'd facilitated a similar relationship forum with a room full of sisters a month earlier. I was pleasantly surprised to discover how emotionally honest the men were. In fact, comparatively, they were more open and transparent than the women had been. They were visibly eager and willing to share their deeper sentiments on love and relationships.

A poignant moment occurred when fifty-six-year-old Marcus, with frustration and pain in his eyes, asked, "Why do black women find it necessary to repeatedly remind us of how strong and independent they are?" The pain in his eyes obvious, he added, "They're the only women I know who do that!"

I asked him softly, "What do you think when you hear a black woman say, 'I'm a strong independent black woman'?"

His answer came quick and clear, "That she doesn't need a man!"

What *do* sisters mean when they declare, usually all in one breath, "I'mastrongindependentblackwoman"? What do they really mean when they utter this string of words? Why do sisters feel a need to make this declaration ever so often? And under what circumstances? Is someone insinuating that she isn't strong and independent and *black*? Has someone had the audacity to even insinuate that she is weak and dependent?

To a sister, this may seem like a fairly harmless statement. While to brothers, it could easily feel like a big wooden stick upside their heads. *Clop!*

Words have power. They can create, cultivate, and sustain closeness and connection. Or they have the power to create confusion and distance between the speaker and listener. Every time a sister snaps, "I'mastrongindependentblackwoman!" there's an impact. On the hearer *and* the speaker. Marcus shared that when he hears a black woman spit those words, it leaves him feeling unwanted and not needed. He added, "How would they feel if every time they turned around a black man was telling them how little he needed them?" I don't know about you, but I heard him say those words left him hurt, feeling dismissed and marginalized. Really, is this how we want our brothers to feel? Do we, really?

## THE POWER OF YOUR WORDS

You might disagree. You might insist that that assertion isn't intended to make the black man feel anything at all, much less inconsequential, irrelevant, and unimportant. You might insist that when you've spoken those words, you didn't intend to hurt anyone. "That black men are hurt by such a declaration is on them," some might say. Let's say you're right. Then, I ask, what do you think is the impact of those words on black men who hear them, regardless of the speaker's intent? Do you think those words make them feel loved, wanted, and needed? Do they draw black men and women closer? Do they foster cooperation, camaraderie, and mutual respect?

Remember, words are never empty; they contribute or contaminate, build or break down. Consequently, we should use them consciously and with care.

Black women make this proclamation when they want a man to get that they don't need them. That they could take them or leave them and be all right. Sisters want the world to know they can make it with *or* without a man. Black mothers raise their daughters to take care of themselves; well, uh, and a whole bunch of other people. The black woman is taught she can not—and therefore, should not—expect a man to take care of her. Men cometh and men goeth. Few stayeth around. So the thinking goes. That's just the way it is. Consequently, sisters learn that men aren't to be relied upon. One sister I know was quite clear when she said she counted on men for one thing and one thing only: sex.

Sisters don't periodically announce their strength and independence because they don't *want* a man. On the contrary. Like any other woman, black women desire connection and companionship with a special man. "I'ma*strong*independentblackwoman!" is a defensive, protective device. It might feel like a sword to a man, but to sisters making that declaration, it is a shield. A shield from the pain of wanting what they fear they can't have— a love they can call their own. A man who will stand by her, through thick and thin, during feast and famine. A man who will be there come what may. "I'ma*strong*independentblackwoman!" are words enlisted to ward off more abandonment, disappointment, and loss. Though they may hurt you, my brother, know that there's hurt and fear behind these words.

## BECOMING THE MEN WE WISH TO MARRY

The black American woman has been the backbone of black families since slavery. With so many black men fleeing from their responsibilities as fathers, many choosing not to marry, significant numbers calling prison home, others marrying outside the race, still others turning their backs on women altogether, black women not only "bring home the bacon, fry it up in the pan," but all too often, sisters attempt to then act as both mommy *and* daddy to their children. When men desert their children, they effectively drop the entire emotional, psychological, social, and financial responsibility for raising their children in the laps of mothers.

I deliberately mentioned "financial" last because raising children is about so, so, so much more than money. Consequently, when a man makes child support payments but shirks the day-to-day rearing of his child(ren), his failure to co-parent is felt by both child and mother and society.

It's no secret that a significant number of black women are single and dissatisfied because they desperately want to be in a loving, committed relationship with a man. When a woman is single for long periods of time, she can get quite adept at juggling her life. She manages a household. Raises children. Holds down a job or runs a full-time business. Takes care of aging parents. Gets advanced degrees. Travels. Nurtures meaningful friendships and family relationships. Works out. Serves her spiritual community. Sends children off to college. Well, uh, you get the picture. Mothers are society's consummate multi-tasker. It takes strength and independent thinking to successfully do it ALL. Shucks, raising children is more than a notion. And doing it well, especially alone, isn't for wusses, wimps, or weaklings.

But here's a question: *Are black women getting too strong and independent for our own good?* What part are black women playing in our being "lone rangers" and raising children solo? And is it really strength and independence that's creating, contributing to, and sustaining the gulf between black men and women, or something else?

## THE BEAUTY OF BEING VULNERABLE

Strength is beautiful and sexy. And so is vulnerability. In fact, it takes strength plus courage to be vulnerable. As the Bible says, there's a time and place for ALL things. There's a time for a stiff upper lip, then there's a time for those same lips to quiver. Even weakness has its place. When a woman is weak she leaves space for her man to show up strong.

I remember when I was too damn strong for my own good. I never let a man see me cry. Then when I wanted to cry, be weak, not fake like "nothing's wrong," my man would say, "I can't stand to see you like this." Like what? See, as long as I was always being strong, he never had to man up and be there for me. He never had to grow up. Be a man. Hold me up. Hold it down. Your pretending to feel strong, when in fact you're feeling weak, vulnerable, and in need of support, does the man in your life and *you* a disservice. How can our men know to be there for us, if we're unwilling to demonstrate that they are needed?

A word about independence. Author Stephen Covey, in his book, *The 7 Habits of Highly Effective People,* says there are three levels of functioning: Dependence, Independence, and Interdependence. Interdependence is the highest level of functioning. It's a myth that anyone is independent. That includes the black woman. Did you make those clothes you're wearing? How about the chair you're sitting in? Did you grow the food you ate today? What about the house you live in, did you design and build it? It's easy to see why interdependence is a higher level of functioning than independence. Interdependence requires skills and strengths that independence doesn't. Here's why. Interdependence often necessitates effective communication, trust, cooperation, working together, agreement, reliance on someone other than yourself, and give-and-take.

When we think independence is the highest level of functioning and resolve to be so, we think and act in ways that undermine true partnership. The woman and man who accept and embrace the truth of human existence, that no one is an island, will be more successful in their relationships. Not just your romantic ones, all of them. If you desire to share your life with another in peace, harmony, and mutual cooperation and support, you've got to let go of the illusion that you're independent. People need people. Embracing this truth gets us that much closer to attracting and sustaining a loving and supportive relationship with our dream mate.

## BLACK WOMAN ANGRY

*"Needing a man is like needing a parachute. If he isn't there the first time you need him, chances are you won't be needing him again."*
—Unknown

Black women are angry, bitter, and hard. At least that's what too many black men are saying about us. Could they be right? Or are *they* just angry and bitter? Not all black women are angry and hostile, and, therefore difficult to love. But way too many of us are. That's just the truth. We might be slow to admit it publicly; still, loads of black women are pissed off. Behind closed doors some of us seethe with anger, while in public, to use the words of poet Paul Laurence Dunbar, " we wear the mask that grins and lies." If you ask a black woman if she's angry she'll likely deny it; still, black women are angry. Angry, and with plenty of good reasons.

So, what are sisters so damn angry about?

There are a multitude of legitimate reasons; let me note some of the obvious ones.

- If she's single, statistically, she has little hope of "finding" a financially fit, gainfully employed, attractive, heterosexual, emotionally healthy brother ready for a loving, trusting, monogamous relationship.
- Since we set foot in America, countless black men have left her to fend for herself, raise children alone, sleep alone at night.
- Black men (and society) act like her brown skin, kinky hair, full lips, and round hips aren't good or pretty enough for her to be placed on the proverbial pedestal. (Even while white women get all kinds of cosmetic procedures in an attempt to look like her.)
- She doesn't feel sufficiently appreciated, adored, cherished, valued, respected, loved, or supported by black men.
- Black men, especially when they join the ranks of the rich and famous, abandon her for white, Asian, and Latina women.
- If she's overweight *and* over fifty, she likely feels invisible or forgotten by black men.
- She's had more than her share of loss, disappointment, abuse, betrayal, trauma, hurt, and heartbreak.
- In the dating game, men seem to have the upper hand, therefore, the power. Feelings of powerlessness often look and feel like anger.
- She falsely believes she's a victim of circumstances beyond her control when it comes to love and relationships.
- For too many, their desire to count on a man for financial, emotional, and psychological support has yet to be fulfilled.
- Too many black men are in prison, gay, or on the down low, marrying outside the race, strung out on drugs or alcohol, not fit for marriage or partnership, unemployed

or underemployed, criminal-minded, emotionally immature or high maintenance, unwilling or incapable of commitment and monogamy and trust.

After a black woman has experienced her share of heartache, heartbreak, disappointment, betrayal, breakups, broken promises, abandonment, lies, and abuse, so often she throws in the towel on love. Some hearts hardens. A hard heart makes for a tough, difficult woman. An angry, don't-fuck-with-me posture is the black woman's attempt to shield herself from another psychic blow, another disappointment, another betrayal, another loss, another you name it.

## BLAME IT ON MEN

When I was in my twenties, I'd see women in their forties, fifties, and sixties who had given up on men and love. Their hurt and disappointment had turned into bitterness and resentment. With my young eyes, I'd look at them with pity and think, "I ain't never gonna be like that!" I simply could not fathom not wanting a man, not wanting to love and be loved by a man. And yet, that time did come. I was in my forties. I hated men, black men. See, I'd tried over and over again to love and be loved, only to be disappointed again and again. Guess who was at fault? Surely not me. I blamed men, which means I took no responsibility for what I was creating in my life. I was a victim, or so I believed until I realized that I was responsible for my happiness. I was responsible for whom I was and whom I chose to occupy the front-row seats of my life. Once I accepted responsibility, my hate for black men dissolved. You see, men can only do to us what we permit them to do. Besides, it is you who attracts and allows any man into your life. Consequently, you have the power to make different choices. Choices that honor you and bless your life.

## THE ART OF BEING A WOMAN

September 2009, I attended the *One Love Women's Retreat* in Jamaica. Nine black women shared five incredible days up in the beautiful mountains of St. Mary Parish. We ate, sang, languished, prayed, meditated, did yoga, laughed, cried, danced, climbed Dunn's River Falls, spent a day at the beach jet skiing, and more. One night a few of us even went to Amnesia, a nightclub in Ochi. I danced like nobody was watching. I had a blast! I can't tell you what else went on there because to get in one must sign a written contract not disclose, divulge or discuss anything that happens in the club. You know, whatever happens in Amnesia . . . stays in Amnesia. *Just kidding.*

Our organizers, Zakiyyah Lana and Shameeka Dream, the two very, very, very able Jamaican cooks, and Fredrick of Juta Tours took care of our every need. The climax of the trip came when we ventured all the way to the other side of the island to St. Thomas, to the Bath Fountain Hotel.

After hours of travel we arrived at Bath Fountain ready to eat, be merry, and experience that much talked about hot spring bath. We were the only guests at this clean, quaint hotel built on a roaring, rushing river. We gathered in the dining room for dinner, where we toasted and celebrated one sister's birthday, comforted and sent off another sister who was forced to cut her trip short to attend the funeral of a dear sisterfriend, and just plain have fun.

Later that evening, some of us gathered in Zakiyyah's room for a conversation about the power and beauty of sex, one of Zakiyyah's all-time favorite topics. The birthday sister already had a taste of the "Mountain Men" massage before dinner. She swooned. Laughed. Glowed. In a sentence, she was delirious with joy. I didn't quite know what to expect, but I knew one thing for sure: *I wanted all of what she'd had!*

I awoke early the next morning, oiled my body down, slipped on my bikini, and grabbed a towel. I met my sisters outside the hotel where it was lightly drizzling. A group of Jamaican men gathered just beyond the gate of the hotel, eagerly waiting for us. Once outside the gate, each woman was paired with a man.

In case you've never been to Jamaica, let me tell you a little about Jamaican men. At this writing, I've been to Jamaica five times, enough times to now jokingly refer to myself as "JaMerican." Well, I've come to appreciate a thing or two about Jamaican men. Other than their physical beauty and charm, Jamaican men are soft-spoken. Even when they see a woman whose attention they'd like to get strolling on Jamaica's sandy white beaches they never raise their voices. "Pst, pst . . . sista, sistaaaa," they whisper. "Sista, respect. Sista . . ." That is, respect them enough to stop and chat.

Not once have I observed a Jamaican man get loud, nasty, or rude because a woman ignored him. Not once. Oh, and they got sweet-talk down to a science; with that characteristically unhurried, sexy Jamaican accent they know what to say and how to say it. They have mastered the art of making a woman feel like she's the sweetest, sexiest, most desirable creature on planet earth. If they want you, they are persistent in their pursuit of you. And yet, no matter how many times you say no and keep walking, they never go Rambo on you like ghetto black American men have been known to do.

I've decided that Jamaica is to black women what Rio is to black men. Only we don't have to pay to play; we get it for FREE!

Okay, there we were, each of us paired with our very own Jamaican masseur. My masseur, Ronald, was a young Bob Marley look-alike! Lawdy. Lawdy. Lawdy. Of course he was tall, lean, and handsome . . . because, uh, he looked like Bob Marley. Did I mention young? Yep, he was young.

Ronald reached for my hand. I obediently placed my right hand in his. He held my hand high, like I was royalty, as he gingerly led me up the rocky mountain path. By twos we headed for the hot springs. Most of us let our Jamaican man take our hand, like the queens that we are, and guide our every step over the rough, unfamiliar terrain. Once we got to the river, our mountain men laid us on rocks or the ground and then proceeded rub our bodies from scalp to soles with their special oil and clay, beat and wrapped us in hot towels, and pour that naturally hot water all over our loosened bodies. It was pure ecstasy . . . and there was no hanky-panky involved.

## SURRENDER DOROTHY

One sister refused her male companion's hand . . . until her foot slipped and she almost fell to her knees. I remember wondering why she preferred to go it alone when right beside her was a man ready, willing, and able to support and guide her to a place he'd been many, many times before. A place she'd never set foot. I remember feeling sad for her. She reminded me of the women I'd seen when I was young and impressionable—bitter women who'd given up on love and men; women who'd grown hard and unyielding.

Another sister ran ahead, stumbling and falling on the rocks. Finally, she sat down and let her masseur take care of her. She relaxed. As I lay there, happily sprawled across my big rock getting the massage of my life, this sister's giggles of delight told me she'd finally surrendered.

Have you forgotten the art of being a woman? Even while we demand that black men be strong, masculine, and decisive, have we forgotten how to be vulnerable, feminine, and yielding? Have we forgotten how to be sassy and sweet, soft and supple, juicy and joyful, magnetic and magical, charming, nurturing, receptive, yielding, fun, and lovely creatures? Have we allowed past hurts and disappointments to harden our hearts? Do we confuse softness with weakness? Do we think being feminine means we've given away our power? Are we too much yang and not enough yin? Are we angry and difficult to be with? Well, I think many of us are. Shoot, I once was such a woman. Back when I went through my I-hate-black-men phase, my anger and resentment toward men made it impossible for me to be happy—with or without a man. Then one day I consciously and deliberately resolved to reclaim my femininity. I knew if I wanted to attract a manly man who was in touch with his feminine side that I'd better return to love and loveliness. Marianne Williamson captures this sentiment in her book, *A Woman's Worth,* when she writes, "Most of us want a masculine man, but there's no way to have one unless we become feminine women."

## WHY BLACK MEN LIKE WHITE WOMEN

Why do black men turn to white women? I think there are a number of reasons. One obvious reason is love. Real love beckons people across racial lines. Love transcends color and race. Brothers are known to say, "I like women. It doesn't matter what a woman's race is. If I like her, I'll date her." I laughed out loud when I heard a brother on Youtube say, "I like ALL women; if she has a vagina, I like her." Unlike the majority of black women, brothers aren't loyal to the black race when it comes to sex, love and marriage. Another reason some black men prefer white women is, simply put, she's white. You and I both have seen brothers with white women on their arms who caused us to say to ourselves, "Now you know, if that woman was black he wouldn't give her the time of day!" These hoodwinked and bamboozled brothers have bought the lie that any ole white woman is superior to even the best black woman. Tsk, tsk! So sad.

Besides falling in love and falling for white skin, I'm convinced that there are other reasons black men gravitate toward white women. Sisters may want to tar and feather me for what I'm about to say, but I'm going to say it anyway. Another reason, I believe, for black male flight is this: *women of other races tend to be more agreeable, yielding, and patient with black men.* In fact, I've talked to, read and heard black men say other race women tend to be easier to get along with than sisters.

I, for one, think it behooves sisters to, at the very least, take a look in the mirror to see if there's any truth to this allegation. What if there's validity to what brothers are saying, wouldn't you want to address this?

Wait! Before you lose your wig, let me finish. I think black women are some of the most alluring, beautiful, magnificent women on the planet. In case you hadn't noticed, I'm a black woman and proud to be one. Sure, I'm biased. So what? I have eyes. I can see. Physically, black women have it all. Full lips, round hips, skin of all hues.

Fortunately for me, I've not allowed white America to brainwash me into believing blond hair and blue eyes are superior to dark and lovely. That said, unaddressed trauma, baggage from childhood and past relationships, parental anger and resentment, unforgiveness, and fear have caused many black women to lose sight of themselves as women—that is, they've forgotten the power of soft, tender, kind, sweet, playful, receptive, yielding, magnetic, and fun. *You,* my sister, may be in touch with your femininity, but many of your friends are jaded, suspicious, inflexible, difficult, controlling, even hostile.

I think I shared a breakfast table with a couple of your friends.

Enoch Pratt Free Library brought the smart and handsome Hill Harper, the author of *The Conversation,* to Baltimore. He was the featured speaker at Pratt's annual Booklovers' Breakfast, which is held at the Marriot Hotel in Harbor East. The ballroom was packed with beautiful people, mostly black women, who are passionate about books. The round tables seated about eight. Though I ran into lots of people I knew, I traveled solo this morning. I took my seat at a table with strangers. The breakfast was fresh and varied; there was something for every palate.

Two full-bodied, well dressed sisters who looked to be in their mid to late fifties sat to my immediate left. Before the event began, one sister summoned the young African American male waiter over to our table and told him what she wanted to drink: a cranberry orange juice cocktail. Her friend asked for apple juice. I sat quietly. When the waiter reappeared, he had two carafes in his hands; one full of orange juice, the other with a small amount of cranberry. He poured cranberry into one of the sister's glass, then looked at me as if to ask, "Would *you* like some?" The indignant grunt of the other sister, who'd requested apple juice, prompted me to direct him to give her the balance of the cranberry juice. He said it was the last bit of cranberry juice in the building.

When the waiter left, the two women grunted and growled about the state of the juice supply, how they didn't believe there was a shortage of the red stuff, and what they should do about it. One snorted as she scanned the room, and then practically shouted, "I *know* there's more juice in this place!" Suddenly she spotted carafes of the precious red stuff across the room at the juice bar. Just then the young waiter appeared. I beckoned him. I'd planned to ask him to bring us more juice from the bar. After all, that's why he was there, right? To serve us.

Before he could reach the table, sister-girl jumped up and flew to the juice bar. She ran back to the table wielding a full carafe of cranberry juice. "Who," she asked triumphantly, "wants juice?" She then proceeded around the table doing the waiter's job, pouring juice into the empty glasses. All with much attitude.

## FEMININE POWER

*Why so much hostility over some fruit juice?* I couldn't help but wonder. Of course, I have a theory. A good one. Long before the young waiter encountered them, these sisters had lost sight of their real power, their feminine power. Maybe as they matured in age they discarded it, thinking they were too old to exert feminine power. Or perhaps an angry ex told them that they were less than and that caused them to lose sight of their feminine power. Or maybe they never knew they possessed such a magnificent, magical power.

Asleep to their feminine power, these sisters reached for the only power that they were familiar with: masculine power. Masculine power is about taking action. Rather than drawing to you what you want, masculine power tells you, when you want something, to "go get the damn thing." This, however, made these sisters unattractive and aggressive because they resented having to go get what they knew they were entitled to have come or brought to them. Had they been awake to their feminine power, they could have had ALL that they desired delivered to them on a silver platter. Literally. By the young male waiter there specifically to serve them.

There are times when masculine power is the "right" power to exert. However, there's something exquisitely alluring about a woman who KNOWS she has magnetic powers. And knows how to use them. Men *and* the Universe gladly respond to this magical creature. There have been times when I felt like these sisters; when I could have been attracting instead I was pursuing. But this was a glorious morning. I remembered I was a woman, and that I possessed something magnetic that I could use that would compel men and the Universe to meet my every desire . . . and enjoy doing it.

## EMBRACING YOUR FEMININE POWER

The sister who embraces her feminine power knows that men, even men young enough to be her son, want to please her. Charm, sweetness, kindness, softness, patience, and a lightness of being are the powers of a woman. They make her magnetically irresistible.

Why were these women so angry? I suspect that these women have been ignored and overlooked again and again by men. Driven by the belief that "there's-not-enough-for-me," they've been fussing and fighting for years to get their needs met. They have likely adopted the false belief that Life, and men, don't support them in having their wants and needs met. They're angry and hostile and controlling because they are afraid.

Afraid of what, you might ask. They're afraid that their experience of "there's-not-enough-for-me" just might be right and thus they really don't deserve the have their heart's desires fulfilled. Their misplaced anger, directed at the young male waiter, was really resistance to their own negative self-talk. Self-talk that would have them believe they aren't worthy; that they don't deserve to have their needs be met with ease and grace.

There's power in being a woman. Why not embrace and use it?

## A SOFTER, KINDER WOMAN

Beneath the hard mask—bitterness, anger, shame, and hostility—there's a softer, kinder, gentler woman wanting to love and be loved. Softness, kindness, and sweet-sassiness are magnetic qualities that create magic in a woman's life. Any woman can cultivate these qualities. Here are my suggestions:

**Let Go of Your Victim Mentality.** You're probably saying to yourself, "She's two kinds of crazy for thinking I think of myself as a victim." Okay, let's see. If you feel like:

- There's a shortage of men, and so they have most, if not all, of the power in relationships
- You're single because men don't appreciate a good woman like you
- All the good men are taken

- All the fine men are on the down low, i.e., gay
- All the successful men want white or light women
- The pickings are slim
- You'd like to be married, but statistically, you're doomed to be forever single
- If not for anger at men you'd feel nothing at all

If any of the sentences above describe your dominant thinking, then you see yourself as a victim. That is, when it comes to men and relationships with them, largely, you feel powerless.

Whether or not you assume full responsibility for your experiences and how men treat you doesn't change this fact: *YOU are the architect of your life.* Even when bad things seem to just happen, in reality, you are attracting, creating, allowing, promoting, or encouraging them. Perhaps you don't like how men treat you. Okay, change that. Remember, we teach people how to treat us. Men are people. Change how you treat yourself and you change how they treat you. Get this: if you lie to yourself, don't respect your time, tolerate maltreatment, accept any old doled out to you, let him treat you like a piece of meat, give, give, give, but don't get much in return, then you can expect no better treatment from a man. Know this: you are not a victim. Men don't hold all the power, while women must subjugate themselves to them so we can have a relationship with one. Women have power too. Equal—in some cases and circumstances more—power when we believe we do. Sister, reclaim your power!

**Forgive Self and ALL Others.** Begin with your parents. If your father left, neglected, or abused you, forgive him. Not by saying, "I really didn't miss having a father" or "I did just fine without him" or "You can't miss what you never had." No, we've got to grieve our losses. That's how we let go of the past and open ourselves to the goodness of the present moment. Grieve the loss of your father.

That means, remember the feelings you had as a child. Yes, feel those painful feelings . . . so you can release them. If you need professional assistance, a sister circle, or a Grief and Loss group, get it.

Maybe your mother was distracted, drug-addicted, distant, cold, harsh, abusive, shaming, and emotionally unavailable. You may be tempted to say, "Well, she did the best she could." You would be right. Still, she hurt you. Mourn the loss of that relationship, of what "might have been." Obviously, you can't change the past. You can, however, change how you feel about the past. With forgiveness, you can let go of the false notion that the past could have been any different than it was. And make peace with what was. As someone once said, "Until you heal your source relationship (the relationship you had with your parents), you're never really in a new relationship."

If you have a pattern of attracting emotionally abusive, physically violent, untrustworthy, cold, cruel, shaming, cheating, unreliable men, and you want to attract a higher caliber of man, you must forgive. Forgive your parents. Forgive all your exes—lovers, husband(s), even sisterfriends—who hurt you. Now let's not forget the most significant person in your life— you. Forgive yourself for everything you did, didn't do, imagine you did or didn't do.

**Find a Sense of Safety and Security Within.** As I've stated more than once, all human beings have both yin and yang energies within them. Although women are wired to express more yin than yang, at least in their intimate relationships, our yang energy, which is masculine energy, is just as important to our well-being. Our inner man is our provider, protector, and source of safety. Sure, we desire a man we can trust. It's, however, our inner man, and God, that we can trust unfailingly. Stop looking *out there* for a sense of safety and security. It's futile. They aren't out there. Notice that as you forgive your parents, exes, and self and learn to re-parent yourself, neediness and clinging begin to dissolve..

Consequently, your expectations of men will change. Rather than expecting a man to make you happy, feel whole, complete, secure, and safe, you'll look to your beloved as your "playmate," someone with whom you can enjoy the journey. Sure, a good man will love, support, and appreciate you. But God is your unwavering, unfailing strength, sustenance, support, and supply.


## THE PAIN IN HER EYES

*"A man has only one escape from his old self:*
*to see a different self in the mirror of some woman's eyes."*
—Clare Boothe Luce


Another reason I think black men turn to white and Asian women is because these women aren't a constant reminder of our painful collective past. Let me expound by way of a story I saw on one of those TV magazine shows that I so enjoy. There was a young white guy and girl who'd started dating. On one of their dates, they drove to a secluded wooded spot on the outskirts of town. While there, a man brutally attacked them. He raped the girl as her date lay tied up a few feet away unable to protect her. Then the crazed attacker forced them into the nearby river, shot them both, and left them for dead.

By the grace of God, they both lived to talk about it. After the attack, the two young people drifted apart. The young man told the camera why. He couldn't keep seeing this woman, he said, because he could no longer face her. The shame that he felt because he couldn't protect her from the rapist was overwhelming. So, rather than endure a constant reminder of his powerlessness every time he looked into this woman's eyes, he chose not to see her again.

Some black men turn to white women because they can't bear to look into the eyes of women, black women, who they feel they have failed, sometimes over and over again. These men don't want to live their lives with a woman who gazes back at them with hurt, pain, and disappointment in her eyes. We're talking generational pain, the pain of our foremothers, blood memory pain, pain that has congealed into disrespect and disdain. Fearful eyes, filled with the expectation of more pain and disappointment. So some black men simply choose to turn away from black women altogether. It's easier. And to be quite frank, I believe it *is* easier for such men.

A hurting woman, of any race, is a fearful woman. A fearful woman can be a difficult woman who is impossible to please. And what does a man need almost as much as he needs oxygen and sex? He needs to feel he pleases his woman; that he makes her happy, that his very presence brings her joy. If a black man must be with a white or Asian woman to feel this way, this is precisely what he will do. Black women, I believe, do have a part in black men turning away from us. And black men have had a hand in shaping the psyches and hearts of black women. Any black man that has betrayed, abused, disregarded, disrespected, abandoned, and/or battered a black woman, has had a hand in making black women who we have become. After all, we are one. Black women are who we are because the black man is who he is.

## WHITE SKIN BLUE EYES

*"When we see a brother with a fat white woman we know he just wants the white skin . . . because if he wanted a fat woman, there're plenty of fat black women to choose from."*
—Twin Brothers

I discovered that Glen's last two long-term relationships had been with white women. I asked Glen, a forty-something-year-old black man, if he'd talk with me candidly about his experience with women, black and white. He agreed. My first question was, "Do you think there are differences in black and white women?"

He sat back in his chair, looked off into the distance, then said, "Well, when there are problems the white woman tends to be more restrained in her response. She'll suggest that we talk about the problem. Black women yell and are quick to blame."

We continued our conversation. I offered this to him: maybe black men treat white women differently, better. This, in turn, supports white women in being calm and cooperative. I asked if this was true. He thought a minute. A light came on in his eyes. He confessed that he did indeed treat white women differently. "Why?" I asked.

He thought for a minute, then said, "Because we think they're special." I just looked at him. I appreciated his candor. I wanted to understand, to learn. We continued. I shared that this confirmed my suspicion, that black men treat white women differently, and that that increased respect, kindness, and gentleness contribute to the peace and harmony in the relationship. He agreed. I conceded that white women just *might* be more respectful, less blaming and shaming when challenges arise in their interracial relationship. After all, white women don't have a history of being disappointed, hurt, betrayed and abandoned by black men. Indeed, it is painful histories, both personal and collective, that make black love particularly challenging.

Author Jimi Izrael, who is black, explains why he finally settled down with a white woman after being married to two sisters. He, however, neglected to mention his contribution to and contamination of those marriages. Did he really value and appreciate those black women? How did he treat them? Did they feel "special" with him? I have no proof, but I'd bet you a week's worth of Dr. Maya Angelou's speaking fees that Brotha Izrael handles white women with more care than he does black women.

Why do I say this? Shucks, the evidence is in black and white, on the pages of his book, *The Denzel Principle.* Every chance he gets he throws daggers at sisters. Nearly all the words that he uses to describe black women are laced with anger, disdain, and contempt. However, when he writes about white women, the tone changes. It becomes delicate and caring and kind.

Let's be real. We live in a society that encourages us—and that's putting it mildly—to place greater value on all things white. Of course, white women included. Or maybe *especially* white women. So wouldn't it follow that black men would tend to treat white women better than they treat black women? Of course, it does.

## THIS SWORD CUTS BOTH WAYS

Black men and women are equally culpable for the shaky state of our unions. It's time both sexes take ownership of the part they play. It's true, black women can be aggressive and blaming and confrontational. It's not just a myth or rumor that sometimes we talk too much. It's not just that black women can be harsh and hard when the situation may call for softness and understanding. It's *how* we voice our displeasures that cause black men to complain that we are quick to anger. We attack. We blame. We can be defensive and confrontational. We close our minds and shut down our hearts when we ought to shut our mouths and open our hearts. We're apt to confuse the present man with the father that abandoned us, with the husband that cheated on us, betrayed our trust, broke our hearts. Yes, black women are as responsible for the contamination of our relationships as black men. How could it be otherwise? Aren't we just as worthy of accolades as our brothers when our relationships thrive? Yes, of course, we are. Well, this sword cuts both ways.

# Herstory of childhood abuse

*"A poor memory is the best response to someone
who has wronged you."*
—Bud Bilanich

**By A. M. Hall**

The beginning is always a very painful place to start, but then, there really is no other place to start, is there? I was the second-born in a third-generational household. Momma had been stricken with a skin disease early in her childhood that was commonly known in the neighborhood as "pigmentation." Just maybe this skin condition caused my momma much heartache and a lot of embarrassment. Sure, I fully comprehend that my mother was emotionally abandoned and ostracized as a child, teenager, young adult, married woman, and adulteress. Yes, I said it. The truth has to be told if you are to fully comprehend my story.

My childhood was not normal. It was a roller-coaster ride of child-molesting babysitters, vaginal, finger-popping stepbrothers, and invasions by a stepfather who was allowed to physically examine my vagina "just to see if any sperm was put there or if the hymen had been broken." Duh!!!

Poor Momma, who, at that time, was mentally challenged, broken, broke, disgusted, abandoned, and mistreated. Get the picture? This is the womb I came from. Do you wonder what happened to my grandmother? Well, as they say, apples don't fall too far from the tree.

My father told me that I was their "love child." I asked him exactly what he meant because I did not want to assume anything. Walking in my shoes hasn't been a journey, but more like a labyrinth. Have you ever wondered about the power of a never-ending cycle? I watched as my mother was abused. Oh yes, society and family can be cruel when you are the so-called "baa baa baa-pigmented goat."

By the time Momma was fourteen, she was married and pregnant with her second child, me. My dad was an active alcoholic. Momma had low self-esteem. And my grandmother ruled with the Word of God, even when it was not necessary. Meanwhile, my grandfather drank Madeira wine every chance he got, and my Aunt Jean openly lived the life of a freewheeling harlot.

All of these women and men unwittingly groomed me to be a green-eyed Jezebel, mistress, audacious adulterer—the Grand Ripper who delighted in destroying the joys and hopes of men.

# Herstory of loving the unavailable man

*"God gave men both a penis and a brain, but unfortunately, not enough blood supply to run both at the same time."*
—Robin Williams

**SassyScribe,** author of *The Party* and *The After Party* and online radio host, tells her story of loving a man who said she wasn't enough.

Maybe it was the way we met, at our coworker's dinner party. It was 1998. At the time I had been living with my high school sweetheart for thirteen years. There was something about him even then. He wasn't the handsomest man I had ever seen, but his conversation sparked my interest, one I knew I couldn't act on though.

Fast-forward to the summer of 1999. He asked me if I remembered him from the dinner party. I immediately said YES! My cousin told me that he wanted to "smash" me. I told her to give him my number. He called. That first night we talked from four in the evening to six in the morning. Many conversations followed. Hell, we just clicked! But I was attached and he was separated, so we didn't actually go out on our first date until February 2000. From that moment, up to December 20, 2004, we were pretty much an item. He, however, deemed it necessary to remind me that he didn't want a relationship but was willing to accept all that being in a relationship entailed: the hot sex, the stimulating conversation, the fantastic home cooked meals, and just being in each other's company was enough, that is, until he decided that I wasn't enough for him.

That night when he came to my house "drunk," I smelled the other woman on him. He was dressed in fresh jeans, a brown button-down shirt, and some Timberland-style boots. Ambivalent is the best word to describe how he seemed to feel about me, and I felt it that night. That is why I told him to leave at six in the morning. That is why I told him to stop at Dunkin' Donuts and grab a cup of coffee to sober up. I didn't believe him when he said he was drunk, because I had seen him drunk and he wasn't that night. He was just tired and didn't want to leave. When he got home I called. He was famous for getting mad at me then not talking to me for days. This was one of the biggest fears that I had when it came to him. His ignoring my calls was like a death sentence to me. So when I saw him online and sent him an IM to inquire about his well-being, he wrote, "I knew you weren't shit . . . and last night you proved it." I never saw him again, at least not for some time.

He told me that he didn't want a relationship. As soon as I began to realize that he really meant it something changed between us. Interestingly enough, he became more attentive to me and my needs. Suddenly he was more than willing to come to my family events, although still reluctant to take me around his family.

As I write this, wondering why he broke up with me when we were never really together, at least not in his eyes, it's perplexing. I recall that time in June 2003, as I worked to complete my book, his friend was going to edit it for me. For the life of me now, I cannot remember what it was that I did or said that pissed him off enough that he would set my manuscript outside of my cousin's house in the rain. Yeah, he wrapped it up so it wouldn't get wet, but that was my "baby" he put on those steps. I should have stopped fooling with him then, but silly me; I thought we could still work it out. But now I know he was only concerned with himself. His aloofness, initially, was endearing. Then it got to be a pain. Again, however, I said nothing because, after all, he would get mad and not speak to me for weeks. I never knew how to handle that, but he gave me an education about men that I will never forget. See, it was his little isms and sayings that were the inspiration for one of the characters in my book, *The Party*. He showed me an arrogant asshole of a man, then was offended that I didn't acknowledge him by name, even while being pissed that I portrayed him that way. How else was I supposed to portray him when that was the man he wanted me to know?

I have him to thank for birthing SassyScribe. Him telling me I wasn't shit. Him insinuating that my body type wasn't the "ideal" sent me on a quest to find myself. I had to take time out to reflect and get to know me, and that I did. His spurning me taught me how to travel solo and take chances that I never would have taken otherwise. He made me a stronger woman, to the point that I know what it is I want from a man now.

But then he had to come and fuck it up. He showed up at my family's annual crab feast in 2006. After two years of no conversation, no communication at all, he shows up at MY family's event claiming, "I just wanted to go to a crab feast." What a lie that was. But it made me feel good to know he had to, was compelled to, come and see me. Rather than show weakness and/or heart, he shows up in a brand-new Jaguar, just like the character portrayed in my book. He even said, "Well, Jacobell Steele had a Jag, didn't he?" How ironic, and how sweet it was that I had a date with a handsome man that day. I even kissed him in front of them. I knew I couldn't stay away.

From July 2006 up to September 8, 2007, we found each other again. We were seeing each other more. He called me every day, sometimes three or four times a day, and we talked for hours. I finally felt like we were back on track. Then one night he called. I asked if he wanted to get a drink. His response was, "Why not?" I should've left it there, but I enjoyed spending time with him—after all, he was the man I loved.

I had no expectations because I remember when we went to Jasper's and I asked him if we were trying to be exclusive and he said, "I don't do relationships." I knew then not to put too much into him. But he called and wanted to see me. Oddly enough, I knew he wasn't attracted to me because he never touched me. In that year we never had sex. Although I performed oral sex on him, he never touched me, never reciprocated, and the two times that he did ask it was like I was just something to do. It hurt, but I justified his not touching me as a sign of me not being attracted to *him* physically.

Little did I know that another woman had tempted him. His appearance when I picked him up from his house was disheveled—his clothes were wrinkled, and his face was unshaven. I asked him if everything was okay, and he answered, "I'm stressed." I didn't say anything, because for the last year I'd taken great pains to show him that there was absolutely no pressure from me when it came to us.

He sat in my car and talked about feeling trapped and not knowing what to do. So, although I sort of prepared myself, when I asked him if he was seeing anyone he said some people had expressed an interest and that he had been out with a couple of people a couple of times. I was devastated, so I asked him what he wanted from me and he said he wanted me to be his friend. I told him that I couldn't sit back and watch him enjoy another woman and give her the relationship that I wanted from him, feeling for him as I did, and he said, "Well, that sounds like a condition."

I now thank him for breaking up with me. It was hard for me at first but I know now that I don't want a man that treats me like a side dish—constantly. I am an appetizer, the salad, the soup, the entrée, the dessert for that man hungry to feast not only on my body, but on my mind as well.

# Black Women Expect too Much

*"Don't be afraid to feel as angry or as loving as you can, because when you feel nothing, it's just death."*
—Lena Horne, *singer*

STEVE HARVEY TELLS a funny story. He was on *The Oprah Show* and a "short and fluffy" woman insisted that a man had to be tall and buffed with a white even smile if he wanted to be with her. Those were just three of her 236 requirements! I thought that was hilarious. I shared this story with my then sixteen-year-old daughter, Adia. Her insightful response was, "Well, she apparently doesn't want a man!" We both broke out laughing. This woman's demands are so utterly unreasonable that I question her sanity. Really, 236 requirements!

Remember author Jimi Izrael? Well, he complains that black women expect way too much from brothers. Let's investigate this together. Maybe Izrael's right. Okay, black women expect respect, integrity, honesty, attention, love, time, support, fidelity, patience, understanding, communication, connection, concern, care. Oh, and did I mention r-e-s-p-e-c-t? Now, tell me what on that list is "too much"? That said, I will meet Izrael halfway.

I think what Izrael means is that black women can be inflexible about what they want. That is, black women want what they want, and that's that!

No, black women don't expect too much. It's just that once a sister has been hurt, disappointed, betrayed, lied to, cheated on, abandoned, beaten, duped, hoodwinked, and bamboozled one too many times, a sister can turn on a brother. On ALL brothers. All black men become suspect. That hurt becomes ATTITUDE. Attitude shows up as impatience, intolerance, suspicion, anger, hostility, closed-mindedness, fear, resistance, hatred, and distrust. I heard a forty-something-year-old brother bitterly complain that he was tired of black women having so much "baggage"! I told a guy friend of mine what this bother had said, whereupon my friend quickly responded, "We made y'all that way!" My friend elaborated by quoting the Honorable Elijah Muhammad, who said, I paraphrase, "Behind every no-good woman is a no-good man. Women aren't bad by nature."

Another brother I know, years later, was still reeling from being cheated on by an ex. One day he paid her a surprise visit. She, he said incredulously, opened the door with another man's cum running down her bare leg. I thought but didn't ask, "So, what did YOU do to her before that?" Not that women are saints—we aren't. But, just like men, if you hurt us bad enough, and one too many times, we can turn on you like a pet pit bull. Maul your face right off.

Trust me when I tell you, this dude had it coming. No pun intended.

Izrael might be right, perhaps black women *do* expect too much from black men. Yep, we've come to expect too much of the "bad" stuff—lies, heartbreak, abandonment, broken promises, disappointment, betrayal, infidelity, and disappearing acts. And yet, with every new relationship, sisters hope and pray for the best, uh, even as they wait for the other shoe to drop.

You know what they say about self-fulfilling prophecies; they come to pass. We get not what we want or hope for, but what we look for and expect. Because our expectations are our thoughts, and thoughts create, over and over again we get the very kind of treatment we say we *don't* want yet believe is inevitable.

Again and again we are disappointed, betrayed, left. . . because our expectations emerge from our beliefs. What we believe, we attract and create. Truth be told, black women have come to expect little good from black men. A woman I know said she would repeatedly accuse her husband of doing nothing to contribute to their family. She, on the other hand, was a go-getter. An entrepreneur who started and runs her own consultancy business, travels extensively for business and leisure, drives expensive cars, and lives in upscale neighborhoods. She expected the best out of herself and produced nothing short of it. Except when it came to her man.

One day after reminding her husband one more time of just how little he brought to the table, he looked her dead in the eye and quipped, "I give you exactly what you expect—nothing!" Both she and I roared with laughter. She had to admit, he was right. She expected nothing, and she got precisely what she expected—absolutely nothing!

Imagine sending your little boy to a school where the teacher expects him to fail. You don't have to imagine this, you say, because every day black parents send their sons (and daughters) to schools where those in charge, those charged to teach them, fully expect them to just "get by," to fail, to flunk out. And unfortunately, many of them do just that, flunk out. Often, by the fourth grade, they have mentally checked out. But doesn't this outrage you that the adults that black parents entrust their children to are oftentimes the very people counting on them to end up a statistic? If it doesn't, it ought to.

We get to see who we are from the light—or disappointment and disdain—in the eyes of the people who populate our world.

When a black man looks into your eyes, who does he see reflecting back to him? Are your expectations of him too high? Too low? Do you *know* he's going to let you down, disappoint you, betray you, abuse you, cheat on you, leave you, break your heart?

Are you succeeding at love? If not, why not? Maybe it's a self-fulfilling prophecy. Remember, thoughts are things. What you think about you bring about. Perhaps we are expecting the men in our lives to hurt, abuse, abandon us like some of our fathers did. Or maybe you were daddy's little girl and so no man ever quite measures up to your expectations.

For sure, black men have a part in how we see, treat, and feel about them. So do we. Humans are powerful, creative beings. Our thoughts not only shape the world, they *create* the world.

# An Interview
## with *Brandy Whyte*, LCPC

**DMR: What do you do?**

**BW:** I am a licensed clinical professional counselor. I work in an outpatient mental health center. I'm also in private practice. I provide premarital counseling and therapy to adolescents, adults, couples, and families. My specialty is blended families, depression, anxiety, stress management, mood disorders, career, and life balance.

### How long have you been in practice?

I have over ten years of experience in the human service field; I've been licensed as a master's level clinician since 2006.

### When you work with couples, what kinds of services do you provide them?

Currently, I provide premarital, marital, and family counseling.

### What kinds of relationship issues do you encounter?

I laughed when I read this question. I thought, is she speaking of my work or my personal life? This time around, I'll keep the focus on my work; perhaps I'll discuss my own relationship journey another time, in another interview. Professionally, most couples have difficulty with the basics: communication, fighting fair, respect. These issues can manifest as infidelity, substance use and abuse, verbal and/or physical abuse, and mental health issues. At the heart of these challenges there is a lack of respect and an inability to effectively communicate.

### Have you seen a pattern or recurring theme, problem, or challenge in couples and singles around love and relationships?

It is no secret that families and family dynamics have changed through the years. With women working and capably "holding it down," there has been a shift in thinking and behavior. While this shift has negatively affected all races, the black family appears to be suffering more. I've observed that African Americans are the last to come in for assistance. When they do, they are usually desperate, have lost respect for their union, and their love for one another is all but gone. This means that as a team, we have to work harder to bring them back to ground zero, where they consider the relationship a source of satisfaction. The things that generally bring couples to therapy are financial challenges, infidelity, sexual dysfunction, and dissatisfaction.

**It is said that three out of four black marriages fail. What are your thoughts about why?**

I agree with Hill Harper, author of *The Conversation: How Black Men and Women Can Build Loving and Trusting Relationships*, when he said as a people, we're not having important conversations, we aren't talking about why some black men are gravitating toward white and Asian women, and why it's so hard for black women to submit to their man. We aren't talking about our hurt and pain and finding common ground to heal. We're not working on self, and then seeking to love and be loved. Given the number of failed relationships among us, like the liquor store in so many urban communities, we should have a support and relationship education group on every corner. We invest in everything but our relationships: weaves, the lottery, clothes, bling, hot rides, big houses. Meanwhile, we're missing out on the most valuable gift life has to offer—unconditional love.

**Why do black women say they leave relationships? Why do you think they do?**

Black women say they leave relationships because they're underappreciated, because of a lack of intimacy and maltreatment, i.e., physical, sexual, and/or verbal abuse. I think most black women have an idea of what they want and need in a man/relationship. Then they meet Mr. Almost Right, make concessions, and settle. These women end up bitter. When they eventually move on, they're weighed down by baggage from the past. This baggage thwarts their chances of meeting Mr. Right.

### What are black women looking for in a man?
Financial stability, love, respect, fidelity, intimacy, and hot sex.

### Are black women's expectations too high?
I wouldn't go so far as to generalize. That said, I believe all women need to examine their expectations to see if they are asking for something they can't give. After all, a relationship is a partnership based on what each part brings to the table.

### If you have any advice for black women about how to make love work, what would that be?
Honestly, I'm still working on it myself, but I think it starts with forgiving yourself and past loves, an open mind, self-evaluation, self-development, and the commitment to working things through.

### If you have anything else to share with my readers about love, what would that be?
When it's right, love is freedom.

# Coping with Loneliness and Loss

*"Pain pushes until vision pulls."*
—Rev. Dr. Michael Bernard Beckwith

LIKE OTHER PEOPLE, black women find ways to cope with loneliness and loss. First, let's define the word "cope." *To cope is to barter, trade, or exchange. To contend against, to deal successfully with, handle, or manage a situation is to cope with it.* When we can't have what we really want or need, we reach for a "substitute." Then we lie to ourselves. We say, "Oh, I'm too busy for a relationship anyway." Or, "I'm happy." We then set out to make ourselves and others believe that our substitute is just as good as what we really desire. Or we deny ever really wanting what we know damn well we do want. If what we reach for evolves us, then I say we have dealt successfully with or handled the matter.

Like other groups, black women engage in healthy *and* unhealthy behaviors and activities to cope with pain, loneliness, and loss.

Breaking up is seldom easy. Where there once was someone to talk to, to hold, cuddle, caress, make love to, laugh with, fuss over and fight with, share hopes, dreams, and disappointments with, now there's a void. There's only one—you. It's only natural if loneliness seizes you during such a time of loss.

When we experience the loss of a relationship, the desire for the pain to stop can consume us. No matter how thorny and rough the relationship had become there will always remain some sweet memories of it. Those memories can taunt and even torture us. Like the death of a loved one, the demise of a relationship can lead to despondency . . . and intensify our fear of the future.

Being dumped, to most, is a blow to the self-esteem. Toxic thoughts consume us: *What's wrong with me? Why can't I find someone to love ME? Something's wrong with me. I'll never find anyone.* We doubt ourselves. We question our worth. We imagine a future without love and companionship. Because we can't possibly see the blessings that await us up the road we tend to cling to the "devil" we know rather than open ourselves to the "angels" we might meet. Translation: We choose to stay in toxic, abusive, dead and unsatisfying relationships rather than move forward solo.

Well, then, how do women survive breakups and the loneliness that often attends them? How do single women manage loneliness, frustration, and fear that they'll never find a love of their own? To what and whom do women turn to cope with loss and loneliness?

**HEALTHY COPING**

Like I said, sisters engage in both healthy and unhealthy behaviors and activities to deal with heartbreak, loss, and loneliness. Meditation, prayer, reading spiritual literature, attending church and personal growth seminars, journaling, therapy, joining support groups, returning to school, spending quality time with family and friends, traveling, pouring oneself into work, career, fitness, taking up new hobbies or interests or revisiting old ones, and volunteering are healthy ways of dealing with and healing emotional pain, heartbreak, and loneliness.

Dating other race men and younger men are also ways in which black women deal with the unavailability of good black men their age.

Healthy approaches can, however, be misused, escape hatches, or become unhealthy when overindulged in. When work and church become avenues of escape, they lead to imbalance rather than increased health and well-being. It's not unusual for sisters of a certain age, after they've experienced more than their share of disappointment and betrayal, now bitter and cynical, to turn to Jesus. Gloria, who you'll meet shortly, is one of those women. Other women pour themselves into their careers, sometimes working themselves into poor health.

## WOMEN LOVING WOMEN

There are other ways in which women are taking care of themselves when landing a relationship with a man isn't working out. Before I proceed, this must be said: *Women loving women isn't anything new.* Black women have consciously chosen to be in same-sex relationships for years. Some of these women might call themselves lesbians, while others may choose not to wear a label. Lesbianism might be something that chose them before they were born, while others might have chosen it. I know a woman who identified as a heterosexual for two-and-a-half decades. During that time she married her childhood sweetheart and had a child with him. Then in her late twenties she consciously and deliberated chose to love and partner with women exclusively.

There was another woman whose husband left her. He adored her, a fact she knew and bragged about. He left her though. Again. Then came back again. He left a third time. Sure he would find his right mind and return to her, she waited. He never did. She took up with a woman. A lesbian. I thought, *an-*

*other woman, fed up with men, has given up on them.* She and this woman have been happily together for years now.

Here's my point, more and more sisters are turning away from men and loving and partnering with women. It's not uncommon for many of these women to bypass labels and simply live and love. One woman I know, who is now happily in a relationship with another woman, says she sees no reason to shun love however it beckons. Echoing author Alice Walker's words, who couldn't see any problem with her sexual choices, "One day you love a man, another day you love a woman." This sister lives by the same edict. She was very vocal, too. I gathered that black men frequently rejected her, that black American men weren't too fond of her very dark skin and rotund body. She was very clear; rather than be alone and unpartnered she would love a woman.

Some sisters are also defiantly choosing to enter into same-sex relationships. As if to thumb their noses at men, *nah . . . nah nah nah nah*, more and more sisters are choosing each other. I can't speak for all "straight" women who decide to couple with another woman, but I can tell you this: I've been so hurt, frustrated, and pissed off at black men that I too have considered changing lanes. As of yet, I haven't. I doubt that I will because I so love the sight, scent, and swag of a man. Like every other woman on the planet, black women want to love and be loved. There are a significant number of sisters who are done waiting for Mr. Right and for Mr. Wrong to act right, and are instead opting to let Ms. Right love them. In a sentence, they are sick and tired of being sick and tired.

## I DON'T NEED A MAN

Everywhere you turn, you see black women coupling. There's the possibility that there really isn't a spike in such relationships; people simply feel freer to be themselves these days. That may be true. I'm convinced that there are at least four reasons why otherwise heterosexual black women are now choosing same-sex intimate relationships:

1. It's a reaction to the harm and hurt inflicted by black men early in life
2. An "eff" you move, "I don't need you! I'm good."
3. Sisters are fed up with black men's shenanigans—cheating, desertion, lying, irresponsibleness, disloyalty
4. A response to the shortage of quality black men

Talk about being strong and independent. Sisters who don't necessarily identify as lesbian are choosing to love a woman, rather than be alone or tolerate black men's disrespect, disappearing acts, and tendency to be unreliable. I say they are taking that "Ima*strong*independentblackwoman" manifesto to a whole new level. And many brothers are bothered by it. A guy friend said as we walked through the throng of people braving the heat and sun to enjoy the Artscape festival, "I'd rather see a black woman with a white guy than do that." He nodded toward a same-sex couple, two black women, walking hand-in-hand. I understood. I also get why some sisters are giving up on black men, no longer willing to live without partnership and love.

Listen, it's not for me to say whether or not a "heterosexual" woman choosing to love and partner with a woman is a healthy coping mechanism or not. Here's what I look at: why? If a woman turns away from men out of frustration, in bitterness and anger, is she operating out of love or fear? If fear is driving her choices, then one might wonder where then will she put her anger and resentment toward men. If it's not addressed and healed, trust and believe, it will show up in her relationships, body, and life no matter who she chooses to love.

**TEMPORARY RELIEF**

Coping behaviors that women turn to in order to feel better, find comfort, lift their spirits, escape, numb out, and check out, such as overeating, drinking too much, using drugs, and having reckless sex, may bring temporary comfort and relief but ultimately lead to despondency, depression, and low self-esteem. According to recent studies, eight out of ten black women are overweight. Emotional eating is at the root of this epidemic.

**WHAT'S EATING YOU?**

*"African American women have the highest rates of obesity compared to other groups in the United States. About 4 out of 5 African American women are overweight or obese."*
—www.womenshealth.gov

I was on the phone with my sisterfriend Deena, who decided that she was going to start attending a 12-Step Program for overeaters. A mutual friend of ours had recently lost more than 80 pounds. Our girl was looking and feeling great as a direct result of attending the program. Our friend said she looked like she had decades ago. Well, Deena's weight had continued to climb. She realized she did not like herself, and yet, she could not control her craving for pasta and potato chips. I asked, "What is it that you're getting from these foods?"

"I just want to FEEEEEL gooooood," Deena said.

I could imagine her clenching her fist as she emphasized the words "feel" and "good."

"What," I asked, "drives this craving?"

"When I lose a relationship or get lonely I want that starch and that salt!"

I understood. I've spoken with and read the stories of other overeaters. One woman reaches for food when she's lonely or feeling abandoned because "food will never leave me," she said rather sadly. Another woman ballooned to 400 pounds after the death of her parents and the disintegration of her marriage.

Good grief!

Yes, *good* grief.

Grieving *is* good and so underrated. When we experience a loss and live with loneliness, our soul urges us to feel what we feel, to cry if we feel like it, to feel sad, to embrace ourselves, literally; that is, to tend to ourselves in mind, body, and spirit. Our resistance to being present to our feelings shows up as addictions. When we are willing to tell ourselves the truth about what we really feel and want and muster the courage to live accordingly, addictions lose their power. So, if instead of sitting down with a quart of your favorite ice cream you would do the things that would make a real difference in your life the urge to numb out would lessen. What if, instead of grabbing that bag of chocolate chip cookies and plopping down in front of the telly you sat down in front of a computer and wrote that book that's been thrumming in your soul for years now? Who knows who you would become. Only God knows.

## IF I CAN'T HAVE YOU

In 1998, I fell in "love" with yet another unavailable man, this time a married man. When that relationship tanked, I was devastated. The pain was overwhelming at times. I, however, didn't realize how much I was hurting until one day I looked up and I was standing in Marshalls checkout line, my arms full of things I didn't need, things that would destroy that zero Visa credit card balance I'd recently achieved. Thing was, I don't remember consciously deciding to go shopping that day. In fact, only weeks prior I'd put myself on a spending diet. *How did I get in that line? What was driving my behavior? What was I unconsciously trying to fix by buying a new dress? More importantly, could I alleviate my pain in less destructive way? If yes, what might I do instead of buying more stuff?*

* * * * * * *

## "Pretending To Be Normal"
## by Jayel Mwangi
### *A Recovering Food Addict*

**DMR: What role has food played in your life and do you consider yourself an addict?**
**JM:** I used food as my comforter, my best friend, to numb my feelings of lack and to make me feel good. My feel-good foods were sugar and flour products in the form of candy, cookies, cake, and, of course, ice cream. Food was so important to me that one year I bought my mother a can opener for Christmas. The one she was using to open my food was rusty, so I decided it would be nice for her to have a new one.

**Would you say there's a connection between your emotional eating and your early life?**
As a child I felt a great void. I felt out of place in my family and in the world. I think it may have been because I was the third of four children, next to the youngest of four girls, and my father was not available to me, first emotionally, then physically. Food was my drug of choice.

As a child, I felt responsible for everything. It was my fault my father was not with us. It was my fault that my mother was unhappy. It was my fault if my sister's favorite basketball team lost the game the day I watched the game with her. I was too skinny. I was too dark. I was too tall. I was too poor. My hair was too short. Give me some candy, some cookies, and some ice cream and put me in front of a TV and the world would become a better place. I was OK then. I forgot for those couple of hours each day that I was not important. That I was not good enough. That I was not loved enough, and that the world was a mean place. I learned at a young age that food could change the way I felt, at least for a couple of hours each day.

**I understand that you lost more than 80 pounds. Have you attempted to lose weight in the past but couldn't or lost it and regained it? What, if anything, did you do different this time around?**

Throughout my life I ate whatever I wanted to and whenever I wanted to. I was underweight during my childhood, teenage years, and as a young adult. I, like my sisters and our mother, did not put on weight until after we turned thirty-five. All the women in my immediate family wear our lives around our waist. Gaining weight around the middle is the most dangerous; it puts you at high risk for diabetes, heart disease, high blood pressure, and stroke.

I smoked cigarettes for a very long time. Before taking up smoking, I had already started gaining weight. When I quit smoking, I put on an additional sixty pounds. When I expressed concern about my weight to my doctor, he said he didn't want to see my weight any higher than 145; I was weighing 142 at the time. My weight ballooned up to 245 pounds. I decided that I would never lose the weight because I had a thyroid problem. Deep down inside I knew I was using that as an excuse. I didn't put into practice all the reading I was doing on healthy eating and nutrition. I would not exercise. However, I would fast for spiritual reasons, hoping to jump-start a diet.

I'd join gyms, pay the money each month, but never go after the first two weeks. I would walk three miles around the track five days a week for a couple of weeks. Buy fruits and vegetables and never eat them. They would spoil, and I'd end up throwing them in the trash.

A couple of times I paid good money for diet pills and vitamin B shots. My last-ditch effort that didn't require consistency or for me to do much except to mutilate my body . . . I considered gastric bypass surgery. I went to a meeting to learn more about it. At that meeting I discovered that I was fifty pounds below the mark that qualifies me for the procedure. I wasn't fat *enough*. Once again, not good enough for what I think I want. Well, I thought, at the rate I'm going I will soon get the fifty pounds I need, then I will be *good enough* to mutilate my body.

## FLOUR, SUGAR, AND SEX

I didn't do anything about my weight problem with even a little bit of consistency. I just *intended* to do something. I didn't have the motivation to do anything about taking control of my life. I was depressed mainly because I didn't like myself, the way I looked, the way I lived my life, the way I felt all the time. Those spiritual lessons I studied weren't working for me . . . because I wasn't using them. I didn't know how to get out of the rut I was in. So I continued to drug myself with flour and sugar products, sex, spending money that I didn't have, holding onto stuff I didn't need, holding onto feelings that did me no good, holding onto people that didn't serve me, hating myself, hating my life. Negative. Negative. Negative. No energy, no good energy. I was done. Something had to give. I knew if I continued on with this life I would end up homeless. There were but so many times that I could disappear from the world for two weeks at a time every six months before I would be fired from my job. Well, I knew I wouldn't survive living on the streets.

So, I'd go to work, eat my stuff, watch TV, have my pity parties in my head, and blame my deceased father and drug-addicted ex-husband, childhood experiences, being born black, picking the wrong family to be born into, my inability to mother my children properly, for my life. Well, there was one thing I was consistent about, that was beating myself up. I was also consistent about not taking care of myself, not taking charge of my life, not creating the life that I *did* want for myself, and not knowing how to change.

## I WAS DESPERATE

My breaking point came when I took a vacation to Jamaica with a group of progressive sisters. I felt so inadequate, not good enough. I was the largest in our group. My self-esteem was very low. My money was low. For a while, I wished I hadn't taken the trip. Well, I ended up having the time of my life. I came back to the states ready to change my life.

One of the women on the trip was Joyce. She shared with us that she had lost sixty pounds. I asked her how, when, where, what's the phone number? I was desperate. She invited me to go to a meeting with her once we got back to Baltimore. I did something that I rarely do; I followed up. I went to some meetings. They were modeled after Alcoholics Anonymous (AA), but the focus was on food, specifically the addiction to flour and sugar. I had found my way. I was always looking for a step meeting; this was for me.

I latched on to a sponsor, and a year later, my Body Mass Index (BMI) went from 38 to 24. I am no longer obese. I am a normal body size. I no longer use my addiction to sugar as an excuse. However, now that I know I am addicted to flour and sugar, I act accordingly. Just like a Crackhead has to stay clean in order to recover from the addiction to crack cocaine, I can never have flour or sugar products if I want to stay a normal, healthy body size. I respect that I have an addiction. I got me a sponsor and did what I was told. As a result, I lost eighty-five pounds in a year.

To do as I am told is not an easy task for me. But I wanted this so badly that I was willing to do whatever I was told so that I could get off this roller-coaster ride that seems to have no ending. I admitted that I am a food addict, and I acted accordingly. I don't eat foods that I am addicted to. I don't use sugar and flour. Today, I weigh between 158–165 pounds. I wear a size 6–8, down from a 16–18.

**Are there similarities and parallels between food addiction and other addictions?**

I have an addictive personality. I have been codependent and addicted to cigarettes, bad relationships, overspending, sex, negative thoughts and feelings, and gambling. If I enjoy it I can become addicted to it. If it keeps me from dealing with life on life terms, it can become an addiction for me. Being a food addict is no different. Addicts use whatever to make them feel different, to avoid feelings and emotions that they don't like. I am one of those people who can't eat just a couple of cookies, a few pieces of chocolate, or just one potato chip, stay married to one man, or work the same job for thirty years. I just can't do those things. (At fifty-six, I believe I can stay married to one man now. I would be an excellent partner. Just had to put that out there.) I used food the same way some people use drugs. I used flour and sugar to alter my feelings. Some people put drugs in their veins. If that was the only way I could get that feeling of comfort, I think I may have injected sugar and flour into my veins. An addiction is an addiction.

**What, if anything, have you learned about yourself since you stopped eating to feed your emotions?**

During the year that I have been in the food addicts program, I have learned to be consistent. Once I removed the drugs from my system—flour and sugar—the fog lifted from my mind. As I lost the weight, I gained confidence and self-esteem. Just as

I learned that I could live without drugging myself with food, I learned that I can deal with life on life terms. I also discovered that I am an immature, middle-aged woman who tolerates too much from others. That I have not been loving myself. That I am afraid of life. That I have little faith in myself, in other people, and in God. When I stopped drugging myself, I discovered that I have a lot of unattended painful business left over from childhood to take care of. I have not forgiven others or myself. Consequently, I am blocked from being the best that I can be . . . until I release this baggage.

Being in a program that promotes self-love and love of others strengthens my faith in my Higher Power. Being with people who have the same problem as I do helps me to appreciate that I am not alone. I am not so weird after all. Even if I am weird, so what? It's okay to be who I am. I embrace the things about me that I like as well as the things that I don't like. By respecting this gift from God, my body, I have learned to respect myself more in all aspects of my life. I no longer act on the impulse to indulge in sex, bad relationships, or foods that I am addicted to. Nor do I throw as many pity parties as I once did.

## I AM RESPONSIBLE

I take care of my mental health also. I take antidepressants now. I suffer from Adult Attention Deficit Disorder (AADD). I take suggestions from my sponsor as well as my doctors. I no longer think I know everything. I am no longer resistant to doing what I need to do to take care of myself. I have learned that I'm okay. I love myself, and I love life.

Don't get me wrong; I still have a lot of work to do. I have a lot of tough choices to make at this juncture in my life. A couple of examples: I really do hate my supervisor at work, and I have too much junk in my home and in my head. However, now I know that I can change any negative area of my life and understand that I am responsible for every relationship in my life, including the one with the supervisor-from-hell. I am getting that I brought that supervisor-from-hell into my life, and I must do the work to remove him. I have learned that it's not my job to change other people; it's my job to change me. I now get that I focus on things that I can't change to keep from focusing on my own stuff. I often pray, "God, grant me the serenity to accept the things I cannot change, the courage to change the things I can, and the wisdom to know the difference." I thank God that I have found this program for food addicts.

**What advice would you give to other women who are struggling with weight?**

If you find that it's hard to give up foods that prevent you from being your healthiest body size, consider that you might be a food addict. Food addiction comes in many different forms— some very severe, some not so severe. Being a food addict means you can't control your impulses to eat more once you have started eating.

African Americans have some serious health issues. A lot of those issues are linked to what we eat and think. Once I started to eat better, I was then able to think differently. If you suspect that you are a food addict, look for a support group or form your own. You may want to model it after a program that has proven to work for people struggling with an addiction to alcohol, i.e., Alcoholics Anonymous.

Go on the web and search for an addiction program. The first step to changing any behavior is to admit that a change is needed. Stop believing the lie that black women are just big-boned and the healthy weight chart is not meant for us. So long as we keep thinking that, we will continue to wrestle with life-threatening health problems at a greater rate than the rest of the population.

**Jayel, have you any final words?**

One "requirement" of being in a 12-Step Program is to give back in service, to others, what you have received. I am committed to spreading the good news about the power of support groups. I know that it is by the grace of God and my support groups that enabled me to lose the weight. The program that I am involved in is not physically accessible to all, which is why I am taking this program to churches and community centers.

If you are not pleased with your current weight or body size, do something to change. It will be the first step toward changing your life. This is a program of attraction and not advertisement. For that reason, I am not able to name it. When I meet you at my book signings, I will share information about the program with you and invite you to let me coach and work with you to get your body back or get the one that you never had but was intended for you. Remember, it's intended that we all be healthy, happy, and addiction-free.

❋ ❋ ❋ ❋ ❋ ❋

## ADDICTION: PICK YOUR POISON

*"I pity the fool who falls in love with you . . . and think you'll be true."*
—Bobby "Blue" Bland

I wrote an entire book about addiction, *Love Addicted,* which chronicles my rocky journey through love and relationship addiction. I, however, cannot in good conscience write a book about breakups and not discuss addiction. Not just love addiction, all kinds of addictions.

We live in an addictive society. Some say 86 percent of the American population is addicted to something—sex, caffeine, nicotine, work, women, sugar, alcohol, men, religion, relationships, worry, prescription drugs, shopping, love, food, cleaning, order, chaos, negative thinking, the past, exercise, TV; you name it, we can be addicted to it. Of course, this isn't an exhaustive list, since we can have an addictive relationship to *anything*. Don't believe me? Consider the reality TV folks who have confessed their addiction to eating toilet paper, ashes, and broken glass. Those compulsions, however, are beyond my realm of understanding so let's just stick with the "devils" we all know, like drugs, overspending, and relationships.

**Some Facts about Addiction:**
- Some types of addictions keep us unaware of what is going on inside us. A way of avoiding responsibility for oneself.
- Process addiction is being hooked on specific interactions.
- Process addictions include accumulating money, gambling, sex, porn, work, religion, and worry. All are processes. They are built-in problems.
- No amount is ever enough for lasting relief or satisfaction.
- We live in an addictive society, which asks us to become comfortable with our own non-aliveness.
- Addiction is usually something we feel compelled to lie about. Ashamed to make public.
- Addictive thinking tells us it couldn't possibly be our fault. Many of us have multiple addictions; they feed each other. Booze and sex. Food and drink. Bingo and pull-tabs. Just some favorites. Casual use moves into abuse. Abuse into addiction.
- We really have a spiritual dis-ease. We feel we must pleasure ourselves in order to be satisfied and happy.
- We must fill that void inside, to satisfy perpetual anguish.
- To recover from addiction we must break free.
- We live in an addictive system. Addiction intervention means we must quit supporting it and allow it to col-

lapse. But, it won't be quick. The addictive system will fight back. It won't quit and go away easily.
- We can no longer label one, or treat one, or see one without acknowledging the presence of all the others.
- We must undertake to treat the system as a whole.
- The problem is systemic. In this, we must take responsibility for ourselves and for our own anguish. Self-responsibility is self-care.
- Breaking our personal addiction is possible.

—www.personal-recovery-tools.com

## IT'LL COST YOU $2,600 A MONTH

"If I want to see him," he said, "I would have to pay him," Gloria tells me, as she looks up at me from her lawn seat. She quickly agreed to his terms. She paid $2,600 a month to see "her" new man two times a month.

I asked, incredulously, facetiously, "Was the sex THAT good?"

Lowering her head, as if the answer was buried in the grass, she thought for a moment, then said sadly, "It was okay." She added softly, "I was stupid."

My curiosity encouraged me. "So, what did you learn from this experience?" I asked nonjudgmentally, fully expecting to hear something thoughtful and profound.

Before she could respond, her friend, my sister jumped in. She learned not to do it again," my sister said.

*Is that all?* I thought to myself.

Gloria, finger pointing toward the concrete, her voice rising, spits in an accusatory tone, "Now my heart is as hard as that!"

I wasn't one bit surprised.

Her heart now closed, she's bitter, angry, hurt, and scared. Men are no longer on the menu for Gloria. All men, she's now convinced, are users and abusers unworthy of her time and trust.

My attempt to coax her into seeing the role she played in the situation was wasted.

Gloria isn't alone; in fact, she's in very good company with loads of women. When our self-esteem is low and we have yet to tackle childhood daddy/mommy issues, it's not uncommon for us to bend over backwards to have a man in our life. Maybe you haven't handed over cold, hard cash to get a few hours of run-of-the-mill sex and some so-called companionship with a gigolo, but I ask you, how low have *you* stooped to get a little male attention?

Have you ever slept with a girlfriend or relative's man? Has a man ever slapped, punched, cheated, disappeared on you, and you kept him around? Have you ever had sex without a condom with a man whose HIV status you didn't know? Have you ever bought a man clothes, paid his car note, footed his rent bill, let him live with you rent-free to ensure that he stayed around? Have you ever hooked up with a married or otherwise spoken-for man? Have you taken a man back even after he did the very thing(s) you said you absolutely would not abide? Have you ever stayed with a guy you suspected, or even knew, was on the down low? If you answered yes to any of these questions, know you are not alone. Women, and not just black women, are famous for compromising themselves to have a man.

But don't despair.

There's hope. You can change.

The power is within you to grow in self-esteem and self-love. As you grow, what you are willing to do for "love" and companionship will also change. Above all else, you will learn to put you and your well-being first.

Gloria hadn't really learned from her gigolo experience. She blamed the man for everything. Blaming him lets her off the hook. Actually, it doesn't. Blaming the gigolo keeps her in the dark. He was bad. Wrong. A user, she told herself. Meanwhile, "Poor me, I was a victim," gets to be Gloria's story. "I'm happy being single," she lied. Single she might have been, but happy she was not! How can a heart as cold and hard as concrete be happy?

"Now I go to church!" Gloria finally announced boastfully. I looked at her. *Another woman,* I thought, *has fallen prey to the illusion that she can escape her miserable, loveless life by going to church.*

## SHE FOUND JESUS

Gloria betrayed herself, and then held the gigolo responsible. She was in her early fifties and sick and tired of being played. Unsure of how to attract the kind of love she so desired, she gave up. Turned to the church. Did what a lot of black women do: she found Jesus. Not as if up until that point Jesus was hiding. Just that she didn't think she needed Him so long as she had a man.

Before you lose your wig, hear me out. There's nothing wrong with going to church, and I'm certainly not against anyone knowing Jesus intimately. But wouldn't it be nice if finding Jesus and having a loving, trusting relationship with a man didn't have to be mutually exclusive? It seems to me Jesus ought not be your Plan B or C. That is, when you can't nail down a satisfying relationship with a man you scamper into church. So, what then happens to your religion if Mr. Looking Right, uh, I mean Mr. Right, suddenly strolls into your world? You gonna stop going to church? Yep, that's exactly what you're gonna do. And you'll be in good company when you do . . . because a bunch of sisters seem to forget where the church is when they get a boyfriend.

To paraphrase comedienne Meshelle, who jokes about not getting to church every Sunday because she likes that uh, well, "whatsaname." Well, some of y'all know what she's talking about. You start getting that "whatsaname" and lose your right mind. Sunday rolls around and still you can't bear to pull yourself away from it. I guess it gets that good to you. Or you're so wiped out from the long night before. Either way, you go MIA, you know, missing in action from church. Tsk, tsk!

We can exploit anything, even Jesus. Anytime we turn to a thing in hopes of escaping reality, we're using that thing, person, activity, entity, or substance as a surrogate for what we really want. Something's just not right about that, to use religion like that. If I were Jesus, I'd prefer that you to come to me because you want *me*, not because you can't land a man and now you're bitter and despondent. I'm just sayin'.

But I'm not Jesus, and so I know Jesus takes us no matter why we turn to Him.

I'm a spiritual person, not religious. My father was a Pentecostal minister. I had a religious upbringing. I spent half my young life going to church. About ten years ago, for eighteen months, I attended an AME church where I witnessed too many people misuse religion. Some women use church like it's pink paint. They pour it over their problems to hide them from others and themselves, rather than asking Jesus to heal them. No worries though, hidden wounds have a way of breaking out of hiding.

There are more than a few Bible-toting-Bible-study-attending Christian sisters who are a clear and present danger to the world because they're so crazy and emotionally unstable. There they are on Sunday morning, speaking in tongues, stomping in the aisles, and shouting "Hallelujah" until they're hoarse and spent. Come Monday, these same sisters don their masks to cover the painful truth that they're angry at daddy, pissed off at momma, hate men, and don't like themselves.

## SISTERS IN THE CHURCH

I'm about to step on some more toes. And yet, I cannot talk about women turning to the church without talking about how too many women view the pastor in these churches.

Before I venture any further into these potentially dangerous waters, let me tell you that I speak from experience. My daddy was a pastor of two small churches; one in Baltimore and one in Philadelphia. So whatever I say about the pastor and his relationship with female congregants, I can say I witnessed it. Because both single and unhappily married women were often so unrelenting in their resolve to get just a bit of my charming daddy's attention, I grew up saying the one thing I NEVER, EVER, EVER wanted to be was the first lady of a church. First Lady of the United States of America maybe. But not of a church. No sir! See, I saw how challenging that role was for my mother, and I want no parts of it.

While writing this book, one day I got into a conversation with a gentleman about the church. Somehow we got on the subject of how women cope with loss and loneliness. I ran down the many ways I've observed women coping, including slipping into the church. Well, it was this gentleman who helped me understand one of the main reason women flock to the church when they are relationally and sexually frustrated: the pastor. "A lot of women see the pastor as their surrogate man," my friend said. I broke out laughing. It dawned on me at that moment that my new friend was speaking from experience. Doggone it, he was a pastor!

"You're right," I said knowingly. I remembered the beguiling women in my dad's churches, who always seemed to have a reason to need "a word" with him right after service. Some of those church ladies were relentless. Even as a little girl, I sensed that some of these meetings weren't about the Women's Day service or the prayer breakfast. One unhappily married woman was shameless in her pursuit of my father's time and attention with her offers to drive him here and there. And yes, from time to time he would accept her "help."

And you know what? I'd bet you a mega church's Sunday offering that a lot of preachers, whether consciously or unconsciously, deliberately or inadvertently, encourage this view of them as a surrogate husband. It's a powerful position to hold. It's decidedly a great ego booster. Not to mention, it undoubtedly helps to keep the tithes and offering baskets healthy. Remember, women are the backbone of the traditional black church. Even as they are "encouraged" to stay out of the pulpit, women take care of the pastor and the church.

## THE PASTOR AIN'T YOUR MAN

Still, he ain't your man. Let me say it again: The pastor is NOT your man. If he has a wife, and most of them do, stay in your lane. If because you couldn't find a husband, frustrated, you turned to the church for comfort and companionship, know this: The pastor is NOT your surrogate husband. He is not your man. He is already taken. And even if he isn't, he's not yours. Just because you tithe 10 percent of your gross income, regularly attend Wednesday night Bible study, is in church every Sunday, organize dinners and bake sales, plan anniversaries, conferences, retreats—doesn't give you the right to get a piece of the first lady's man. So, if you're in a church right now where you're eyeing the pastor funny, where you're a bit too taken with him, where you're fantasizing about the pastor in ungodly ways, where your dependence on him is inappropriate, you need prayer . . . because you know God don't like ugly.

If your being saved and sanctified and filled with the Holy Ghost haven't extinguished your desire for a man, maybe it's because you're still a woman. You're a spiritual being having a human experience. In our humanness we naturally desire to share our life with someone special. Get real with yourself. Let go of the false notion that you're unlucky in love; that there's no one for you or it's too late for you now. Those are just stories you're telling yourself. Tell yourself a new story and you'll create some new and improved experiences.


## CHOOSING HEALTH OVER HAIR

Did you know that more than 40 percent of black women say they don't exercise because they don't want to mess up their hair? Can you believe that? Well, you know 4 out of 5 black women are overweight or obese, right? That's 80 percent of us!

We can prevent many of the illnesses that plague African Americans, like strokes, diabetes, hypertension, heart disease and cancer simply by managing our weight. I know we are sometimes tempted to complicate matters but truth is we manage our weight by consistently doing two things:

1. Eating less and
2. Moving more

That is, we have got to exercise. When I talk to younger women about exercise I often say, "It's easier to keep it than it is to get it back." In my youth I cultivated a habit of taking care of my body by eating healthily and exercising. In so doing, exercising became a part of my lifestyle. And because I grew to appreciate the benefits of exercise—looking good in my clothes and naked, feeling strong, increased confidence, a sense of empowerment, and the ability to turn men's heads—I kept it up. If you're young and shapely, don't lose your figure by overeating and lack of exercise. While you're young acquire a taste for exercise by making it a priority. Make exercise a part of your daily routine like you do going to work and eating. Don't pencil it into your schedule; ink it in. If you wouldn't think of letting someone talk you out of going to work, don't let laziness, inertia, your hair, distractions, family or friends interfere with your daily workout.

The Mayo Clinic offers us:

## 7 BENEFITS OF REGULAR PHYSICAL EXERCISE

### No. 1: Exercise controls weight

Exercise can help prevent excess weight gain or help maintain weight loss. When you engage in physical activity, you burn calories. The more intense the activity, the more calories you burn. You don't need to set aside large chunks of time for exercise to reap weight-loss benefits. If you can't do an actual workout, get more active throughout the day in simple ways — by taking the stairs instead of the elevator or revving up your household chores.

### No. 2: Exercise combats health conditions and diseases

Worried about heart disease? Hoping to prevent high blood pressure? No matter what your current weight, being active boosts high-density lipoprotein (HDL), or "good," cholesterol and decreases unhealthy triglycerides. This one-two punch keeps your blood flowing smoothly, which decreases your risk of cardiovascular diseases. In fact, regular physical activity can help you prevent or manage a wide range of health problems and concerns, including stroke, metabolic syndrome, type 2 diabetes, depression, certain types of cancer, arthritis and falls.

### No. 3: Exercise improves mood

Need an emotional lift? Or need to blow off some steam after a stressful day? A workout at the gym or a brisk 30-minute walk can help. Physical activity stimulates various brain chemicals that may leave you feeling happier and more relaxed. You may also feel better about your appearance and yourself when you exercise regularly, which can boost your confidence and improve your self-esteem.

### No. 4: Exercise boosts energy

Winded by grocery shopping or household chores? Regular physical activity can improve your muscle strength and boost your endurance. Exercise and physical activity deliver oxygen and nutrients to your tissues and help your cardiovascular system work more efficiently. And when your heart and lungs work more efficiently, you have more energy to go about your daily chores.

### No. 5: Exercise promotes better sleep

Struggling to fall asleep? Or to stay asleep? Regular physical activity can help you fall asleep faster and deepen your sleep. Just don't exercise too close to bedtime, or you may be too energized to fall asleep.

### No. 6: Exercise puts the spark back into your sex life

Do you feel too tired or too out of shape to enjoy physical intimacy? Regular physical activity can leave you feeling energized and looking better, which may have a positive effect on your sex life. But there's more to it than that. Regular physical activity can lead to enhanced arousal for women. And men who exercise regularly are less likely to have problems with erectile dysfunction than are men who don't exercise.

### No. 7: Exercise can be fun

Exercise and physical activity can be a fun way to spend some time. It gives you a chance to unwind, enjoy the outdoors or simply engage in activities that make you happy. Physical activity can also help you connect with family or friends in a fun social setting. So, take a dance class, hit the hiking trails or join a soccer team. Find a physical activity you enjoy, and just do it. If you get bored, try something new.

### The bottom line on exercise

Exercise and physical activity are a great way to feel better, gain health benefits and have fun. As a general goal, aim for at least 30 minutes of physical activity every day. If you want to lose weight or meet specific fitness goals, you may need to exercise more. Remember to check with your doctor before starting a new exercise program, especially if you have any health concerns.

## EXERCISE EMPOWERS YOU

Exercising makes you feel more empowered, too. My trainer, Chauncey D. Whitehead, Owner of CDW Health and Wellness, LLC said when his female clients get fit and strong they not only grow more confident but more assertive. They take less off of folks, personally and professionally. They learn how to say "no" to nonsense. I can speak to that. Being physically fit makes me feel more confident, capable and in control of my life. And another thing, when a woman loves herself enough to take good care of her body the man in your life is less likely to think he can take her for granted. A woman's ability to turn heads helps to keep her man in check. When you look good your man isn't so inclined to think if he should leave you that you'll be all alone. He knows better than that. Having a strong and beautiful body is a source of power. Why not enjoy this power for as long as you can? Exercise. It's truly the fountain of youth.

## I Let You

When I see you I start to go backward
I become the me that I was with you
the me that would do anything for you

You used me
hurt me, changed me and abused me
And I let you

Because I wanted you to love me too
In the same way that I loved you
You said you cared
that you'd always be there
And I believed you

Because I wanted you to love me too
In the same way that I loved you
You took all I had
And gave me nothing back
And I wanted you too

Because . . .
You know why
It took me awhile
to look at your smile
The smile you smiled at someone else
the smile I wanted for myself
And now as I look back
I realize you never looked at me like that
Never.

And I deserve better
But it's my fault because I let you
Because I wanted you to love me the same way that I
love you.
Correction: loved you.

—*Adia Ricks Cummings*

## Nuggets of Wisdom from
### *Marian Johnson*

**DMR: Tell us a bit about you.**
**MJ:** I am a sixty-five-year-old retired, divorced mother of one son and grandmother to three granddaughters. I am not having the life I envisioned as a young woman, but largely, I am living a content, full life.

**Can you share some of your relationship journey with our readers?**
My relationships with men have run the gamut. I have had four deep and loving relationships. The first of these relationships was with my husband, who I believed would be the only man that I would love. I never saw it coming, us growing apart. As I grew professionally and socially, he remained the same; consequently, we had less and less in common. I had little or no patience for waiting for him to catch up. In retrospect, I realize that my impatience cost me and launched my endless search for "Mr. Goodbar." (He does not exist. Trust me. I have looked thoroughly!)

Subsequent relationships, although they proved to be meaningful, loving, learning opportunities for me, somehow missed the mark. Today, I am in a comfortable relationship with a man I adore, but this relationship lacks something important. Nonetheless, because I am older, I am less likely to leave this relationship to pursue something new. I have learned to settle a bit more—I am not sure whether this is good or bad.

### What were some of your mistakes?

I made plenty of mistakes. The most glaring mistake was loving my men more than I loved me. I was open and vulnerable. I revealed my weaknesses, and the men used that to control me and direct the relationships to their advantage.

Fortunately for me, the men I have been involved with have basically been decent types who, for the most part, did not have my utter destruction in mind; nonetheless, I went through all the game playing that unhealthy relationships go through. Another thing, I believed that if the sex was good everything else in the relationship must be good too. So, I often operated the way we accuse men of operating; I'd think with my loins instead of my brain.

### Do you see other women making these or other mistakes?

Of course! Look at the teenage pregnancy rates; listen to the misogynistic rap lyrics directed at women; look at the statistics for brutality and homicide and other crimes against women. Much of these social anomalies are due to the poor self-image girls and women have of themselves. We must, as those who allegedly know better, continue to enlighten our younger and not-so-young sisters. Many of them have very destructive behaviors that cause them to fall into the arms of men who do not have their best interests at heart.

### What have you learned?

I had enough experiences with men to discover what I

wanted and what I did not want. I know that a truly, loving relationship has trust, communication, and compassion as key components. All the components may not be present initially, but they should eventually emerge.

**What was your relationship like with your father? How did that relationship shape you and dictate how you showed up in relationships with men?**

My relationship with my father was somewhat complicated. Up to the point when I started school, we had the typical endearing daddy's little girl relationship. There were Sunday rides, ice-cream cones, and sitting on my daddy's lap. When I went to school I grew more independent, and consequently, I was less dependent upon my father. As I grew with my own thoughts and opinions, I noticed that much of my thinking did not agree with my father's old-fashioned ways. I started to despise my strict, often unreasonable upbringing and father. I had to get to a point in my adult life where I let the past go, forgive my dad and myself, and move on.

**A lot of black women are unpartnered and in search of a satisfying love relationship. What are your opinions about being a woman and single?**

As I explained in some of my other responses, I am a single woman who has been single for more than thirty years and have been partnered nearly all of that time. One day a close friend said, "You don't know how to be alone without a man." Although I believe I *could* be alone, I do not *want* to be alone and without companionship. It's a choice. I also believe that love for self and God ought to come first; love for a man, if it is meant to be, will follow.

**Women over fifty want and need love and sex too; any words of wisdom for them?**

Yes, we do. I believe that love is something that takes time to grow, but sex is needed by most women to stay emotionally and physically healthy. It is my intention to keep that part of my life vital for as long as possible. To that end, I will strive to maintain caring, trusting alliances in my life.

**What advice/insights would you offer young women about attracting a loving, trusting relationship?**

Young women should keep education as the centerpiece of their growth and development. As they evolve, they will have a better chance of attracting the right kinds of men. Again, this is where having enough experience to know what you want and don't want comes into play.

**Do you have any final words for our readers?**

My final words are to my young sisters, our daughters and granddaughters. They should learn to value themselves and dwell in the teachings of God and their elders. Seek truth and wisdom that will help them cultivate the skills to relate well to people and eventually a loving, trusting relationship with a man will follow.

# The Way Forward

*"Our culture sanitizes or satirizes any emotion that
might slow us down or, God forbid, connect us
to the pain of others. But grief is healing."*
—Elizabeth Lesser, author of *Broken Open*

*"Sometimes you just gotta be your own hero
and save your own little heart.
Because sometimes the people you can't
imagine living without can actually live without you."*
—Author Unknown

YOUR RELATIONSHIP TANKED. What now? Where do you go from here? In a conversation with a sisterfriend, she expressed her utter frustration at women for succumbing to anger and bitterness after a breakup. "Why can't they just see the good in what they had and move on?" she demanded.

I understood her thinking. But I disagree. Anger is a natural emotion. Anger rears its defiant head when someone violates our boundaries, disrespects us, takes us for granted, or deny us something that we want. Anger is also a natural response to loss. What, however, is unnatural and unhealthy is to stay angry. Anger that isn't expressed and released becomes bitterness. "Anger," I said to my friend, "is one of the stages of grief." As we move through the grieving process, we'll finally reach the final stage: acceptance.

That is, if we do the work to move ourselves through this process.

If you're going through a breakup and you're seething with anger, no worries. Anger is not only okay; it's healthy. You're feeling something, which means you're at least not numb. You have a right to your anger, so long as it doesn't lead to violence or retaliation.

If, however, it's been years since a relationship has ended and you're still angry, then you're stuck. You aren't doing the work to heal that ultimately leads to acceptance and peace. Well, it's time to get unstuck. Until you do, you're destined to repel love while you attract pain. Why? Because we draw to us what we think about, believe, and radiate. If you're not radiating love, then you can't very well attract love.

A sister at a financial literacy seminar that I attended in Puerto Rico suddenly had a light bulb moment. "I realize I've got to forgive my ex-husband . . . if I'm going to forgive other men," she said slowly. This woman finally got that so long as she was angry with her ex, she was blocking her blessings and repelling love.

Dr. Elisabeth Kübler-Ross, psychiatrist and author of the groundbreaking book, *On Death and Dying*, dedicated her life to helping dying people transition with grace and dignity. Dr. Kübler-Ross noted that there are five stages of grief. We go through these stages whether our loss is through death or desertion. As you may know, when someone you love leaves you, it really can feel like a death. And, in a sense, that loss *is* a death. It's the death of a dream and future with your ex, someone who you may still love. Even if it doesn't feel like death, a breakup is a loss that deserves our respect.

How do we show respect? We respect any loss by acknowledging it and the pain that we feel. We live in a society that too often discourages the acknowledgment of losses. That's an unhealthy approach. To grieve and mourn our losses is to respect them and ourselves. Grieving clears a place within us, creating a clearing for the possibility of something new and wonderful to come in.

## THE FIVE STAGES OF GRIEF ARE:

- Denial—this isn't happening to me!
- Anger—*why* is this happening to me?
- Bargaining—God, I promise I'll be a better person *if* you'd make this stop happening.
- Depression and despair—okay, I don't care anymore.
- Acceptance—I can live with what is and be okay.

When a man leaves you, even though you may feel as if you're absolutely powerless, you actually have a choice about how to handle that loss. The wrenching pain coursing through your mind and body can feel like it'll go on forever. You may even imagine that you can't go on without him. Your mind might tell you he was your last chance for love, for happiness, for partnership. Or that no one else can possibly love you like he did.

After a breakup, what you say to yourself can be the difference between moving through the grieving process and getting stuck somewhere between denial and depression. Or worse, getting so depressed that you attempt to take your own life. *Whatever you do, don't resort to a permanent solution for a temporary painful problem.*

If, after years of separation and no healthy signs of his desire to reconcile, you still "hope" he'll realize his mistake and return, you are living in denial. If you are blaming or consumed by conversations about your ex years after his departure, your anger has now become resentment. If you continue to call him long after he's made it abundantly clear that he has moved on, hoping to entice him into giving your relationship another chance, you're stuck. If you lost interest in the things that once brought you joy, no longer care about your appearance, often feel fatigued, overeat, overspend, drink excessively, self-medicate with street or prescription drugs, you have probably sunk into depression.

If you are in the throes of a breakup or can't seem to fully recover from a relationship that ended some time ago, I strongly encourage you to try these things:

1. Turn within to a Power greater than your pain.
2. Pray. Meditate. Journal.
3. Reach out. Join a loving and supportive spiritual community/church. Talk to a trusted friend or family member.
4. Seek professional counseling or therapy. Get into a support group.

Whatever you do, don't pretend you're okay when you're hurting. It's time to tell on your pain, to expose it. You owe it to yourself to be 100 percent. Healing is possible, but you must do the necessary work. What you do or don't do can affect the healing process greatly.

First, I want you to know that I know and understand. I realize that heartache from a heartbreak can sometimes make you wish you were dead. Any battered woman can tell you this: *Emotional blows are every bit as painful as any physical assault.* They say the emotional abuse can keep on wounding long after the black eye has faded. So, it's natural and human to sometimes resort to unhealthy means in an attempt to escape from painful emotions. It's not uncommon for hurting folks to drink too much, overeat, spend mindlessly, fall into a new relationship too quickly, bed bounce, gamble, and overwork in an attempt to numb themselves against the loneliness and loss.

But there's another, better way. Notice I didn't say easier way. I said better way, as in a healthier, life-enhancing way to mend a broken heart. I offered several of them above. Later, I provide you with some additional tools.

## HENNESSEY, VALIUM, OR A NEW LOVER?

A few more words about grief and grieving. When we lose someone through death, divorce, or their departure, our mind, body, and spirit register that pain. If we give in to the temptation to ease the pain with a bottle of Hennessey, Valium, or a new lover, though we may experience some immediate relief, we've only put a Band-Aid on our wound. That is, our "solution" is only temporary. Pain that's numbed, ignored, pushed down, and buried in our psyches and bodies waits for our attention. While waiting, it can morph into physical dis-ease, addictions, and mental illness. Nor does it go away just because you've chosen to act as if it doesn't exist.

So many relationships falter because the parties aren't emotionally and psychologically fully present. They aren't ready. They haven't taken the necessary time and space required to heal the pain, shame, and tendency to blame that attends a breakup. Too often, they've fallen into another relationship way before they've sufficiently grieved, reflected upon, and emotionally released their last relationship. The hurt gets piled high and deep. People lose the ability to distinguish one lover from the next. Emotional baggage burdens and taxes the new relationship. The weight of the past causes the new thing to collapse. Then these two people scurry off in search of yet another human balm for their pain. And, oh, what a futile search that is.

We live in a society that recoils from sorrow and grief, as if those emotions kill. We tacitly allot people a nominal amount of time to mourn their losses, even the big ones. We are quick to push a grieving person to "get over it and get on with your life." Their grief, we fear, will put us in touch with our own unresolved issues.

I told a friend of mine about a nasty breakup that I was going through. Shoot, before I could put a period at the end of my closing sentence she was insisting that I get over him and move on. But what if my mind, body, and spirit weren't quite ready to move on? What if I still had some grieving to do? What if my broken heart had yet to heal? What if I had more tears to cry? Was I required to get over it in a designated number of days, weeks, or months? Besides, why was she so invested in my moving on, even if that meant I did so with an achy-breaky heart? "Why prolong it," you might ask, "when you don't have to?"

Grieving is a natural, necessary process for optimal mental and emotional health. Don't wallow in sorrow and sadness, but by all means do honor your unique grieving process. To grieve is to release, to heal. As my father would frequently quote from scripture, "There's a time and season for all things." That includes a time to be sad, sorrowful, melancholy, even grief stricken. Emotional and psychic pain, which can eat away at the body like maggots, seek full expression. Love can't survive, let alone thrive, if you've not yet grieved and thus, let go of, say, the fact that your father abandoned you. You can't be available for love so long as you have yet finished crying over the cruel, drug-addicted mother who neglected, ignored, or discarded you. Marianne Williamson once said, "If you have eleven tears to cry and you've only cried six of them, then you have five more tears to cry." Give yourself permission to cry *all* your tears.

We owe it to ourselves, our loved ones, our children, our families, our communities, our country, our world to take care of our emotional and psychic hurts and wounds. Nobody's going to do it for us. If you broke your right arm, you would get thee to a hospital for some medical care, wouldn't you? You would tell the doctor the truth about what happened so you could get the most appropriate care and treatment. Then you would cease to use your right arm until you thought it was healed and strong enough to lift, pull, and throw things. Right? Well, give your heart the same degree of care by tending to it when it's bruised and broken. Then when it's strong and clear, you're ready to get back in the love game. It need not be 100 percent, but your awareness of this fact and ability to communicate openly and honestly with your new beloved makes up for any left over bruising. You'll be in good company because, to some degree, all of us are wounded.

## DENIAL

When we experience a sudden loss, like a breakup, often our first reaction is denial. *This can't be happening! Not again. Why? Why me?* If we could only steel ourselves against the truth, our mind tells us, then maybe we can escape the pain that comes with our new reality. Denial, though it has earned a bad rap and reputation, has a purpose, a valuable one. Denial is a protective device. It acts as a shield, to keep out information that we're not ready to fully digest. Denial is the mind's attempt to give the system—mind, body, and spirit—time to grasp shocking new realities. Denial, therefore, is a normal and arguably necessary reaction to "bad" news. It's resistance to an unwanted change in the status quo.

Denial is characterized by shock, numbness, and confusion. Let's face it (no pun intended), change can be hard. It's especially challenging when it's sudden and unplanned and unwanted.

Be ever so gentle with yourself. You've just embarked upon the grieving process. So long as you don't get *stuck* in denial, in time, this too shall pass. And yet, before the sun comes out tomorrow, you may be gripped by another unwanted emotion—anger.

## ANGER

My husband left me. It was August 1, 1987. I'd stayed out all night with my boyfriend. (Yep, you read it right, my *boyfriend*.) Even before I put the key in the door, I knew my husband had moved out. It was woman's intuition. Initially, all I felt was a sigh of relief. *Phew! He's gone. Now I can have some doggone peace,* I thought, as I scanned the now messy apartment for my things. Things had gotten so crazy between us. By the end of our fifth year together—two of which we'd been striving mightily for the ever-elusive wedded bliss—all I craved was peace. After all, all we had by then were our arguments. We fought about everything. Our sex life dried up, which was, in my opinion clear, incontrovertible evidence that we were through. Now Avery had moved out, leaving our lovely eighth-floor apartment overlooking Druid Hill Park and its reservoir all to me. *Lucky me,* I thought. *Now I don't have to find another apartment.* I was young, single, and free! Uh, at least I had two out of three. I was childless, single, uh, and almost free. I was still legally married, and more significantly, I was not free because anger, resentment, and fear held me hostage.

If you are seething with anger or, seemingly out of the blue it rises up and slaps you in the mouth at the very thought or mention of your ex, don't be alarmed or embarrassed. You're simply moving through the grieving process. Let no one tell you that you have no right to your anger. You do. Anger is as natural as fear. Your anger isn't justified because your ex was wrong or bad to choose as he did, but anger is a natural human response to hurt, betrayal, disappointment, and boundary violations. When my tumultuous marriage ended, I was consumed by anger for months. I was angry with myself for marrying the "wrong" man and livid at him for not measuring up to the man I needed him to be so I, not him, could be happy.

People who *express* their anger in healthy ways aren't angry people. It's stuffed anger that ferments into resentment. Resentment is a seething poison that eats away at your life force, blocks your blessings, and blinds you to your possibilities. This is where a support network comes in. Every woman needs to surround herself with people who love and support her. Talk out your anger with your friends and family; pray, meditate, journal, cry. Anger can cloud your thinking, so avoid making important decisions while you're pumped up with anger. If you articulate your angry feelings, you can neutralize them and thus, stave off resentment. Resist the urge to seek revenge. Since the best and only revenge is the well-lived life. Take care of you. Do it well.

Grieving isn't a linear journey from breakup to acceptance. It's chaotic and confusing and, at times, protracted. You loop back and forth through the stages. One minute you're pissed off, the next you're begging for another chance to make a relationship work that deserved to die.

## BARGAINING

Wading through the mourning labyrinth can be excruciatingly painful. Is it any wonder that "good" women are known to beg "bad" men to take them back? And you know when "bad" things happen we bargain with God. "God, please, please, pleaasssse, make him come back to me. I'll be a better wife. I'll be more loving. I'll go to church more. I'll . . ." We so want the pain to stop, by any means necessary.

## DEPRESSION

Yes, depression is one of the stages of grief. Go through it; don't get stuck there. If you fall into despair after a breakup reach out to someone. Maybe you need to talk things through. Do that. Whatever you do, don't be okay with being depressed indefinitely. Though relationships are eternal, they do change forms. That change can turn your world upside down. I'll say it again; reach out for help. You deserve it.

**ACCEPTANCE**

The scripture says, "Weeping may endure for a night, but joy comes in the morning." No matter how wrenching the pain, in time, this too shall pass. How you speak to yourself can either expedite your healing or prolong your suffering. Remember, there's not just one person on the planet for you. Okay, even if he was wonderful, know this: there are more wonderful men out there. Accept what is. He's gone, but you're still here. You're here because you have more life and love to experience. Acceptance brings peace. Getting to acceptance, however, might require you to forgive.

Black women *are* angry. So are black men. Both black men and women are angry. But for vastly different reasons. In an earlier chapter we addressed sisters' anger. Now let's talk about the black man's anger. I believe black men are angry about their "outsider" status in America. They're challenged by racism on a daily basis, no matter their accomplishments or profession. Black men's effort to achieve socioeconomic and political equality is thwarted on many fronts. For some reason, more than a few black men blame black women's success for their failure. "Those jobs that black women got should be ours!" some brothers rail.

In relationships, it's not uncommon for brothers to compete with sisters. Not for a particular job but for status and success and recognition. I was involved with a brother who said to me one day, "It's as if we're competing with each other." I thought that was interesting. So there he was competing with me. Meanwhile, I was behaving as if we were on the same team. I was committed to supporting him in achieving his dreams, while he secretly competed with me. Actually, now that I think of it, his competing with me wasn't a secret after all. This was the brother who resented me calling my daughter when I was with him. The same man who tried to pull me away from a speaking commitment when his car broke down on the road. The same man who chose to spend Thanksgiving with his friends instead of me.

But for what, I wondered, was he really competing with me for? We weren't even in the same business or industry. Sadly, he saw my success as some sort of threat to his. Unfortunately, he didn't get that we live in an abundant world, so there's enough success to go around.

## THE ANGRY BLACK MAN

If black men are angry with black women, and I'm convinced that they are, how does this anger look and get expressed? As already mentioned, anger can show up as competition. A guy friend of mine said, in one of our many conversations about relationships, that one way black men indirectly express their anger toward black women is by cheating, mistreating, beating, disrespecting and hurting them. I agree. To this list I will add down-low behavior, i.e., men sleeping with men. It's yet another way some black men attempt to tell black women, "You are dispensable! See, I can even get my sexual needs met without you."

Black men's anger at black women also shows up in their music. Much of rap and hip-hop music do what? Degrades and denigrates black women. Black men are the ONLY race of men that do this in their music. Why? Because they are ANGRY at black women.

This anger that the sexes feel is unconscious, historical anger. If you were to ask a brother, "Are you angry at black women?" they'd likely look at you funny, but never answer the question. And yet, a lot of their thinking and behavior toward black women is laced with anger. The brother who insists he's done with black women is angry.

## THE "SIXTH STAGE" OF FORGIVENESS

*"How willing are you to forgive your brother? How much do
you desire peace instead of endless strife and misery and pain?
Forgiveness is your peace."*
—A Course in Miracles

*A Course in Miracles* says there are but two emotions: *love* and *fear.*
If one isn't giving love, then he is seeking love. What you might
observe is some form of fear masked as anger. Anger is often a
mask for hurt. Think about it, men aren't allowed to say, "You hurt
me." But they can say, "Bitch, why you carrying me like that?"

At a book signing I did for *Love Addicted,* a distinguished-
looking, mature black man, salt-and-pepper beard, expensive
suit and overcoat, briefcase in hand, said to me after reading
the title of my book, "Black men have to forgive black women."
I waited for him to elaborate. "They must," he added, "forgive
black women for surviving." This man's words are forever etched
into my mind. I knew then what I know now: he spoke truth.
Let me add this truth: black women must also forgive black
men. We must forgive black men for all the things we think they
should have done but didn't do, like protect us from the slave
master's lust and lash. We must forgive black men for all the
things that they did do, like abandon us to raise children alone,
leave us to fend for ourselves, and too often, fail to be the caliber
of men that we need them to be.

## A TIME TO HEAL

It is time to heal the chasm between black men and women.
We've been angry and hurt much too long. It is time to step up to
the plate and forgive. It is time to heal. Nothing heals like forgiveness. We must forgive each other collectively and individually. If

we don't heal ourselves, and each other, tell me, who will heal us? It is time to bury the hatchet. It is time to forgive. Without forgiveness there is no hope for us and our precious children are doomed to repeat the cycle of distrust, hate, and violence.

Sister, will you forgive the men in your life? Will you forgive your father? Will you free yourself and forgive your husband, lover, boyfriend, baby daddy, brother, uncle, cousin, and *all* your exes? Your forgiveness of just one man brings healing to our planet. You become an example of what is possible as you add more light to our world.

It takes courage and surrender to forgive. The ego, which stands for Edging God Out, would keep you in bondage. The ego wants you to believe you are separate from your brother. It doesn't want you to know and trust that you and your brother are one. But we are one. This is why when you hurt another, you feel that hurt. Even as you deny it, you hurt. This is also why when you are angry at someone else, it is *you* who feels the heat of that anger. It is time to heal. Will you forgive?

Brother, are willing to forgive your sister? And free yourself.

## GETTING OVER HIM

*You can forgive . . . even as your heart continues to pine
for The Departed. Now, are you ready to get over him?*
—DeBora

Too many women are hurting, stuck, and angry because they have yet to get over a man who is long gone. I bet you know someone in that predicament, don't you? Well, uh, it could be you.

I'll admit it, getting over someone, no matter how the relationship ended, can be difficult. It's especially hard if you are still in love with him. You've not only lost his presence, attention, affection, love, and companionship, but your plans for a future with him have been shattered. You miss him. You miss time together, even the rough patches. The conversations, lovemaking, and laughter are no more.

No matter how ugly things got, still there were sweet moments. Tender times together. No matter how bad he was, he wasn't *all* bad. If you've not yet attracted a new relationship, and he's with someone new, that fact can contribute to your feelings of not being good enough, of betrayal and loss. If he walked off without saying good-bye and you pine for closure, that fact can add to your feeling stuck. Maybe he betrayed your trust, cheated on you, abused you or simply decided he no longer wished to be married to you. Now you're angry. Hurt. Sad. Confused. Lonely. And you just can't stop thinking about him. A song comes on that conjures him up, and your heart sinks. You drive by his house and sadness washes over you. You can't watch a love scene in a movie or on TV without your heart breaking.

Yes, getting over him can be hard. It can take time. And work. *It, however, can be done.* Indeed, if you want to live and love again then you must find a way to get over him. As long as your heart remains shackled to the memory of one man, you make yourself unavailable to the new man that the Universe wants to send you.

I've been left, cheated on, and dumped. My heart has been broken more times than I can remember. I, however, know how to get over a man. Just ask my friends. My friend Georgia said she admired this ability of mine. "One day you're talking about how much you're in love and that he's The One. Next thing I know you're moving on. Not like me, who took thirty years to get over my ex," she said laughing. She's right. I have learned how to get over a man. I had to learn if I was to live a passionate, purposeful life open and available to love. So, I offer you six steps to getting over him. But first, let's see how my friend Vickie got closure.

## DESPERATELY SEEKING CLOSURE

Remember Vickie? Let me refresh your memory. Vickie was seeing a guy who quietly slipped away without a trace. One day she ran into him, he who we shall call Jack. When Vickie saw Jack, memories of how she'd felt when he disappeared resurfaced. Vickie had burned a load of brain cells wondering what had happened. What had gone wrong? What had she done? Remember her New Year's resolution was to take more risks? Every day, rain or shine, she would take one risk. Her risk for the day, Jack, awaited her. After some small talk Vickie asked him, "Why did you stop calling? What happened?" She then stood there waiting for his response. Vickie needed to put a stop to the wondering. If she was going to do that she needed closure.

Jack stared back at her. "Do you really want to know?" he asked slowly.

"Yes," she said softly, "I do. I really want to know."

"Okay." Mr. Departed told Vickie that he wasn't physically attracted to her. He liked her, as a friend, she just didn't turn him on.

So, he went back to dating his type. Well, to each his own. Jack likes what he likes. We all have preferences. And yet, the very least Mr. Departed could have done was to tell my friend that he was no longer interested. That he wouldn't be calling anymore. Coward! I know, I know, it isn't easy ending a relationship, even a brief one. Things can get messy. So what? Who said love and relationships are supposed to be nice and easy? Any flower as deliciously layered and beautiful as love and relationship inevitably comes with some thorns. If only Jack had manned up and shown another human being the kind of respect that she, and the situation, warranted, he would have spared Vickie some anguish. Sure, had he told my friend sooner it might then have caused her anguish. And yet, is it too much to ask a man who we've shared our time, energy, body, and affection with to treat us with respect and regard when what he does impacts us? I don't think so.

Being willing to have courageous conversations with the people in our life is a part of being an adult. See, Vickie was once overweight. Then she set out to get physically healthy and consequently lost more than a hundred pounds. I admire and am inspired by my friend's maturity and confidence. She was neither deflated nor discouraged by this man's admission. Instead, she was optimistic and undaunted. She finished our conversation on a high note when she said, "I know there's a man out there who will love and accept me . . . just as I am." And you know what? Vickie's absolutely right. Every woman should be so confident that there's someone somewhere who will love and accept her for who and what she is and for who and what she is not.

Vickie sought answers, that is, closure, from the man who'd disappeared. When a relationship ends, whether abruptly or gradually, a part of us naturally seeks closure. What is closure? Dictionary.com defines closure as "the resolution of a significant event or relationship in a person's life or *a sense of contentment experienced after such a resolution.*" Closure isn't about *what* happened, the ending of a relationship; rather, closure is about how complete we feel about what happened. Closure is about achieving a sense of peace after a loss. Vickie sought answers from Mr. Departed because she believed those answers would bring her a degree of peace.

## GETTING CLOSURE

Why do we need closure? What does closure do for us? Getting over a man isn't a linear process. That is, after a loss, we don't necessarily move through the grief process—from anger to acceptance—in a nice straight line. Instead, our emotions tend to oscillate. One moment you accept that it's over because he cheated on you. Minutes later, you're seething with anger because he cheated on you and forced you to kick his ass to the curb. Closure brings peace. We desire the things that we think will bring closure because we desire peace. We seek closure because it closes one chapter of our life and open us up to new chapters.

How do we get closure? How do we experience peace when our heart is shattered? How do we find contentment when we're still seething with anger? How do we achieve closure when we secretly hope it's not really over? How do *you* move on without him when he refuses to help you understand what happened, what went wrong?

We cannot get closure so long as we are pining for yesterday. Closure demands something of *us*. Not him. If we're to get closure, we must be willing to let go of some things. As essential as hope is to living a vital, vibrant life, it, however, only keeps you tied to your ex and the past when a relationship tanks. Stop hoping he'll come back. Let go of anger and the need for anything from the departed. You have the power to give you closure. Closure is an inside job. When a man leaves you, even as your heart aches, you hold the key to the gate that leads to peace and contentment. This may come as a surprise to you, but it's the absolute truth: You don't need any particular person in your life to experience peace, wholeness, or happiness. You don't need for any situation or relationship to go as you hoped it would for you to experience peace and contentment. You have all that you need, right here, right now. Be willing to let go of anger, hope of reconciliation, and him coming back.

I know the ego, the false self, will have you believe that that man, the one you loved from the depths of your heart, is the only one for you. The ego will tell you that without him, or at the very least, some words of clarity from him that you cannot possibly move forward, that you can't possibly know peace again. Nothing is further from the truth. God, who abides within you, IS peace. Turn within. Be still. Be willing to forgive your ex.

And yourself. Bless and release him to the Universe. Be willing to embrace what is and the Universe will assist you in getting to acceptance. Closure, that is, a sense of peace, will come. In time, you will know a peace that surpasses all understanding.

## SIX STEPS TO WHOLENESS AND FREEDOM

**Step 1. Tend to Your Pain**—The worst thing you can do with pain is to deny and repress it. Cry. You owe it to yourself to cry. Crying purges and strengthens and heals us. In other words, grieve your losses. Proper grieving has the power to take us from anger to acceptance. Feel what you feel without making yourself wrong for feeling it. There are no wrong feelings. It's only what we do in reaction or response to our feelings that can be deemed right or wrong. You might be tempted to try to escape the pain—don't. Sit with it. Tend to it. Ask it questions. Treat you like you would a small child who has lost a pet she loved. Hold you. Caress you. Talk sweetly to you. Take good care of you.

**Step 2. Pray**—Prayer changes things. "God, deliver me" is a simple prayer that works for me. God's got you. No matter how bad it hurts, God's got you. If you're like most people, when heartache knocks, you can't help but call on God. Whether you open your mouth or not, remember, every thought is a prayer. I, however, encourage you to pray out loud. Hearing your own words will have a profound affect on you. As the Bible says, "Weeping may endure for a night, but joy comes in the morning." Remember, God won't heap onto you more than you can handle. Trust me when I tell you, this too shall pass.

**Step 3. Meditate and Journal**—Meditation is one of the oldest spiritual practices. We still use it because it works to calm and clear our minds. You need not meditate for hours though.

Sometimes I'll meditate for five to ten minutes and feel as if I've been sitting for hours. Journaling has saved my life. Journaling helps us to see our part in any situation, brings clarity and calm. One young woman said journaling helps her to forgive. Negative thoughts and feelings are like poison; they eat away at our bodies and minds. Rob us of our peace. Writing down negative thoughts and feelings gets them up and out of you. You'll notice a calm that overcomes you after writing down your troubling truths. One caveat. Don't beat yourself up if you don't write every day. Even if you write two to three times a week, your mind, body, and soul will thank you

**Step 4. Reach Out to Others**—Every woman needs a sister circle/loving community that she can count on when life throws her curve balls. I don't know where I would be without my women friends and spiritual community. When we attempt to recover alone, we slow down the healing process. Talking is therapeutic, healing, and revealing. But don't just talk—do as one of my spiritual gurus and bestselling author Iyanla Vanzant urges us to do, "Tell the *absolute* truth!"

**Step 5. Trust that Life Is Abundant**—Okay, he's gone. Now what are you going to do? Are you going to just sit there wallowing in self-pity, sadness, and anger? Or are you going to face the fact—that he's gone—and move confidently forward with your life, knowing that life and love are abundant? You get to choose. Which will it be? He was just one man. *One* man. Not the only man on the planet.

**Step 6. Know Your Worth**—We women are too hard on ourselves. Rather than see ourselves as the beautiful, powerful, glorious creatures that we are, too often we focus on what we perceive to be our flaws and shortcomings. Is it any wonder that the men we attract mistreat, berate, belittle, criticize, disrespect, and disregard us? Their treatment of us is but a mirror image of how we see ourselves. Sisters, it's time we know our worth.

Regardless of your past, whether you have an advanced degree, a house, luxury vehicle, or a mate, you are worthy of respect, love, attention, abundance, prosperity and joy. If you're not already standing in this truth, begin to do so today. Stand in front of a mirror every single day and tell you something beautiful. Tell you that you love you. Call your name and say, "_____, I love you. I love you very, very much. Because I love you, I will take good care of you in mind, body, and spirit."

# Why Can't I Be Okay?

*"How wrong it is for a woman to expect the man to build
the world she wants, rather than to create it herself?"*
—Anais Nin

A SISTERFRIEND TEXTED me. "Why can't I be okay with myself?"

"Huh?" I texted right back. I hadn't talked to my friend in a few days and didn't know what exactly provoked this question.

"It was just suggested by my sponsor that I not be in a relationship during this first year of recovery. I know it's true, but I've been asking for balance and companionship, and now that's being taken away as well as the food I love. Which brings me to just me . . . I don't like being there," she texted back.

"Don't like being where? Alone with you?" I texted.

"Yes."

"That's precisely why you need to do it then," I texted.

"Yeah . . . well, I guess that is part of my problem, and it's scary to think I will end up like my mother and aunties . . . old and by myself . . . still working on how to be with me . . . that's depressing."

That text exchange warranted a call. En route to afternoon court, I phoned her. I discovered what provoked those texts. My friend was supposed to call her sponsor at 4 o'clock, to check in.

Well, this Sunday, she was hanging out with a man and completely forgot. Whenever this man called and wanted to see her, my friend always made herself available. When she did report to her sponsor, the sponsor said, "You need this time to focus on you. Don't be in a relationship for at least a year."

Ouch!

By the time I'd called, she was in a better place. She'd reached out to another Food Anonymous member. I understood my friend's pain. I've walked in her shoes. For years. You already know my story. I'm a self-confessed love junkie in recovery. I'm inclined to say I'm healed from love addiction, but I won't say that because I don't want to invite a test from the Universe. Today, I do, however, know how to be single and satisfied. I love men. And yet, I don't *need* a man in my life to experience joy, peace, and wholeness.

So I talked to my friend. Through sobs she told me how she has always dreamed of getting married and growing old with a loving man.

"How many times have you been married?" I asked, knowing the answer already.

"Three times." *Sniffle, sniffle.*

"You've been married three times, and some women haven't been married once," I said calmly.

I asked that question about marriage for several reasons. One, I wanted my friend to realize she had indeed been married. Those marriages didn't last forever, but she'd been down the aisle three times; three times more than a bunch of black women. Second, I wanted my friend to see how she'd tried to avoid being alone again and again, unsuccessfully. However, the Universe doesn't support us in hiding out in relationships, and maybe she might consider a new approach.

What would a new approach to living and loving look like? What if no one comes right away? What if Mr. Right, The One, your soul mate, gets stuck in traffic and never gets to you?

Could you be okay? Could you live a full, vital life if Mr. Right never comes? Do you think it's possible to live a vitally good life without a man? Is it possible for a heterosexual woman to be single—not even have a friend with benefits—and be happy? That is, can a woman be happily single? Can *you*?

This is an important question for a multitude of reasons. For now, I ask this question because I want you to examine your thoughts regarding being single. I hope you'll look at how you feel about being single. If you nurse disempowering thoughts and feelings that cause you to feel less than, inadequate, or like a failure, I support you in yanking them up out of your psyche by their very roots. Even as we pray for the right and perfect man to walk into our life, it's important that we learn how to be happily single.

## WHY YOU HATE BEING ALONE

If you don't like your own company, how can you expect a man to enjoy it? If this is you, you're not alone. You're in good company with women (and men) from all walks of life who hate being alone with themselves. In fact, because the yearning to append ourselves to another is an emotional and psychic wound, it hardly matters how professionally or intellectually advanced you are. How much money you make, the titles you hold, and the number of fancy letters behind your name will not heal emotional and psychic pain. But self-love does. Before we talk self-love, however, let's talk about why you hate being alone.

I don't know anyone whose childhood didn't bruise or nearly break them. Our parents, God bless them, did what they knew to do. They loved us as best as they could. To paraphrase Dr. Maya Angelou, "Had they known better, they surely would have done better."

Females grow up with the message that we're not enough alone. A man will complete us . . . so we are led to believe. Yes, even black girls get this message. Sure, black girls are encouraged to have their own, and yet, messages abound that *real* women are skilled at getting and keeping a man. Little girls watch women in their families and communities pine for, seduce, endure, and suffer men. Cheating, beatings, lying, disappearing acts, disrespect, man sharing are tolerated to avoid being a woman alone. "A good woman" stands by her man, no matter what. A woman that can't keep a man is pitied. Looked at sideways. Remember terms like "spinster" and "old maid"? These were derogatory terms given to women who never married, even relatively young ladies. Though those terms are no longer fashionable, the thinking behind them is still en vogue.

Along with the unspoken messages, there are verbal ones. If your wounded father pummels you over the head with, "You'll never amount to anything!" and your mother insists that, "You ain't shit!" what kind of self-esteem do you think you'll have? You guessed it—low, low, *low* self-esteem. Women with low self-esteem tend to reach for stuff, like designer clothes, expensive shoes and bags, and men to make them feel significant.

Old tapes die hard. And yet, they can be destroyed. You have the power to kill those old tapes that would have you believe you're nothing without a man and replace them with the truth: *I AM whole and complete. I AM enough.*


## LOVING THE ONE YOU'RE WITH

I hated being alone. With a passion I hated it. If you read *Love Addicted*, you'd see how much I hated myself. How my self-loathing was at the root of my addiction to men and relationships. Boy, was I determined to have me a man! The Universe, however, didn't support that escape plan. Instead, I was supported in learning how to be alone because men kept leaving me. Or doing something that justified my kicking them to the curb. To use the words of singer will.i.am, "It's a new day!" Thank you very much.

I'm not in a relationship as I write this. Today is Tuesday. On Saturday, I woke up excited about the day that stretched like a lazy yarn before me. My daughter was gone for the weekend. I had time on my hands. First, I spent some quality time with God in prayer and meditation. Then, I did some journaling and reading. Next, I studied and played with my new Webcam. When I was bored with that, I dressed and went to the lake and walked around it three times. Then I did laundry, went shopping for a baby shower gift, cleaned my house, wrote more of this book, showered, and recorded videos for *YouTube*. I made no calls and was pleased that no one called me. I thoroughly delighted in my own company. I'm healthy. I'm living on purpose. I'm jetting to Paris in June. Life is GOOD! Why? Because I'm single and satisfied, because I love the one I'm with—me.

Do I desire to share my life with a loving, kind, smart, financially fit, funny, spiritually grounded, energetic, accomplished, clean, sexy hunk of a man? Absolutely! A man who will complement my life, not complete it. And I know, when I'm ready for that committed relationship, I will attract the right and perfect man for me.

## THE BEAUTY IN BEING SINGLE

There's a calling on every life. Yours included. An emotionally mature man knows how to be in a relationship *and* keep his eyes on what matters to him. If he's "forced" to choose between you and his vision for his life, well, uh, you'd better get ready to jump back into the dating scene. Seriously, secure men don't look to a woman for approval, identity, and validation. In fact, studies indicate that men actually do better in their careers when they are married. Which suggests that men, when married, are even more focused on their careers and success.

Women are nurturers. Whatever we love we support. We take care of the people that matter to us, especially our men.

Sadly though, we quite often take better care of our men than we do ourselves. If we're codependent, and many of us are, it's not uncommon for us to put our man's needs before our own. Women are apt to put desires, dreams, and needs that appear to be inconsistent with their role of lover, wife, and mother on the back burner where they simmer and eventually burn for lack of love and attention. Even in the twenty-first century, some women have no identity apart from that of their husband or man.

Women are known to lose themselves in their men. I know from experience. I was one of those women. Until I decided to honor my needs, dreams, and desires, even in the face of my man's griping that I wasn't available enough to him. I realized the problem wasn't that I took care of me; the problem was that he was insecure, controlling and unreasonable in his demands. He was ancient, i.e., chauvinistic. Per his ancient paradigm, a man is ought to be the center of a woman's life. His attempt to hoodwink me into believing I was not a good woman because I sought to tend to mine and my daughter's needs, as well as his, failed. Not initially though. Initially, I tried too hard. Then I woke up. Thank God, I woke up!

If a woman loses herself, where do you think her needs, desires, and dreams end up? Remember my friend who was advised by her sponsor to stay single so she could succeed at changing her relationship with food? She needed to focus. On herself and on the work ahead. Not on a man. So long as my friend's attention was out there, on a man, she shortchanged herself and undermined her ability to achieve her goal. There are times when we simply don't have the time, energy, or space for a man. That's okay.

Our sacral chakra, which is located at the base of the spine and at the upper and back part of the pelvic cavity, is the seat of both our sexuality and creativity. Sure, we can be both sexual and creative. However, so many people, brothers included, pour gallons of their sexual energy into sex and relationships when they ought to be building a career, writing a book or blog, painting a picture or house, teaching some children or themselves, coaching a little league football team or a younger brother, growing a relationship or family, raising their sons and daughters, serving their spiritual community, meditating, praying—you name it. I hope when you are single, you are able to be okay with it. It's this okayness that frees you to pour yourself completely into interests, work and people that matter to you at any given time in your life.

## LETTING GO IN LOVE

We don't just want to let go. We want to let go in love. Why? Because when we "let go" in anger, resentment, blame, and judgment, we haven't let go. We are still attached! We are linked to our ex in dis-ease. As long as we harbor negative, hostile thoughts toward someone, that someone controls us. He, though physically gone, is still very present in your life in a negative, unproductive way. Consider this:

- **Stand for What You Want**—If you desire a monogamous, loving relationship with a faithful man, then you must decide to walk away from the man who isn't that. There are women who live what you want. Why not you? But you can't both settle *and* expect to attract your right and perfect divine partner.
- **Release Him with a Blessing**—You can leave in love. Anger, bitterness, hostility, resentment, and judgment will attract more anger, bitterness, hostility, resentment, and judgment. Is that what you want? We attract *with* what's in us, in our minds, hearts, and bodies. Our thoughts and feelings pull people into our life that match our thoughts and feelings, about ourselves and the world. Consequently, if you're carrying around thoughts of anger, you will attract anger into your life.

We don't get what we want but who we are. Be love and love will be your companion, inside and out there. Remember, you are not a victim. No matter the choices that your ex made that don't comport with what you want, he did nothing TO you. What he did revealed him to you. His actions showed you what he was thinking and who he was.

When we hold our brother and ourselves hostage with thoughts of anger, attack, and revenge, we are the ones who will experience the pain of those emotions and the consequences of those thoughts. Those thoughts and emotions are those of a victim. If he left you for another woman, she is not your enemy. Just like you, she wants and deserves to be loved. Even if your man cheated on you with her, she is not your enemy. Love and bless them both.

- **Pray. Meditate. Journal.**—Your doing the leaving does not protect you from a broken heart. You may wish it was different, that you could stay together. You may have wanted him to leave another woman and be with you. He stayed though, with her. He might have cheated on you, again, and you felt compelled to say bye-bye.

    Prayer indeed makes a difference; it can help you to remember that your source of unconditional love and comfort is not a man but God. The Universe supports you in right action. Go within, into the silence. Meditation opens you to hear God's will for your life. In meditation, you reconnect with that still small voice. Remember, journaling is a marvelous tool for those who want to know themselves and their thoughts better.

- **Invite Support**—Enlist your family and friends in your process. I'm blessed to have friends, female and male, who espouse love. When I was going through a breakup and tempted to see my brother's guilt instead of his innocence, a couple of my women friends helped me see the folly of my thinking. If your friends support you in being angry and unforgiving, maybe you need new friends. Seriously though, angry friends who encourage your anger support you in closing your heart. A closed heart isn't going to attract love but repel it. If your family and friends can't help, find a spiritual community that teaches only love.

- **Expect to Miss Him**—You can miss someone *and* still let go. You loved this person. Y'all had some good times and bad times together. For some reason, you decided to part. As I heard someone say, "it's called breaking up because it's broken." You can miss him and still move forward without him.

- **Live a Sweet and Juicy Life!**—It's harder to let go of a man in love when you're unhappy with yourself and your life. If you don't like your life, then do something about it. Remember, YOU are the architect of your life! Nobody's going to hand you a better life on a silver platter. But you can. If you've made a man your whole world, his leaving will absolutely devastate you . . . because your frickin' world is gone now.

    Live a sweet and juicy life! Spend quality time with children, family, and good friends. Travel. Skydive. Go whitewater rafting. Learn a new language. Read. Work out. Do something that scares you. Take up a new hobby. Revive an old interest. Take classes. Revamp your look. Reinvent yourself. Color your hair. Go dancing. Serve others. Rediscover what matters to you and spend time doing it. Live! Laugh! Love!

- **Cry if You Want To**—Grieving is a process. I reiterate, it's not *linear*. That is, you can be in acceptance, then go back to denial. Cry if you want to. Don't deny what you feel. To the degree that we can feel sadness we can also feel joy. This too shall pass.

- **Keep the Faith, Baby**—What's for you is for you.
  The time you shared with your ex wasn't wasted. You
  touched his life, and it will forever be changed. His
  presence changed you. Know that love will come again.
  If you can let go in love, you will radiate love, for you
  will *be* love. Have faith in God and your future. Have
  faith that someone just right for you will soon appear.
  Stay in love.

Remember, we teach men how to treat us. No man is going
to elevate you to where you think you belong. You've got to elevate yourself!

# Know Thyself

*"Knowing which changes are best for you comes,
always, from assessing what you feel."*
—Martha Beck, *author & life coach*

There I was cruising toward the courthouse, Amos Lee playing in my ear when it came to me what kind of man I want. *"How could you be so careless? How could you be so careless? How could you be so careless . . . with her heart?"* Lee crooned. I know what kind of man I desire. The man right for me is tender, loving, communicative, monogamous, heterosexual, spiritual, smart, financially stable, emotionally and physically healthy, sexy, fit, adventurous, caring, passionate, progressive, well-read, and self-motivated. He loves to laugh, make love, and travel! The man right for me cares about my heart. My feelings really matter to him.

April 2008 I decided to write a narrative of the kind of career life I dreamed for myself. I talked about how much money I desired to make and how I see this book taking off. Just for good measure, I thought I'd better note what kind of relationship I desire with a man. Here's what I wrote: *"The man in my life loves who I am. He's proud to call me his woman. He's self-assured and secure in who he is. Sometimes we travel together. Our life together is fun, exciting, supportive, loving, tender."* I've since embellished this story because I realize we can't very well attract what we want if we aren't crystal clear about what it is that we want.

What kind of man do you want? I'm not asking you to tell me what kind of man you think is available to you. Nor am I asking you to think about what kind of man might want you. I'm asking you to think of your ideal mate. What kind and caliber of man do you desire to share your life with? What kind of man do you dream of? What kind of man, if you could design him, would you fashion? My friend PeaJae didn't make a list of the characteristics that she was looking for in a man; she made a spreadsheet! She was very specific.

Just don't be ridiculous and over do it like the woman I mentioned in Chapter Nine, who had 236 requirements for her ideal man!

## YOUR DEAL BREAKERS

> *"By becoming a conscious choice-maker, you begin*
> *to generate actions that are evolutionary for you."*
> —Deepak Chopra, *bestselling author*

What are your deal breakers? First, what is a deal breaker? In politics or business, a deal breaker is any issue or factor that is so significant that once discovered, all bets are off. Deal breakers bring negotiations to a screeching halt. Deal breakers are things you won't tolerate under any circumstance. They simply aren't negotiable. In relationship "negotiations," a deal breaker is any issue, factor, characteristic, trait, quality, behavior, attitude, or thing that you absolutely cannot abide . . . no matter how fine he is. No matter how good he looks in his Mercedes. No matter what other wonderful qualities he possesses, a deal breaker is just that. It breaks the deal.

Because our eyesight can get bad when we're lonely and horny, we can overlook unacceptable habits, character flaws, or traits. In the beginning. Then we wake up one day, and it's no longer tolerable. That is, when we're not so lonely or sex starved or depressed, suddenly, we can now see the light. And in the light of day he ain't looking so good anymore. That uneducated, underemployed, undisciplined guy ain't nearly as fine as you initially thought he was. Now that you're seeing a bit more clearly, you're able to see the red exit sign too. Your need for something more, something better suited to who you are and what you really want has resurfaced with a vengeance.

I went on Facebook and asked women to tell me what their deal breakers were. Before I could barely finish writing the post one woman wrote, "Oh, that's easy! I'll private message you." She wrote, "OK, if someone lives with their parents or relatives, they gotta go." Another young woman responded with, "Physical, mental, psychological, and financial abuse, inattentiveness, thoughtlessness, and incompatibility . . . to name a few" were deal breakers for her. Another thirty-something year old said her deal breakers are "lying and insecurity." They just kept coming, fast and furious.

Here are more Facebook posts:

- He lacks vision and integrity. Doesn't have an open mind
- Alcoholic and finds no reason to quit!
- I broke up with a guy for saying we could get married in about ten years. Needless to say, he didn't last long after that. I had already wasted about five.
- I can't stand a cheap man! OMG!
- Ambitionless, rude, godless, or egocentric (one and the same), possessive, dumb and/or ignorant, whorish . . . yeah, I have a few. Oh-oh-oh and . . . boring!
- Deeply angry, violent, criticizes below the belt
- I would agree with the theme here, inauthenticity (if that's a word). If I find that a man can't even be real and true to himself, then I promptly put him in the proper lane. He lacks a basic awareness of self and is not interested in finding the truth of who he really is.

Think about it. Be absolutely honest with yourself. You've got to know your deal breakers, if you're going to honor yourself. Write them down. What turns you off about a man? What can't you abide, no matter how good he smells? What grinds your gears? What are your must-haves when you're considering entering a committed relationship? You need to know your deal breakers so you can honor them. By honoring them, you honor YOU! Knowing what you WON'T tolerate and CAN'T abide helps you avoid wasting your precious time with a man that's not right for you and ain't never gonna be right for you. And perhaps avoid another unnecessary disappointment. If you're trying to decide what your deal breakers are AFTER you're already involved, then you're late. Before you know it, you've fallen under his spell. Your hopes are up. You start to rationalize about why what you said you desired isn't all that important really.

So, write down your deal breakers so you can check your list and check it twice. Do this before your head is in the clouds and your knees are in the air.

## ARE MEN BECOMING OBSOLETE?

I love men. I'd like to be in a juicy, succulent, loving relationship with a man one day, too. And yet, I've got to be frank, after my last few relationships and reading *Men Don't Heal, We Ho,* I don't know. I'm wondering if this is possible for me, especially with a black man. Let me explain what I see as the problem, which is why I'm asking: *Are men becoming obsolete?*

Once upon a time women needed men to provide for and protect us. However, as women increasingly take charge of our financial lives, evolve spiritually and mature emotionally what we need in and from men also changes. If I can buy my own home, finance my own travel, and buy a home security system to protect all my stuff, for what do I need a man? Well, I don't.

Still, I want a man. I want a man I can connect with emotionally, one I can expand and evolve with spiritually. That's what I want with a man. I think that's what the majority of today's women desire with a man. Sure, there are still women looking to a man for protection and provision. That's the old paradigm. Maybe some men and women continue to operate out of that paradigm. The modern woman, however, doesn't lean on a man financially. What's troubling is this: while many women are evolving financially, emotionally and spiritually too many brothers are losing ground. That is, too many men have yet to learn how to be emotional and spiritual partners.

Consider this, a lot of brothers simply aren't able to provide for a woman financially. And from what would a woman need protection? If a man can't provide and doesn't need to protect his woman and he's unavailable emotionally and spiritually immature, then what is he good for? Maybe it's time for men to redefine themselves, their roles and identities. Even if they make loads of money and therefore could provide for two or three women, maybe it's time men embrace a new reality and be willing to become men that women can connect with emotionally and spiritually. This might be scary. But the alternative is scarier—experiencing the fate of the dinosaur, becoming extinct.

Seriously, both men and women might want to seek to better adapt to our changing times and roles. I'm not suggesting that black men cease to provide for and protect or want to do these things. I'm merely asking that we be more open-minded and flexible about how we get to relate, love, and be together. Our unwillingness to embrace change is only making our relationships far more challenging than they have to be.

Couples break up and marriages disintegrate because one or both of the parties are unwilling to adapt to a changing world. In the new world women make as much, and in many cases more, money than their man. A man who handles this reality with emotional, psychological, and/or physical violence isn't a man a woman can afford to keep around. Brothers' unwillingness to embrace new ways of being in relationship as partner, supporter, friend, lover, and confidant, I think, have been major deal breakers for many sisters. I've ended a relationship or two primarily because the man didn't know how to give of himself in ways that were meaningful and significant to me. I know I'm not alone. Many sisters are choosing to be alone rather than settle for men who simply don't measure up emotionally and spiritually.

## YOU COULD BE CHOOSING TO BE ALONE

If you have a list of 200 things that a man has to possess, like a young sister I saw on Youtube, you're really telling the Universe: *I don't really want man.* You might want to rethink and rework your requirement and deal breaker lists. C'mon now, if you're not EVERY single thing that you demand of a man, then what gives you the audacity to make those demands? Really.

Okay, stop reading right now and make a list of your deal breakers. When we know there is no lack and limitation in anything, including love, that the Universe is abundant and generous, we will cease to settle for what we don't want.

## THE BETRAYAL OF SELF

### 50 Ways to Leave Your Lover

The problem is "all inside your head," she said to me
The answer is easy if you take it logically
I'd like to help you in your struggle to be free
There must be fifty ways to leave your lover . . .

You just slip out the back, Jack

Make a new plan, Stan
You don't need to be coy, Roy
Just get yourself free
Hop on the bus, Gus
You don't need to discuss much
Just drop off the key, Lee
And get yourself free

Paul Simon's cute little song, "50 Ways to Leave Your Lover," has always made me smile. And isn't it so fitting for a book on breakups? This little tune inspired me to consider the many ways women leave, abandon, and betray *themselves*. Even as we demand that others treat us with respect, keep their word, honor their vows and commitments, be faithful, have integrity, in big and small ways we leave and betray ourselves.

First, let's define our words. To *betray* is to deliver or expose to an enemy by treachery or disloyalty; to be unfaithful in guarding, maintaining, or fulfilling; to disappoint the hopes or expectations of; to be disloyal; to deceive, misguide, and corrupt; to desert. To *abandon* is to give up with the intent of never again claiming a right or interest in or to withdraw protection, support, or help from.

Now, I offer you *50 Ways to Leave You*, i.e., ways you betray and abandon yourself.

Not knowing your worth; not loving yourself; saying "yes" when you want to say "no"; suffering toxic relationships; giving away your power; losing yourself in a man; overworking; living out of balance; criticizing and belittling yourself; overeating; eating too much junk food; neglecting to eat whole foods, life-enhancing, nutrient-rich foods; spending every penny you have (not saving and investing); not getting enough sleep and rest and relaxation; sleeping around; having sex without a condom with a man whose HIV status you don't know; having sex with a man who sleeps around; having too little fun; tolerating abuse and mistreatment; not forgiving self and others; abusing substances; not regularly seeing a doctor; living amid clutter and chaos; judging; caretaking others and putting yourself last on your to-do list; arguing for your limitations; giving up on yourself and life; "living" in debt; having bad credit.

And if these are not enough, how about not speaking your truth; not living your truth; comparing and competing with others; not thinking for yourself; living someone else's life; engaging in any self-sabotaging thoughts and behaviors; carrying around guilt and shame; not tending to your spirit; acting like you're powerless; procrastinating; not finishing things you start that are good for you; looking for someone else or something else to make you happy; living in F.E.A.R. (**F**alse **E**vidence **A**ppearing **R**eal); blaming your circumstances, failures, and unhappiness on your gender, race, age, marital status, income; making excuses; excusing abuse; waiting for something out there to change so you can be fulfilled/happy; holding onto the past; giving up on love; dumbing down to hold onto a man; not believing in yourself; not trusting self and God; not living your values; not speaking up for yourself; not believing in you; giving too much; declining to receive.

# *H*erstory of love and attraction

*"It doesn't interest me what you do for a living . . .*
*I want to know what you ache for, and if you dare*
*to dream of meeting your heart's longing."*
—Oriah Mountain Dreamer

**By Daphne**

We danced late into the night in my mother's basement. I was celebrating my twenty-fifth birthday and wanted to make sure the atmosphere was just right. I had the lights down low and the music was nonstop. I put on my favorite songs; songs I envisioned would be perfect for that right moment. Everyone was slow dancing to the Commodore's latest hit, "Zoom." I wanted to be taken far, far away in my Prince Charming's arms. I looked at him as we held each other, then I asked him to kiss me. I didn't care who heard me or thought negative about my aggressiveness. He responded without any hesitation or question and kissed me. After everyone left we sat out back looking up at the stars.

You see, I was still married to another man at that time—but only in name. I married at eighteen. Yes, I was still a baby then, and believe me, that's a *long* story. I had made that choice because I wanted to get away from a certain "situation," i.e., my parents, who created havoc in my mental, physical, and spiritual life. I found out that it takes love of self before you can embrace another person's so-called love. It took a while before I could forgive myself and others so that I could move on with my life. I began to trust again. I was able to open that door just a wee bit more to begin another journey.

When I first met Willie in January 1976, I was pregnant. I never let on that my marriage was all washed up on the ragged rocks of despair. There was something about Willie that told me I would know him for a very long time. Our relationship began as friends. When people saw us together they would insist that we were going together, but we would exclaim, "No, we're just friends."

During my separation from my first husband I began seeing other guys, but they just didn't fit with my persona. Something just wasn't quite right. Little did I know that who I was looking for was right under my nose.

Another year went by before Willie and I took that step forward. I wonder now what happened that night we sat under the morning sky after my birthday party. I gave myself another birthday party that following year. It was going to be a small gathering of my closest friends. I asked Willie to come. He came over about 9 o'clock, and we sat on the dining room floor and just talked. It was getting late when we realized no one else was coming. Willie still teases me about it now, saying I hadn't invited anyone else—that it was all planned. Seriously, though, I did invite people over, but I believe our Creator had other plans. Yes, that was the night the magic happened. A new bond was formed in our relationship that evening.

As we continued to build on our relationship, I realized how blessed I was. I thought I would never meet someone so caring and loving. It takes a special person to embrace another man's children. Willie helped raise my children as if they were his own.

We now have two girls, two boys, and eight grand-children, and there is no separation. They're ours together. As a matter of fact, my children from my previous marriage have more of Willie's traits than mine.

Everyone who has ventured into Willie's life has also been blessed with his presence. In all our years together, the one thing I didn't know was that he gave his leave time to his coworkers. I didn't find this out until his supervisor acknowledged him for it at his retirement luncheon. He never bragged or boasted; he just gave from the kindness of his heart. Believe me, my husband loved time off from work. He despised work and to give his leave to others really touched my heart. He's so special to me, our family, and to others, and I love him so much.

## SEX AND RELATIONSHIPS

*"Women need a reason to have sex. Men just need a place."*
—Billy Crystal, *comedian & actor*

How important is sex to the health of a relationship? If you ask any man, it's right up there with oxygen and water. They need it. Gotta have it. And. Want. It. Often. If they don't get it regularly with their woman, it can register as rejection. And rather than do without, they'll get their needs met elsewhere. Can great sex sustain a relationship? No, it cannot. Both women and men agree on this point. And yet, a sexless relationship or marriage is a recipe for disaster. Couples must communicate; sex is a form of communication. A man might stay in a sexless marriage or where sex is rationed, but know this: he's got a chick on the side. Or two. Simply put, most men are more committed to their penis than they are to their partner or vows. I'm just sayin'.

Can scrumptious, delicious, out-of-this-world sex make a man commit to you? No. Absolutely not! So quit sleeping with a man in hopes that you'll seduce him into becoming your man. Every man I've ever spoken to about this assures me that great sex, though important, will not make him love you. Sure, a man wants the sex to rock with the woman he plans to spend the rest of his life with, but sex alone won't make him do that.

Now, if he finds in you the many qualities that he's looking for in a woman *and* the sex rocks his world *and* he's ready to commit, then it's a go because you're the whole package. A fine brotha I know who was looking to settle down told me about the pretty forty-something-year-old woman he stopped seeing. She was all that he wanted in bed, but she didn't have her "program" together. She had no car, house, or job. She'd called one time too many asking him to pick her up from her mother's house so she could spend some quality time with him. Finally, he told her, "Baby, this just isn't working out."

Men aren't women with deeper voices. When it comes to sex, for most men, it can be recreational or a release after a long day. He can then get up, put on his pants, leave you in the fetal position, and never call again. So I repeat, do NOT have sex with a man you barely know, expecting to make him fall in love with you. Great sex does not translate into love. Don't confuse the two.

However, if you desire more than a sexual relationship, then before you lie down with him, make sure you know what you want with him. Your head is clearer when vertical. Once a man sleeps with you, outside of a commitment, it's tougher to get him to see the benefits of making a commitment to you. If sex is all you want, just know that. Don't pretend you can handle casual sex if you can't. If you know sex with a man causes you to fall head over heels in love, then you're not cut out for casual sex. If, however, you just want to get laid and you don't need to hear from the man later, suit yourself. I don't recommend it, but you're grown. You gonna do what you want, no matter what I say. Make sure he uses a condom though.

Oh, also know that every time you sleep with a man you bond with him. It's NOT just physical. Sex is also emotional and spiritual. Even if he doesn't ejaculate in you, he leaves some of his spirit in you. This explains why women who have multiple sexual partners are often crazy.

## WELL, I WANT A DIVORCE

Someone once said this about sex: "When it's good, it's about 5 percent of the relationship. But when it's bad, it's about 95 percent of the relationship." Like I said, sex is a form of communication between couples. The quality and quantity of sex matter. Like not being understood by and understanding your significant other when the two of you talk and attempt to work through conflict, incompatibility in the bedroom is not only frustrating and confusing, but it can leave one or both people feeling unloved, unfulfilled, and even inadequate. Such feelings, when they are triggered, can't help but stress and even weaken the bond.

Sexual incompatibility doesn't mean two people don't love each other. And yet, it can leave one or both people feeling unloved. If that feeling persists, the discontented will often reach outside of the relationship or marriage for what he or she needs and wants. I'm reminded of a funny story a sisterfriend told me about relatives of hers. One day the husband asked his wife of thirty-two years if she would be so kind as to give him some head. Her quick response was, "Absolutely not!"

"Well, then," he said, "I want a divorce!"

The wife was beside herself. She couldn't believe it. "How could he end a thirty-two-year marriage over oral sex?" she hissed. Here's how. Uncle probably woke up one morning fed up with not being sexually satisfied in his marriage.

"Why should I," I imagined he fumed, "have to get Sally in the alley to suck my dick when I've got a perfectly good mouth right here at home?" Did this husband end his three-decade-plus marriage for oral sex? Not likely. Chances are there were many other reasons he was unhappy at home. There were likely more than a few ways his wife was uptight and stingy, in bed and out. Brotherman just got fed up with being underfed.

This story leads me to another question.

## ARE BLACK WOMEN SEXUALLY REPRESSED

Are black women sexually repressed? If you ask the black men that Hill Harper interviewed for his book, *The Conversation,* then the answer would be yes. They say sisters have sexual hang-ups. Some sisters do. Some white and Asian women have sexual hang-ups too. But we're talking about black women at the moment.

A sister I went to college with confessed that she didn't like sex. When she was twenty her favorite uncle seduced her. A dozen years later, when we met, she had yet to forgive *herself* for having sex with him and liking it. Her punishment, I suspected, was to deny herself the pleasure of enjoying sex thereafter. She also grew up Catholic. Per her religious upbringing, sex was dirty and, if indulged in outside of marriage, a dreadful sin.

A lot of black women have experienced sexual trauma. Incest. Molestation. Rape. Trauma can leave a woman, well, uh, traumatized. I've talked to more than a few brothers who said their woman was molested or raped in their youth; consequently their sex life is challenged.

If you've been raped or molested and can see how your sexual health is being compromised because of it, I strongly encourage you to seek professional help. No matter how long ago the violation occurred, if your life today is negatively impacted by it you own it to yourself and your partner to seek help.

## THINGS YOU WON'T DO IN BED

Well, are you sexually repressed? Are you turned off by sex? Do you think sex is dirty and sinful? Do you frequently have a "headache" when your man reaches for you? Do you make your grocery list or wonder what you'll fix for breakfast while your man's on top of you? Is there a laundry list of things you won't do in bed? Are you a "pillow princess," that is, do you treat sex like it's a spectator sport? If you could would you just eliminate sex from your life or relationship altogether? If you answered yes to any one of these questions, and you're in a relationship, then know that your relationship could be at risk. No matter what else you're doing for or with your man—cooking, cleaning, having clever conversations, giving him back massages—baby, if you're not sexing him up, he's not happy at home. He doesn't feel loved and wanted by you. Someone once said men give love to get sex while women give sex to get love. I happen to think both men and women who love sex need a regular dose of it to keep love hot and juicy.

He'll leave if you don't want him sexually. He may not leave physically, especially if you're married, but he'll step out on you if you ration out the booty. I know a man who's been married twenty years. He stepped out on his wife two years into the marriage. The wife, even today, is still angry about her husband's infidelity. She expresses her anger by withholding sex. She's cutting off her nose to spite her face because unless she's got a hunk on the side, she's not only denying her husband pleasure, she's denying herself! Why would she stay with the man if she is never going to forgive him for his transgression? Why would a physically healthy woman settle for a sexless marriage? Maybe she's sexually repressed and merely hiding behind her husband's infidelity. Hmm. Just a thought.

When you're not having sex your relationship suffers. There's a disconnect that nothing but sex can fix. Great sex helps you and yours to better weather the inevitable storms that every couple has. Sex helps the relationship bend, rather than break. Sex brings two people closer together. It's the balm that heals after you've talked all you can. Shoot, sometimes it's the healer before you talk.

## MEN AND SEX:

- He's gotta have it! Men see no honor in or reason for going without sex. So they won't. If they aren't having sex with you, their mate, trust and believe they're having it with somebody else
- Most men want to be with a woman who loves sex
- Men want a lady in the street, a freak between the sheets,

in the kitchen, in the hall, in the guest bedroom, in the . . . well, uh, you get the point

- Men are visual creatures, so it's important for a woman to keep her appearance tight, fresh, and sexy
- Men love to please you in bed; that makes them feel connected to you. Pleasing you pleases them
- Sex makes your man feel loved. When you withhold sex from him, this can leave him feeling rejected and unwanted. Feelings of rejection translate into emotional instability in men
- If you want a happy man, love, love, *looovvve* his Member, and do it often
- If your physically healthy man isn't interested in sex with you he's either gay or getting it elsewhere

## FACING HARD FACTS

The Centers for Disease Control and Prevention estimates that 1 in 16 black men will become infected with HIV in his lifetime; 1 in 30 women will become infected with HIV in her lifetime. In the U.S., 9 out of every 10 new HIV infections among women are black women. Black women now account for almost 70 percent of all female cases of HIV, and the numbers keep going up. Largely, when black women contract HIV, it's through heterosexual contact.

What does all of this mean, really? Plain and simple, it means having sex can forever change your life. It also means black women aren't doing such a good job of protecting ourselves. Black women aren't taking charge of our bodies by practicing protected sex. It could mean black women are too casual about sex. These statistics tell me black women must, if we intend to arrest the spread of HIV, take back our power. We must stop living in denial and stupidity and exercise our God-given power to take good care of us.

Dr. Michael Zollicoffer, a pediatrician and health advocate, said the greatest health threat to the black community is black men going to prison. Estimates are that the rates of HIV/AIDS in correctional facilities are three to five times higher than in the general population, and approximately 15 to 40 percent of inmates are hepatitis C-infected.

Sure, it's tough having to face hard facts, but face them we must. On any given day, more than 1.5 million black men call prison or jail home, while another 3.5 million are on probation or parole. One ex-offender, a brother, told me that prison feels more like home than any place else does. Given the large number of black men who cycle through the penal system—jail, prison, probation, jail, prison, parole—it appears this brother is in good company with a bunch of black men. Men who do long sentences in prison will often be "gay for the stay," though few will ever admit to having been another man's boyfriend or bitch while incarcerated.

More than 95 percent of the prison population will eventually return home. These men, whether they're screwing other men or being screwed, then return home to girlfriends and wives to live as heterosexual men. With them some bring HIV. That's a fact.

## KEEPING IT ON THE DOWN LOW

Then there's the brother on the down low. Some of these men were once incarcerated, but many of them weren't. Incarceration isn't a prerequisite for down-low behavior. I could name five to seven men that I know personally who are on the down low. How do I know? They certainly didn't tell me. Observation and intuition and questions, that's how I know. We have five plus one senses. With our eyes and ears wide open we can learn much about a man. If it doesn't stack up, well, then, it doesn't stack up. A man can't always be trusted, but can always trust our intuition. Just because we wish something wasn't so, doesn't change reality. People tell us who they are, says Dr. Maya Angelou. We can believe them or not. Regardless, a man is who he is whether you approve of it or not. Men tell us who they are with their actions and words. When we trust what see more than what we hear, we make better choices. Choices grounded in reality, rather than in what we wish was so.

Yes, I intuit these things. You too have one of the most reliable GPS devices known to humankind. The down-low brother, like many incarcerated men, engages in high-risk sexual behaviors that pose a threat to your physical, sexual, and spiritual well-being. Like the formerly incarcerated man who sleeps with men, the down-low brother is in deep denial about his sexual proclivities and orientation. "I'm not gay, I just like doing men," he lies. Nor is he bisexual. He just likes sleeping with men. Really? Besides, does it matter whether he's gay, straight or bisexual . . . if your man sleeps with other men . . . you've got a problem on your hands.

Many of these men sleep with men without a condom, then come home to you, his wife or girlfriend. A young openly gay man who once prostituted to support a drug habit told me that all kinds of so-called straight men paid him for sex. When he cross-dressed, when his johns discovered that he was not a real woman, they would shrug their broad shoulders and say, "It doesn't matter," and proceed to have sex with this male prostitute. Most often, without a condom!

We can curb the spread of HIV simply by taking charge of ourselves. Sister, let's take back our power!

## WHAT'S LOVE GOT TO DO WITH IT

I got to confess; there was a time when I took stupid risks with my sexual heath and well-being. I've had sex without a condom with men whose HIV status I didn't know. I've been in relationships with men who fell into one of the high-risk groups. In 1988, I was involved with a recovering drug user. After we broke up, I heard through the grapevine that he was HIV positive. I was finally about to become a lawyer, a dream I'd secretly nursed since I was ten years old, and now this? To say I was petrified would be an understatement.

I went to the Red Cross and got tested. The nine days that I waited for my results were pure hell. I couldn't eat, so I lost weight. Sometimes in the middle of studying I'd break down crying. Fortunately, I was not alone. My new man drove me and my sister to the Red Cross for the results. The three of us rode in complete silence, like we were going before a firing squad. I'd waited nine hellish days to get those results; I was beside myself with fear.

My guy stayed in the car while my sister Ayo accompanied me into the building. My sister and I walked to the dark office, took seats across from a desk and waited. A woman came in and sat behind the desk and placed a sheet of paper in front of her. She looked across the desk, at me and said slowly, "You're HIV negative." My sister and I leapt into air, into each other's arms, our tears flying about the room.

Still, I wasn't free. Even after getting the good news I continued to live in fear. One time I was in the law library studying when fear rose up and slapped me in the face. Next thing I knew, I was roaming the aisles sobbing and praying. Back in the '80s, we knew much less about HIV/AIDS. Nobody seemed to know the incubation period. It was hard to decipher the truth from rumors, myths, and untruths.

I've since been tested many times. Each time I've been blessed to be HIV negative. The last time I was tested, I decided I would never contract HIV because from there on out I will love myself enough to do everything in my power to stay HIV negative.

Recently, a sisterfriend asked me incredulously, "You mean you don't have a maintenance man?" You see, I'm single. Not in a relationship. Not even dating. Me, one who loves herself a man. But you know what? I now love me more than I love any man. I certainly love myself too much to lie down with a man who isn't my man just for a few moments of pleasure. In this day and time, you mean to tell me a woman thinks having casual sex makes good sense? You gotta be kidding me! If you're HIV negative, there's no reason why you have to become a statistic.

It's time we take charge of our lives, ourselves, our bodies. It's a matter of self-love, self-respect, and self-preservation.

* * * * * * *

## A Conversation with Zakiyyah Lana on *Women and Sexuality*

**DMR: Tell us about you. What inspires you to speak and write about women and sexuality?**

**ZL:** I discovered some time ago that women know very little about our bodies, sexuality, and sexual healing. Many of us don't know the true value of our sexuality and the benefits of sex. I noticed when I started learning more about my own sensuality and sexuality and engaged in discussions with my sisterfriends, it would generate powerful positive energy, laughter, and deep reflection. Many aha! moments took place as women talked about how they feel about themselves, relationships, and sexuality. They would uncover deep emotional stuff that was preventing them from fully expressing themselves sexually.

Largely, we were never taught the true meaning of sexual intimacy or the physical, emotional, psychological, and spiritual benefits of sex. We have no idea how powerful and positive sex can be. We know the pleasure of sex, but there is so much more to discover about the health benefits of sexual energy, like its ability to heal illness, slow the aging process, and rejuvenate us in body, mind, and spirit.

**Just how important is sex to a woman's mental and emotional health?**

Interestingly, I noticed how I neglected my body when I wasn't in a relationship. I didn't take as good care of it. I didn't take time to give it massages or speak endearing words to it. I didn't have a mate to share my body and express my sexual self with so I did what many women do; I stuffed my feelings. I stuffed them with food, doing too much, anger, depression, and self-pity. I was unhappy, unfulfilled, and physically sick.

One day I went to see an energy healer for a massage. It was the most amazing thing I could have done for myself. My healer moved energy through my body, releasing negative energy and clearing blockages. I had orgasm after orgasm, cried, and released all kinds of emotions. And all of this happened without any direct contact with my genitals. After my session, I felt the most amazing freedom, healing, and lightness of being.

I now desire this experience for all my sisterfriends because so many of us have emotional, mental, and physical issues. Our bottled up emotions and blocked energy are making us sick, depressed, bloated, fat, angry, bitter, resentful, and ashamed.

My healer gave me two books about women and sexuality from ancient Asian and Tao traditions, Mantak Chia's *Sexual Reflexology* and *The Sexual Teachings of the White Tigress* by Hsi Lai. *Sexual Reflexology* teaches couples how to heal themselves using their sexual energy. I had never considered sex a healer. I knew sex felt good and could relieve some pain, like headaches, but I never knew about pressure points and areas inside the vagina and in the penis that are connected to our energy centers that, during lovemaking, movement, touch, massage, can heal our body and help promote optimal health. These ancient teachings speak to the affect of sexual energy, orgasm, and the sexual relationship as healing, rejuvenating, and youthfulness enhancing. So, yes, I imagine the emotional and mental benefits are just as significant.

Chia writes in *Sexual Reflexology* that, "You can visualize a god and goddess above your head making love. Feel the sexual energy of the universe in harmony with your own sexual energy. Allow the intimate connection between yourself, your partner, and the universe to pulse through your entire being."

Now, if that doesn't promote mental and emotional healing and well-being—with the exception of meditation, prayer, and sharing love—I don't know too many other things that will. Sex has to be better for us than prescription drugs that are supposed to relieve anxiety, depression, and an assortment of mental and emotional disorders.

According to these ancient tantric teachings, "The orgasm is a person's most intense experience. *No other experience is as totally focused or concentrated, providing not only a great sense of pleasure, release, and relaxation but also a powerful enhancement of all of one's senses.* The orgasm emits sexual energy from the body, not only in fluids, but also as a substantive psychological force."

### How significant is sex to the well-being of a relationship?

Sexual energy is nourishment for our total selves—body, mind, and spirit. It replenishes us. Making love is more powerful than most of us have ever imagined. I now realize I'd been cheapening the sexual experience and missing out on the full benefits of it. When women and men recognize and practice sexual healing, rather than just "doing it," they and their relationships will experience increased health and well-being.

There has only been one time in my life that I felt that wonderful divine connection. I felt enveloped in love. I didn't realize then that a spiritually bonding experience was taking place between me and my lover. As we know, sex can be the glue that holds a relationship together. It's amazing how much love can pour from within when we share this sacred union. Thus, when a man or woman feels their mate withholding sexually, it can create feelings of hurt, rejection, and abandonment. When there is no sexual release or expression, our energies can stagnate and become blocked. Unhappiness, anger, frustration, and illness may follow. We may then turn to food, drugs, and alcohol to fill the void. We may also fall into a depression. Many will step outside of the relationship to meet their sexual needs, which, of course, can lead to the dissolution of the relationship.

Imagine being with a lover with whom you share an intensely gratifying sexual relationship. You reach orgasmic ecstasy and feel an unimaginable closeness. You feel alive, energetic, happy, loving, and peaceful. Your hormones and chemicals heal and replenish your body temple.

I was absolutely floored by *The Sexual Teachings of the White Tigress*. No one, not in my fifty-plus years of being on the planet, ever told me about the benefits of sex to a woman's health, longevity, and youthfulness. *The Sexual Teachings* contends that, "oral sex is a necessity. Nothing has as much influence on our health and psyche. Oral sex can be a woman's portal to realizing not only her spirituality but also the very force that *retards aging.* Semen (which is primarily protein) draws fresh blood acting like an astringent in the generation of new skin cells and tissues." Fresh semen also contains high amounts of vitamin C, phosphorous, calcium, and iron, and it even has antibiotic properties. These teachings also say, "semen spread over the face . . . will tighten and shrink wrinkles, feed skin cells, and leave the skin feeling light, clean, and smooth."

I know, few women are ready for this. I shared this information with two sisterfriends. "Ewwwww, that's nasty. I ain't putting no sperm on my face!" they both said. I guess I should have expected that reaction, given that most of us have been raised to see bodily secretions as revolting. But look at it this way. God made semen and endowed it with all these wonderful vitamins and minerals that help to create new life. So why is it just okay for the vagina and making a baby but not okay to put on our face? We would rather spend hundreds and even thousands of dollars on facials, chemical peels, and exfoliants to slow the aging process, vanish wrinkles, and rejuvenate our skin, rather than the semen from our beloved. And it's FREE. Just think about it. It's certainly something to consider. If it worked for women in ancient Asia, it can certainly work for us. We just have to get past it being nasty.

*The Sexual Teachings of the White Tigress* also says, "When a woman takes a man's penis in her mouth it is in one instance a symbol of both control of and power over a man." Think about that, my sisters! Had that ever occurred to you? Now men, who once complained that their mate won't perform oral sex on them, will now be delighted by their newly enlightened women. Women who are more open and willing to pleasure their man with oral sex because she knows it will not only make him happy but will enhance her health, keep her young, *and* make her feel powerful! It's a win-win proposition! We are supporting each other in being healthier, happier, more peaceful beings; especially when our sexual union is with someone we deeply love.

**Western experts agree, sex is good for our health. What do you suggest unpartnered women do to take care of themselves sexually?**

Sexual health is just as vital and important to our overall well-being as physical, mental, and emotional health. Many single women hit the gym to improve their physical health. They go to therapists, counselors, psychiatrists, and support groups to enhance their mental and emotional health but will neglect their sexual health because few have been taught the importance of sexual health and well-being. It is this lack of education and understanding that keeps us from exploring our options to maintain sexual health.

Some religious and spiritual doctrines insist that women practice celibacy. Self-pleasuring is deemed unacceptable, even wrong. I was raised under such teachings. I respect everyone's beliefs and traditions. What I offer here is for the woman who is open to learning more about how to achieve and maintain sexual well-being while respecting her spiritual beliefs.

Let's take a look at what I consider to be the most unique and beautiful part of a woman's body, her "yoni." The correct term is vulva, and most of us grew up knowing it as our vagina. I won't get into all the technical terms (biology is not my forte), but I heard the term *yoni* and fell in love with it, so that is the word I have chosen to use.

## ZAKIYYAH TALKS SEX IN JAMAICA

In 2005, I was facilitating a workshop in Jamaica with a group of women, and I asked them, "When was the last time you told your vagina, 'I love you'?" The room got so still you could hear a pin drop. Eyes opened wide, mouths dropped, then giggles and laughter filled the room. It was an amazing and enlightening moment for me. The whole tone of the workshop shifted. We were talking about how to love ourselves and what are some of the things we do to show ourselves love when the next thing I knew I was asking this question and getting this response. No one said, "Yes, I talk to my vagina every day and tell her I love her and thank her for serving me so wonderfully."

I then asked, "How often do you look at your vagina, caress her, touch her, other than while bathing?"

Most of the women answered "not often" or "not at all." I said to my Jamaican sisters, "Why do we allow our sexual partners to pay more attention to our vaginas than we do?"

When we are with our partners, and they are touching and caressing our yonis, and we are feeling the pleasure that comes with that touch, and the pleasure of the sexual union, that is when we acknowledge the goodness and magic of our yoni, and then, when it's all done, we go back to forgetting all about her.

Why? Why don't we pay attention to this part of our body?

We look at and pay attention to our breasts, which we are told by the medical profession should be examined every month to check for lumps. Maybe this is so because we put on bras every day and, if we are nursing mothers, they nourish our babies. We feel them bouncing around when we exercise, and during our menstrual cycle we notice how sensitive they can become. Or we might be consumed by how small they are and wish they were bigger or imagine they are too big, so we long for reduction surgery.

Our legs and thighs get our attention. "Oh my cellulite! My thighs are so fat." We pay attention to our stomachs, whether to count and curse our rolls, or we take pride in how flat it is. We *and* brothers pay attention to our butts. We're either proud of our firm "booty-licious" buttocks or disgusted by its jiggle when we walk. We spend exorbitant amounts of money on products to make them larger or smaller. Even our arms get some play, whether they are soft and fluffy or strong and muscular. Need I mention how much we pour into our hair, skin, hands, and feet with all kinds of attention that money can buy? Meanwhile, our yoni, the gift from God that brings forth human life, is all but ignored.

I encourage you to take more time with this precious part of your body. Tend to her, talk to her, massage her often, tell her how much you appreciate and love her. Remember, our bodies are alive. We are energy and our cells and tissue hear how we feel about them, and feel what we think of them.


## PLAY WITH YOUR YONI

As a little girl, the one thing I could do to put myself to sleep was to play with my yoni. It was comforting and relaxing, and it worked. Later I learned as a preteen that when a boy played with my yoni that it also felt good, warm, and tingling. In fact, it was an indescribably pleasurable feeling. As time went on, playing with and massaging my yoni became an invaluable part of my sexual experience with a lover; it made lovemaking more satisfying. I started to realize this was not just "a thing" between my legs, but she really serves a healing purpose, not to mention she had the power to bring forth new life.

Unfortunately, many women were raised to believe that their vaginas are bad and dirty, or just for a man's pleasure. Many women won't talk about their vaginas, and even dislike them. Even when they clean it, have sex, or have a baby, the vagina gets little thought. Perhaps, however, when they experience some gynecological condition that requires their attention they may think of this part of their anatomy.

Lots of women have been sexually abused as children, raped, sexually assaulted, or molested and have learned to shut off feelings for their vaginas. Incredibly, some women wish they didn't have this "thing between their legs" that has caused them so much pain because of someone else's sick and perverted behavior. For these women, it may take a while to feel love for their yoni. Some may even require therapy or a support group. My prayer for my sisters is that one day they will heal and come to love and honor their yoni as a precious gift from our Creator.

Single women need not believe they can't achieve sexual health or pleasure without a man. That's just not true. There are an abundance of sex toys available, from the smallest bullet-shaped vibrator to the large penis-like gadgets, lubricants, hot oils, tingling potions. You name it, it's available. These are all wonderful; they work and are fun too.

But there is nothing like your own touch. Your healing hands are perfect for your yoni. You get to really discover everything about her, and if something's not quite right with her, you can feel that too. I've heard therapists say we are responsible for our own sexual healing and pleasure. Yes, we hope to have a lover who knows all our erogenous zones and what brings us pleasure; but if he doesn't, it is our job to show him and even demonstrate what we like. We learn what we like through our own exploration.

*So, what, you ask, can single women do for their sexual health?*

**1. Love your body, all of it.** Look at its beauty, talk to it, every part of it, and tell it something loving and kind on a daily basis. Make it a good night prayer. Tell your body how much you appreciate her and how she serves you so well. Pay attention to your yoni. She is your jewel, your treasure chest, your closest girlfriend. To send healing, stress-relieving energy to yourself, fondle your body often.

**2. Make a date with yourself.** Light candles and unwind in a nice hot bubble bath while listening to some good mood music. Give your body a gentle massage from head to toe using scents like lavender or peppermint or whatever turns you on while telling your body how beautiful and wonderful and sexy she is. Use your healing hands to gently massage your yoni and take yourself to ecstasy.

If you are open to sharing your love and sexual energy with someone, get yourself a sexual healing partner who is just as committed as you are in the healing art of lovemaking. Let me pause here to say this: If you are blessed to find that man who wants to join you on this journey to wholeness, give thanks. Brothers who will go that deep with you are rare. Most men won't because, unfortunately, they do not know how, and few are teachable. Most brothers have sex for the pleasure of it and couldn't care less about learning the art of healing through lovemaking. Attracting a lover who wants to learn about the benefits of sexual healing, one willing to learn and grow with you, is truly a God thing.

*Sexual Reflexology* says, "With the proper guidance, the sexual energy can be a rich treasure of joy, happiness, and passion. It can be a tool to create and maintain optimum health and vitality, transforming a mediocre life into an exceptional one, changing a stress-filled unhappy life into one filled with success and fulfillment. It is simply that powerful." Isn't that magnificent!

**Many men shy away from marriage because they say women stop wanting sex after marriage. What do you think is really going on in these marriages?**

I know men who complain that sex decreased after they said, "I Do." There are many reasons for this. Men who have experienced a decline in sex in one marriage are then reluctant to go through that again in another marriage. The amount of sex two people have can undergo a change when children arrive. After a woman has a baby, her body experiences lots of hormonal changes that can lead to a decline in her libido. It is suggested by many therapists that women seek medical attention to remedy this problem. Additionally, men need to be educated about how a woman's body changes and be willing to offer his partner love, support, patience, and pampering so as to prepare her for a special time of lovemaking. Remember, she didn't make this baby by herself; he has a responsibility not only as a father but also as a husband to find out what his partner needs and support her in having it.

Also, once children come, a woman's energy level can take a dive. She has more responsibility and less time. If she's a working mother, she has both a job and family, which often means her day doesn't end at five or six. Very often, she still must fix dinner, clean the house, do laundry, help the children with homework, bathe them, and prepare them for the next school day. Now it's 10 or 11 o'clock at night, and all she longs for is some sleep so she'll be rested enough to repeat the routine all over again the next day.

So what happens when he reaches for her and she withdraws? She feels compelled to make excuses: "Not tonight, honey; I have a terrible headache." Or "My stomach is bothering me." Or "I'm coming on my period." Anything that says, "I'm not interested." Then he complains, "She never wants to have sex." Well, it's not that she doesn't desire him or sex. Most women do want that intimate connection; in fact, we need it. But when we are bone-tired, sleep trumps sex, so we opt out. I'm not saying it's right; it's just what happens.

There, however, is a simple solution that works most of the time.

Brothers, step in and help your woman. Help prepare the meal with her, and while doing so, give her some kisses and pats on the butt, or a little feel here and there, or a nibble on her neck and ears to help her relax and feel good. Wash the dishes while she helps the kids with homework or help with homework and bath time while she cleans the kitchen. Once the kids are in bed, take a relaxing shower together and begin the foreplay while gently massaging her body with soap and your hands. Kissing is an amazing thing; it can get those juices flowing. While kissing her, gently massage her yoni. Your lady will be ready to give herself fully and completely to you.

This is for men: Really appreciate the importance of foreplay. It is vital if you want a woman that is receptive. You have to learn her body like you would learn to put together one of your toys. Your woman is your instruction manual. Ask her what feels good. Take your time. Learn her pleasure centers. How does she like to be touched, caressed, and fondled? Don't base it on what you have done with other women (although some of what you did in past relationships may work well with her). If she doesn't respond, ask questions.

Give each other a massage that will relax the two of you and prepare you to experience the ultimate sexual pleasure and treasure of lovemaking.

If the problem is that the two people have stopped communicating with each other or the "thrill is gone" because of neglect, financial challenges, work, too much time with other people, or TV, and too little quality time with each other, this too can be resolved through open and honest communication, through really sharing your feelings. This, we know, can be challenging for men because they're generally uncomfortable talking about feelings and listening to women talk about their feelings. Getting counseling or therapy can help, especially since these issues are causing problems in the bedroom.

## WOMEN WANT SEX TOO

Most women want sex as much as a man. And when he does it right, she will not usually resist his overtures. Women love being pleasured, especially when she knows how to achieve an orgasm. Sisters, please learn how to achieve orgasm. It is vital to your health, and you will feel spectacular! It takes two to make a relationship work. And it is essential to the sexual relationship when the two people care enough about each other to want what's best for their mate.

Because women are nurturers, we want to nurture our man. We also desire to feel nurtured by him. We want to make sure he is happy and feels good, *but we aren't inspired to do this with a man who doesn't honor, respect, and appreciate us. Or with a man who doesn't make the effort to learn how to pleasure us.*

So, men, if you wish to keep your sex life hot and juicy, pay attention, be tender and loving, help your woman with the children and household chores, listen to her, communicate with her, and let her know she is appreciated. Write her a note and put it in her purse. Buy her flowers. Kiss her often. Hold her hand when you are out together. Show affection, even when you are watching sports. Say, "I Love You." Take her to a movie. Or out to dinner . . . or both. Venture out to a concert or just for a walk by the water. Let her know how important she is to you and how much you love her, and do this often, and sex will be plentiful.

There are some women that have a stronger sex drive than their man. This may be a delight for some men, and for others, not so much. Emotional intimacy can be just as satisfying. Besides, intimacy is what women yearn for. Yes, we love sex, but intimacy with our beloved is what makes us want to make love. So, brothers, learn how to be intimate with your woman and do it often. She will love you for it.

I have spoken mostly to the brothers, but I have a word for my sisters too. Sisters, we have the power between our legs. It can make or break a relationship. If you want to keep your relationship alive and your man's hands on you and not on some other woman, then learn to love him and make love with him often. Initiate sex. His body needs touch just as much as yours does. Learn his pleasure centers and how to massage his lingum (penis). Wear fragrances that are appealing to him; and look as sexy as you can (I know that isn't always easy because we sometimes like to put on our flannel PJs, especially in the winter). But a few times a week, especially when you want to make love with your man, bring out the fancy stuff.

Offer to give him a massage, ask him to talk about anything on his mind. While he's in this vulnerable position, he may just open up to you about what's going on in that mind of his. Men need to be loved and touched and appreciated too. They may not need the same kind of attention as we do, so learn what it is your man craves. If you don't, somebody else will. Don't take for granted the things he does for you. Let him know how much you appreciate him for thinking of you. Take an interest in what he likes to do. If he watches sports, watch it with him (even if you don't like it).

Remember, whenever you can get some time with your man, it's good to take it. Just sitting together close to each other you are sharing your energy with each other. Showing an interest in what he likes will keep things flowing in your relationship. Initiate sex with him in other places besides the bedroom. In between commercials give him oral pleasure; it's to your benefit as well as his. Remember, his semen contains the fountain of youth. So blow for it!

"My woman doesn't initiate sex" is one of men's major complaints. This is a big deal, ladies. Men want to feel attractive and sexy to you too. When you take the initiative, it makes him feel desired. He will love it. Remember, other women are out there and many have no problem letting your man know how handsome, sexy, and appealing he is. You want him to feel that at home so "out there" won't be a temptation.

**Again and again, I hear or read that black men think black women are sexually repressed. What are your thoughts about this?**

Personally, I have a hard time understanding why black men say this. Black women have been sexually liberated for centuries. We've been "working girls" since way back when. We have worked in brothels, and on the street, in adult clubs, been mistresses and "massa's" sex toy. Today, sisters own their own businesses marketing adult toys. I think, largely, black women are sexually alive and expressive. They love getting their freak on just like other groups of women. Black women are sexy and voluptuous, and in the right circumstances, they can give a man the ultimate pleasure. We may not be as into multiple partners during the sexual experience like some women . . . but we know how to handle our business in the bedroom.

I, however, did hear a fine black man say he would never go back to being with a black woman because "they have too much drama with them" and that he "preferred Asian women because they are less inhibited sexually." This saddened me. But he's right. *Some* sisters are sexually repressed. I think it's because we are ignorant about sex, sexuality, and the true gift of the sexual experience. Black women weren't encouraged to be sexually expressive. Religiously, we've been taught to be ashamed of our bodies and our sexual urges, to repress them, especially if we aren't married. Once these ideas are imbedded, it can take years to discard, even if we are blessed to have a loving and patient man willing to help us heal. We have old tapes playing in our heads about what's "proper" to do with a man. We can still hear our mommas saying, "Good girls don't do so and so," or "a man only cares about one thing" or "once you give him some, he'll leave," all of which can make it difficult for a woman to relax and fully savor the sexual experience.

**Zakiyyah, have you any final thoughts?**

When we learn we have the power and are the power and how using our powerful sexual energy can help us heal ourselves and our men, I believe we will grow more and more open and willing to experiment, enjoy, and embrace our sexuality in all its power and beauty.

* * * * * * *

## THE 90-DAY RULE

Okay, now that I've warned you of the dangers of unprotected sex and Zakiyyah Lana has enlightened you to the benefits of sex—like its ability to keep you young—let's talk about when and with whom we ought to be having sex. If you want to see a room full of women divide, ask them to share their views on how soon a woman should sleep with a man. Several of my sisterfriends think if a woman feels like hopping in bed with a fella on the first meeting, she should.

I disagree.

Here's why. It doesn't matter how soon you sleep with a man if all you want to be to this man is a body, a thing of pleasure, a booty call. If all you want is sex with this man, then I say, go for it. Dance on the table. Swing from the chandelier. If you don't mind risking your physical, emotional, and spiritual health and well-being for a few hours of pleasure—or what you hope will be pleasure—then I say get naked. Go on, do the doggone thang. Get busy. If you don't care what he'll think of you in the morning, then every time you feel amorous with a new guy go ahead and express yourself. If you don't mind being a "Jump-Off," being thought of as a ho and thought even less of after he finishes getting off, then go ahead have sex with him before you even know his middle name.

I so disagree with those who claim it doesn't matter when a woman has sex with a man. Ask any man; it matters! Well, uh, to a good many it does. Listen up, if you want the man you're dating to see you as commitment and marriage "material," then do not have sex with him on the first, second, or third date. I'm not telling you to *play* hard to get, I telling you to actually *be* hard to get.

Let me share with you some of the reasons why I suggest that you take your time having sex with a man. If you need me to be more specific, here's a good rule of thumb: *no sex in the first 90 days.* Of course we know it takes much longer to really know a person. However, 90 days of observing a man from an upright, rather dispassionate posture gives you just enough time to see whom you're dealing with. Even the masks of most experienced players and predators, masquerading as sincere, emotionally healthy, commitment-ready men start to crack in 90 days.

All right, here are five reasons why sex can, and certainly should, wait:

1.  When a woman has sex with a man she tends to lose perspective. Sex is an emotional investment for most women. Once invested, even if that man does some pretty cruel, disrespectful, and thoughtless things to her either she won't see them for what they are or she'll deny them, make excuses for his behavior, *and* stay with him. Are you familiar with the hormone known as oxytocin? Oxytocin, nicknamed the "cuddle hormone," is released during sex. Dr. Beverly Whipple, Secretary General of the World Association for Sexual Health, says oxytocin is released into our bloodstreams in response to breast or vaginal stimulation. Oxytocin has been found to increase our levels of trust and make us feel more connected with people. That is, women, even more so than men, bond with the people they sleep with, especially if the sex is toes curling good. But what happens when you sleep with a man who doesn't deserve your

trust because, quite simply put, he isn't trustworthy? Well, now you've fallen for a man that you'll trust and cling to despite that he isn't worthy of your trust and loyalty. Yep, sex is that powerful!

2. Let's say you're dating. Dating means you go out with, hang out with, have fun with, talk on the phone to several men simultaneously. We date to have fun. We also date to gather information about the men we're dating. Don't sleep with any of them. If you're looking to get in a committed relationship with one of these men, don't sleep with any of them. Have fun. What happens once you sleep with one of them? Ever heard "once he gets your parts he'll get your heart"? Well, it's true. By the way, now your decision-making abilities have been seriously compromised. Once you were clear-eyed and levelheaded; now you're crazy in love. And it could be with a nut.

3. While he gets your heart, you get his spirit. Even though our society has all but reduced sex to a sport and recreation, sex really is so much more than two people rolling around on sheets, grunting and panting. Sex is a sacred, spiritual act. A man makes deposits into your body when he penetrates you. Once he withdraws, he leaves inside of you not only his sexual juices but parts of himself. If you're sleeping with more than one man then you have all of these men's essences colliding inside of you. Is there any wonder that you're confused and your life is chaotic?

4. Sex doesn't mean the same thing to men as it does to women. If you have sex with men in hopes of getting their love and commitment, stop it! It doesn't work. It has never worked— ever. And it will never work. Not ever. For men, sex is a sport. It's a release. They use sex to release the stress of a hard day. A man can have sex with you five nights in a row and still not love or want you. What he wants he's getting—the use of your body.

Consider the male anatomy. Now think about the female anatomy. No mistakes there. The man's sex organ is outside of him like an arm or leg. It's a tool that he uses to get what he wants: pleasure. When a woman sleeps with a man she hardly knows, she's not lying down with a man who cares about her. You could leave his house, get run over by a truck and he not even attend your funeral. Why? His heart isn't invested in you. Remember, you were just a means to an end: a nut. Now, like I said earlier, if you don't mind being a Jump-Off, go ahead jump on it.

5. Last but certainly not least, if you're sleeping with a man after the first date you don't know his HIV status, do you? You've not demanded that he get tested, have you? You probably haven't even broached the topic of STIs, have you? Well, then, you're stupid. I can call you that because I've also been stupid. My mother's prayers protected me, and God had mercy on me. Now I'm being smart. No test, no taste. No commitment, no yoni. Even a condom won't protect you from some sexually transmitted infections. And it sure won't protect your heart from being broken from being effed and forgotten.

If a woman's going to risk getting HIV or herpes, shouldn't that risk at least come with love and commitment? Here's what I mean. If you've done all your homework to get to know the man you sleep with, including took your time to lie down with him, but up the road you contract something, at least you don't feel like a fool. Like you gave up so much for so little. Stuff happens, even after people do their research. Take it slow; demand that your partner use protection. You might even go get tested together.

Sisters, you've got to be smart. That's your body temple. It's precious. Protect it from diseases. Guard your heart from men who don't give a damn about you. Such men don't belong on top of you, inside of you. Teach men how to treat you like the Goddess that you are, by treating yourself that way.

## Being Easy Ain't Easy

Baby girl, being easy ain't easy,
believe me.
You'll spend tons on doctor visits and pharmacy
prescriptions trying to get rid of that itch homeboy
neglected to mention.

Pay attention to not just your motives but his intentions.
Stop looking for affection in penises erected,
then find yourself neglected, infected, and rejected.

I'm just sayin', being easy ain't easy.
At the end of the day it takes a lot of work to be sleazy.

Trying to keep up with the lies
cause you the girl on the side.
You tell him you love him then get mad at his reply
(man's voice) "Baby girl, it is what it is, and you knew that
when it started."
He sees you catching feelings so he quickly departed.
Now you all brokenhearted
and you behave as though he did it.
When he told you from the beginning
he just wanted to hit it.

Reflection should reveal you played yourself.
The situation created . . . you designed yourself.
If you don't like the results then redefine yourself.
And if you feel like you lost, then go and find yourself . . .

Cause,
Being Easy Ain't Easy.

—*Shvilla M. Rasheem*

## THEIR STORY OF MAKING LOVE LAST

*"It matters not Who you love, Where you love, Why you love,
When you love, Or how you love, It matters only That you love."*
—John Lennon, *singer*

One Valentine's Day, after I heard that Jamie had been happily married to for ten years, I congratulated her. With a wide smile that lit up her face she said, "It feels like it was yesterday that we met." Curious me asked, "What's your secret? How have you made it work all these years?" That question launched a 45-minute conversation.

Jamie told me that once upon a time she would repeat the same relationship missteps again and again. Then one day her therapist suggested that she not get into another relationship until she healed her own wounds, or at least stopped looking to a lover to complete her. She was advised to give herself everything she'd want another to give her. That's *everything*. By doing this, she would then inevitably attract someone into her life that also takes care of *himself*. Now you have two whole and complete people, together. Rather than two half people, as Marianne Williamson says, "joined at the hip."

When we enter relationships operating from our wholeness—since we're already whole whether or not we know or feel it—rather than seeking to get something, instead, we're out to give something. We've stopped looking for someone to save us for we no longer see ourselves as victims. "And you know what victims attract?" Jamie asked.

"Victims attract Knights in Shining Armor," I answered.

"And you know what Knights have?" she asked and followed with a quick response, "They have a dark side."

"How well I know," I chimed in.

Jamie went on. "And what do Knights like to do?"

I knew from personal experience the answer to that question. Knights like to rescue. And when a woman no longer needs to be rescued, what do they do? They leave.

"Knights leave when they no longer have anyone to save," Jamie added.

That had so been my story for so many years. The proverbial damsel in distress. Oh, how I pined for a Knight in Shining Armor. The last Knight that I had, Adam, whom I write extensively about him in *Love Addicted,* was a case in point. Sure enough, once I finally blossomed into a full-blown woman, the relationship folded. I left him. The relationship served its divine purpose, which was to help me get to a place where I no longer felt I needed to be saved. At last I had learned to save myself.

How do you know you're acting like a victim? Victims move through life looking for people to take care of them, save them, complete them. They're whiners, complainers, always upset about this or that. The world is never good enough. Somebody's always mistreating them. You, their beloved, never gives them enough. You treat them unfairly. You don't care enough. Somebody's always hurting them, letting them down, not living up to their expectations. They're never pleased, never happy. Nothing's ever, ever good enough. If you ask them what's wrong, why they aren't happy, they'll tell you what somebody else did to or didn't do for them. They're emotional parasites. They suck you dry. They leave you exhausted and drained and frustrated because no matter how much you give them they always need more.

And please, don't try to make them happy. Don't bother. It's a waste of time and energy. You see, their very identity is that of a victim, although they're likely oblivious to this fact. If you take their complaining and whining and unhappiness from them—as if you could—they won't know who they are or how to be in the world.

By the way, if you're in a relationship with a victim who you are bent on making happy, chances are you are a rescuer;

you're invested in saving others. That is, YOU are the Knight in Shining Armor.

Back to my conversation with Jamie, who shared that another secret to longevity and happiness is that when things get challenging, they know how to bend, rather than break. Resiliency and tenacity can take a couple a very long way indeed. Forgiveness of others and self makes you supple and pliable. When the difficulties come, and they most certainly will, the two of you, together, can bend instead of break.

# Herstory of lost and found love

*"It is a funny thing about life; if you refuse to accept anything but the best, you very often get it."*
—W. Somerset Maugham

## By Cassandra-Nkem Nwosu

If someone had asked me two years ago why my ex broke up with me I would have cringed at the very thought of sharing my insecurities.

We worked together for about a year. We always knew the physical attraction was there, but relating at any level other than professionally was a no-no. He left the company first; I left a few months later. January 2000, the turn of a new century, he called me on my cell phone.

"John who?" I asked. It had been at least six months since I had heard his voice. We agreed to meet that weekend, over dinner. It snowed that entire weekend, which set the stage for three days of some serious lovemaking—really; it was more like four if you include Monday morning. As I dashed off to work, I thought, *that was a hell of a weekend.* Still, I knew deep inside that he was not The One. That didn't stop me though from spending the next five years trying to convince myself that he was.

I distinctively remember the day he called me, unexpectedly, after yet another breakup. The phone rang about 8:00 Saturday morning. On the other end was a familiar voice, but the phone number was different.

The voice said, "Hey, babe . . ."

"Who are you talking to?" I asked.

"Do you know who this is . . .?" the voice asked.

"Huh, I do now."

He thought of me, he said, while tuning in to *The Audrey Chapman Show*. He went on to say a woman came on the air exclaiming how confident she was, but she was puzzled as to why she could not attract a good man or relationship. In his opinion, if she was so confident, then why was she lonely and miserable? I thought to myself, *Who you talking about? I know you ain't talking about me.* Yeah, he *was* talking about me. We dialogued a little on the topic. Of course, I held my own. But at the end of the day, he won. You see, he had mastered every emotion. He knew me like no other. He knew that all he had to do was push a button, create dialogue, subtly pick a fight, and just like that, I would fall. It didn't matter that it was emotionally draining; he knew I would never give up a chance to win at anything. I couldn't win his heart, so I had to win intellectually. And there it was, a way for him to reenter my life. Another three months of passionate lovemaking, brutal arguments, and violent outbursts that would eventually lead to *the* breakup.

We loved and hated each other for five years. The relationship was an emotional roller coaster—not the updated, pimped-out kind you find at a newly opened amusement park. No, it was more like the kind you find at one of those traveling carnivals. You know, the kind that makes you wonder if the bolts will give way any minute. Yes, it was that bad. Yet, I painted it in my mind to be so damn good. All my friends loved him, often commenting, "So what, girl? *At least* you *got* a man!" I always thought to myself, "Really—I don't!" What I had was physical while what I needed and desired was spiritual.

After years of trying to make it work, I simply let it go. No, for real this time, I let it go. Even today, when I hear his voice it does nothing for me. If anything, I think to myself, *"What were you thinking?"* I then embrace myself knowing that that relationship taught me what it truly means to love. Because he was the opposite of love, real love now had meaning for me—he gave it texture. I could now at least conceptualize what I thought it was, what I believed it to be. Because I could see it and feel it, I now felt empowered to create it!

The greatest lesson I learned through that experience was the importance of simply being. My determined efforts to find the lesson kept the experience alive until I decided to open my eyes and really see it. Today, I am in a spiritually centered relationship with a man who creates and expresses love through every touch, conversation, and interaction. I am being love for I can be no other way. Because I *am* love, I now attract love. No other energy but love can live here with me.

It always amazes me to hear sisters say, "Love yourself first." I happen to think it's deeper than that. We are not here alone; we need to love ourselves *and* others. Ultimately, this creates the energy or the presence of love and invites it to pervade and take permanent residency wherever we plant our feet.

Words to the wise and those who seek love: practice loving and being love in all you do. Share a hug with a perfect stranger. Greet someone on the elevator you wouldn't normally talk to. Pray for that coworker who gives you a dose of hell every day and wish him or her well. And most importantly, thank the Being and every experience that brought you to this point. You have arrived here for a reason. Be present to it, enjoy this moment for what it is, and if it ain't working for you, shift your thinking until it becomes evident that the path you've chosen has now chosen you.

Affirm: I Am co-creating. I Am being love. Love has permission to express in me each and every moment of the day.

# Honoring the Call on Your Life

*"Sometimes a breakup is a breakthrough in disguise."*
—DeBora

I'LL SAY IT one last time, there's a calling on your life. There's a calling on every life. Sometimes we aren't meant to be in a relationship. Not because we tend to lose ourselves in our intimate relationships, but, quite frankly, too many of our relationships are toxic. Draining. Exhausting. Distractions from what's really important, like serving the world with our gifts. You've got bigger things to do than babysit some man. And to be quite frank, some men are adult-babies. Yeah, I said it. They are emotionally unstable, verbally abusive, needy, codependent, lost, and, therefore, a drain on your life force.

## THE GOOD MAN

A good man is a partner. A good man is resourceful. A good man is emotionally stable. A good man is someone you can turn to for strength and comfort when life gets messy and challenging and scary. A good man doesn't pull you down but build you up. A good man brings something of value to the table of love. A good man supports you in being the best version of yourself. He applauds your successes. He has his own path and honors it. A good man walks with you, not in front of you, not behind you. A good man has flaws, foibles, failings, and fears but doesn't make you a target for his anger and frustrations, nor your enemy when life challenges him. You're his confidante, friend, partner, lover, and teammate. Will he stumble? Sure. Will his shadows sometimes come out of the dark? Of course. But the scales of love, support, and respect must outweigh the ugly stuff.

Are there any good men left? Absolutely! It's up to you to be a magnet for them. The "man" who drags you down keeps you from living with power and purpose. You can't afford that.

Whatever you do, please, please, please, don't expect a man or relationship to completely fulfill you. You've got to answer your Call and live on purpose if you desire to live a whole, full, and vital life. Don't seek to hide from your destiny in a relationship, either. And for goodness' sake, let NO man rob you of your dreams, destroy your self-esteem, or keep you from answering the Call on your life. God won't like that. Nor will you be happy and fulfilled.

You want to be happy, right? You want to be fulfilled, eh? Then live your life with power and purpose, whether you travel with a companion or solo. God bless you!

# *Acknowledgments*

I HAVE THE great pleasure of thanking some very special people who gave themselves to this book in a significant and meaningful way by contributing a poem, story, interview, ideas, or support. Without you, this book would not be. Thank you Essa Ali, John Barnes, Ellen Wright-Besenski, Jackie House-Bey, Constance Delores Burrell, Patsy "PeaJae" Cannon, Adia Ricks Cummings, Shameeka Dream, Eyitayo Enitan, Christopher J. Gross, A. M. Hall, Saundra Harris, Merci Hunt, Cynthia Jackson, Marian Johnson, Kenyatta, Zakiyyah Lana, Azya Maxton, Allan Van Johnson, Neecy, Cassandra Nkem-Nwosu, Shvilla M. Rasheem, Barbara Redfearn, Sadé, Babatunde Enitan Salaam, SassyScribe, Jeanette Taylor, Kim H. Walker, Angel Richardson Whitehead, Kiara Whitehead, and Brandy Whyte.

Thank you Alanna Boutin, my editor, for your commitment and dedication to this project.

To every woman and man who contributed to this book I say, "thank you, thank you, thank you!" You entrusted me with your beautifully honest stories, and for that I will be eternally grateful.

To the Spiritual Empowerment Center (SEC) I say thanks from the depths of my heart. I am who I am because you embrace, love, and support me in being fully self-expressed, powerful, and free. A special thanks to Reverend Michele K. Synegal, SEC's spiritual leader, for her powerful example of limitless living, dynamic Sunday lessons, and commitment to walking her talk.

I thank my many teachers, gurus, and soul companions who show up in my life as authors, associates, friends, and family.

To my dear mother, Mattie S. Ricks Hairston, I say, "thank you" for giving me life and for quietly supporting me in all that I do. I must thank my daughter, Adia Ricks Cummings, twice, because she is so nice. Adia, I love, adore, admire, and respect you for, indeed, you are one of my most powerful teachers from whom I learn much about life and love. Last but certainly not least I thank God, my Source, Sustenance, Strength and Supplier from whence All that's good, sweet, and wonderful in my life comes.

# About the Author

DeBora M. Ricks is an author, speaker, facilitator, writing coach and publishing consultant, radio and TV personality, executive producer of a radio show, and proud mother. She has worked more than a decade with abused and battered women as an attorney, advocate, coach, and counselor in the criminal justice and civil systems. She is passionately committed to helping women take charge of their lives, heal after a breakup, and let go in love. She has also worked three and a half years in a residential drug and alcohol program helping men and women untangle their legal issues.

DeBora is the editor of more than ten books, nonfiction and works of fiction. In 2010, she realized a life-long dream to do a book reading and signing in Paris, France. She currently lives and works in Baltimore, Maryland.

To buy additional copies of **Why Did He Break Up With Me?** and **Love Addicted,** or to contact DeBora for a book reading, signing or talk, go to her web site at www.DeBoraRicks.com.

17576444R00162

Made in the USA
Charleston, SC
18 February 2013